THE MEANING OF
THE LIBRARY

King James Library, University of St. Andrews. Photograph by Peter Adamson.

THE MEANING OF
THE LIBRARY

A Cultural History

❧

Edited by Alice Crawford

PRINCETON UNIVERSITY PRESS

Princeton and Oxford

For Robert, Lewis, and Blyth

CONTENTS

❧

LIST OF ILLUSTRATIONS

ACKNOWLEDGMENTS

I am most grateful to all the people and institutions who have contributed to the production of this volume. In particular I must thank the academics and librarians who made the pilgrimage to St. Andrews to deliver the King James Library Lectures, which were the original inspiration for these essays, and the audiences who so enthusiastically received the talks and confirmed our feeling that lots of people still love libraries and want to know more about them. It is good to see these discussions of "the meaning of the library" now opened up to an even wider public.

Jon Purcell was director of Library Services at St. Andrews in 2009, when the book and lecture series were first suggested, and most generously provided library funds to launch the project. Deputy director Jeremy Upton and John MacColl, who succeeded Jon as director in 2010, continued to make that funding available over several years until the project was complete. They have my sincere thanks—this book would never have happened without them.

The contributors and I gratefully acknowledge Faber and Faber and W. W. Norton & Co. for permission to quote from "Casting and Gathering" by Seamus Heaney, and from "Memorial" by Alice Oswald. We are most grateful, too, to Penguin Random House for permission to quote from Andrew George's translation of *The Epic of Gilgamesh* (Penguin, 1999) and to the Agencia Literaria Schavelzon, Barcelona, for permission to quote from Alberto Manguel's *The Library at Night* (Yale University Press, 2008).

We would also like to thank the following for permission to reproduce illustrations: Peter Adamson (frontispiece); the Musée archéologique de Sousse (figure 1.1); Professor Richard Gameson (plates 1, 14 and 22); the Biblioteca Medicea Laurenziana (plate 2); the Archivio dell'Abbazia, Montecassino (plate 3); the Biblioteca Apostolica Vaticana (plate 4); the Bibliothèque nationale de France (plates 5, 8, 9 and 19); the Bibliothèque municipale, Le Havre (plate 6); the Dombibliothek, Cologne (plate 7);

the Universitäts-und Landesbibliothek, Darmstadt (plate 10); the Archives nationales, Paris (plate 11); Freiburg-im-Breisgau University Archives (plates 12 and 13); the Musée Condé, Chantilly and the Réunion des musées nationaux (plate 15); the British Library Board (plates 16, 17, and 21); the John Rylands Library, University of Manchester (plates 18, 23, and 24); the Detroit Institute of Arts and Bridgeman Images (plate 20); the Trustees of the British Museum (plate 25); the University of St. Andrews Library (plate 26); Punch Limited (figure 10.1); HathiTrust (figures 11.1 and 11.2).

Ben Tate, Ellen Foos, and Hannah Paul at Princeton University Press have guided and helped with tact and consideration at all stages—I am most grateful to them and to my wonderfully patient copyeditor, Kathleen Kageff, who has saved me from many pitfalls. My indexer, Blythe Woolston, has done a superb job, for which she has my warmest thanks.

Those at home—Robert, Lewis, and Blyth—know most about the trials and tribulations that have accompanied the book's long gestation. Their support and encouragement throughout have been invaluable.

A.C.

UNIVERSITY OF ST. ANDREWS LIBRARY

March 2015

INTRODUCTION

🐝

Alice Crawford

. . . with bewildering optimism, we continue to assemble whatever scraps of information we can gather in scrolls and books and computer chips, on shelf after library shelf, whether material, virtual or otherwise, pathetically intent on lending the world a semblance of sense and order, while knowing perfectly well that, however much we'd like to believe the contrary, our pursuits are sadly doomed to failure.

Alberto Manguel, *The Library at Night*

Any consideration of the meaning of the library must acknowledge Alberto Manguel's compellingly candid assertion that as a construct it is "doomed to failure."

All the essays in this collection tell the story of how, from earliest times, human beings have with "bewildering optimism" amassed collections of books and created buildings to put them in; how they have striven to assemble, encompass, and contain the materials on which the world's knowledge is recorded in the vain but determined hope that they will somehow, ultimately, be able to gather it all into one coherent, ordered space.

Each essay enacts in its own way the paradox of that dynamic, the confrontation between the drive to build the all-embracing überlibrary and the acceptance that the endeavor will fail. They are essays full of oppositions. Just as the history of libraries charts the perpetual ups and downs of their growth and disintegration—libraries throughout the ages have constantly been built up with gusto, destroyed by malice or neglect, then rebuilt by a hopeful new generation—so the essays here reflect the continual ebb and flow of that impulse. Tensions complicate and enliven them all. They show how libraries can be both hugely purposeful and dangerously useless; how they can channel both order and chaos and house both print and digital, old and new; how they can both control and liberate the knowledge they contain. Each author in this collection enjoys the tangle of paradox and teases out the snarl of oppositions in an effort to articulate his or her sense of the many meanings with which "the library" as a concept seems to resonate.

The essays were collected between 2009 and 2013, against a backdrop of economic stringency that has seen many public libraries throughout the United Kingdom close. Figures from the Chartered Institute of Public Finance and Accountancy confirm the closure in 2010–11 of 146 branches, with the number increasing to 201 in 2012.[1] Numbers of librarians have fallen in line with branch closures, decreasing by 8 percent in the year to March 2012, as have visits to libraries across the UK, which in 2012 were down 2.4 percent to 306.6 million compared with the previous year. Campaign groups have blossomed, raising their voices in pressing support of an embattled institution. UK organizations such as Speak Up for Libraries, Voices for the Library, Shout about Libraries, and the Library Campaign are all engaged in a newly necessary crusade to protect libraries, their staff, and their readers.[2]

These essays were written, too, at a time when technological change has created the popular perception that there is no longer any need for libraries or librarians since, with a good search engine and the ever-increasing proficiency of the keyboard-tapping digital native, "everyone's a librarian now." With the loss of their traditional role as intermediaries between information source and user, librarians seek new purposes for their skills, and new arenas of usefulness. The questions "Why libraries?" and "What are they for?" are beginning to be asked with increasing urgency.

Happily a more nourishing local context has inspired the collection and supported its development. The essays were originally launched as a series of lectures offered by the University of St. Andrews Library to mark the four hundredth anniversary in 2012 of the founding of its historic King James Library, an event that coincided with celebrations for the six hundredth anniversary of the university as a whole. Internationally renowned figures from the academic and library worlds were invited to talk about what the library as an institution has meant to civilization in different historical periods and to set out visions of what it might mean now and in the future. The series was inaugurated in June 2009 by the librarian of Congress, Dr. James H. Billington, who drew movingly on his many years of experience managing the world's largest book collection to consider the library as a force for freedom in his lecture, "The Modern Library and Global Democracy." Ten further lectures followed in which the idea of the library was variously explored by people who had used, led, worked in, studied, or simply loved libraries.

Advertised as the King James Library Lecture Series, the lectures' association with St. Andrews's King James Library (shown in the frontispiece of this book) has been apt. In use continuously for four hundred years, this is a library that has itself been many things and had many "meanings" over time. Founded in 1612 by James VI and I, it had a protracted and difficult birth. A roofless building till 1618, it remained an empty shell till eventually furnished and stocked with books in 1642. In 1645–46 it was the home of the Scottish Parliament, its lower hall used for meetings when there was an outbreak of plague in Edinburgh. In the early 1670s it was the laboratory of astronomer James Gregory, who perhaps worked there on his invention of the first reflecting telescope. In the eighteenth century it was a place where geological and zoological specimens were luridly displayed ready for the natural history or ethnographic experiments of the university's Enlightenment scholars. Between 1710 and 1837 it was one of the select group of copyright deposit libraries entitled to receive a copy of every British book published, a privilege that was eventually surrendered when the difficulties of claiming large quantities of books from London became too great. For Samuel Johnson, visiting in 1773, it was an "elegant and luminous" book room, and for novelist Margaret Oliphant its blocked-up North Street façade was the inspiration for her ghost story "The Library Window," published in *Blackwood's Magazine* in 1896.[3] In 1940 it was the victim of Second World War bombs, and in the 2010s it has been variously a space for a display of modern art, a catwalk for a fashion shoot, a backdrop for the filming of celebrity interviews, and the surprising venue for rock group the *Lost Todorovs'* "secret gig."

This library has worked out its meaning through many manifestations —as empty shell, and stylish book room; as a parliament hall and a science laboratory; as a museum for the university's "artefacts and curiosities," and as a sought-after venue for cultural events. Now in 2015 it is a valued social space for concerts, exhibitions, poetry readings, fashion shows, and parties but remains, most importantly, a much-loved study room where students set up their laptops for twenty-first-century scholarly endeavor.

All the essays in this collection consider "the library" as a changing and organic entity, something that is constantly adapting and becoming something else. Through the lens of these lectures we see it like a kaleidoscope image, forever nudged into new versions with each turn of the cylinder; a concept endlessly and energetically reinventing itself.

Lots of books have been written about libraries and their histories. *The Cambridge History of Libraries in Britain and Ireland* is the benchmark publication on the subject, but the appearance on our shelves in 2013 of James W. P. Campbell's superbly illustrated *The Library: A World History* attests to current and continuing lively interest.[4] So too do Michael H. Harris's *History of Libraries in the Western World* (1995), Martin Lowell's *Enrichment: A History of the Public Library in the United States in the Twentieth Century* (1998), Matthew Battles's *Library: An Unquiet History* (2003), Lucien X. Polastron's *Books on Fire: The Tumultuous Story of the World's Great Libraries* (2007), and James Murray's *The Library: An Illustrated History* (2009).[5] Volumes of Konstantinos Sp. Staikos's *History of the Library in Western Civilisation* have continued to appear since 2004 while Simon Eliot and Jonathan Rose's *A Companion to the History of the Book* in the *Blackwell Companions to Literature and Culture* series has covered similar or parallel territory since 2007.[6]

This collection of essays, however, will approach the life of libraries in a different way. Although they are arranged to follow the library's development through history, the essays aim to offer simply glimpses of what libraries were like at these times rather than a comprehensive historical overview. They focus on what libraries were used for, why they were needed, why they were meaningful to the various communities from which they emerged, and provide impressions rather than analyses of their value in the changing chronological contexts. "The library," we find, "means" many things over time and throughout these essays. It is a collection of books, a center for scholarship, a universal memory, a maze or labyrinth, a repository of hidden or occulted knowledge, a sanctum, an archive for stories, a fortress, a space of transcendence, a focus of wealth and display, a vehicle of spirituality, an emblem of wisdom and learning, a mind or brain, an ordainer of the universe, a mausoleum, a time machine, a temple, a utopia, a gathering place, an antidote to fanaticism, a silent repository of countless unread books, a place for the pursuit of truth. A concept that has inspired many metaphors, the library as an idea has appealed to the human imagination throughout the ages and continues to do so today. The writers of these essays suggest why this is so.

The book's first section, "The Library through Time" begins with Edith Hall's "Adventures in Ancient Greek and Roman Libraries," in which her consideration of the relationship between libraries and cultural creativity leads her to examine the library at Alexandria's iconic bid for completeness in its collections. Embarking on the Herculean task of preserving Greek literary output in its entirety, this library's scholars were the first to attempt, perhaps with Manguel's "bewildering optimism," to obtain copies of every known work of their time. Saluting them in this mammoth undertaking, Hall argues that their achievement was not just a vast collection of works but the introduction of a whole new concept for the library as an institution. They paved the way, she suggests, for the library to be seen not merely as a place where individual records are left by individual writers, but as something far more transcendent and ambitious. It can now be viewed as "an instrument designed to preserve intact the memory of humankind." The scholars' attempts to collect everything ever written in the history of the world "changed our mental landscape forever," lifting libraries to a symbolic level on which they represented "a cosmopolitan and tolerant ideal."

Importantly, however, Hall does not recognize this striven-for wholeness as an unadulterated "good thing." By conceiving the idea of completeness, she points out, the Alexandrians necessarily conceived the idea of its opposite also. If the library could contain the whole memory of mankind, the possibility had to be confronted that that memory could be lost: encased within man-made walls, the entire memory of the human race could be "vulnerable to complete erasure." The underlying paradox of the library as an idea emerges early. Strong in its pursuit of the whole record of civilization, it is nevertheless unavoidably susceptible to disintegration and decay. Hall's essay opens on the image of a library in tatters—the scholar Euripides (in a scene from Aristophanes' *Acharnians*) sitting among the shredded pages of his own discarded plays—a tragicomic visualization of the essential mismatch between the library's ideal and its reality.

Bravely, too, Hall suggests that the influence of the library in ancient civilizations may not always have been benign. The library is, she reminds us, "a tool that can both liberate and oppress." She notes its frequent association with imperialism and control and considers the possibility that "the emergence of great libraries of literature [may have] had a hand in killing off innovation and experiment in Greek poetry" by allowing poets to immerse themselves too comfortably in the poetry of the past, stifling the imaginative drive to produce something new.

Richard Gameson articulates a similar ambivalence in his attentive consideration of the depictions of libraries by medieval and early Renaissance artists in "The Image of the Medieval Library." Among the many images he considers that carefully portray libraries as emblems of wisdom and learning or vehicles of spirituality for fostering goodness and holiness, there lurks memorably the foolish bibliophile in the woodcut for Sebastian Brant's *Das Narrenschiff* (1494). As the fool sits vacantly amid the many volumes in reckless disorder around him, we see that his folly consists of amassing the "useless books" of the picture's caption—useless because they are unread. In medieval, as in ancient, times there was no consensus that the library meant something unassailably good.

In his "The Renaissance Library and the Challenge of Print" Andrew Pettegree suggests one reason why some sixteenth-century books might have been unread. Libraries in the Renaissance were beginning to decline, their role as places where great men gathered to display their wealth and books undermined by the affordable new printed items deluging the market at this time. With an estimated 180 million print volumes suddenly available for anyone to buy, books and libraries began to lose their attraction as status symbols for rich private collectors, who turned their attention instead to purchasing paintings, tapestries, and other objets d'art. Glutted with books yet with a sparsity of libraries, the sixteenth-century book world was a strangely paradoxical place. We enjoy Pettegree's opening account of the disintegration of Italian nobleman Gian Vincenzo Pinelli's fine library—of books lost through theft, appropriated by pirates, cast overboard into the sea, their rescued pages used as draft excluders or to mend boats—and recognize it as a colorful synecdoche for what was happening to the great Renaissance collections throughout Europe as a whole. In contrast to the powerful "energy to amass" that drove the great library at Alexandria into existence, the dynamic was now downward, toward fragmentation and dispersal. The library's meaning became obfuscated, its role unclear.

The downward trend was not terminal, however. Pettegree traces the library's retreat from this nadir to its reemergence in the seventeenth century "as a physical space with a new role, as a center of scholarship." He shows how the Renaissance book *trade* rather than its book *collectors* supplied the coherence contemporary libraries were failing to deliver, establishing a "pan-European integrated market" for Latin books, which ensured that these were produced in a small number of places well situated for distributing them along Europe's main trade arteries. He looks forward, too, to how the digital scholarship of the twenty-first century will make possible the reintegration of items from the dispersed Renaissance collections, recapturing those that have been tracked down to six thousand or so libraries and archives worldwide and drawing them together into secure databanks such as the Universal Short Title Catalogue.

"[B]ooks were meant to travel," writes Pettegree as he describes the distribution practices of the sixteenth-century book trade. Robert Darnton continues the trope of the travelling book in his "From Printing Shop to Bookshelves: How Books Began the Journey to Enlightenment Libraries," in which he follows eighteenth-century bookseller Jean-François Favarger on his adventure-filled sales trip across the mountains from Neuchâtel to Marseille then northward on to La Rochelle. His foray into this later book world is salutary in its depiction of how lives were risked to deliver books to buyers. Favarger sets out on horseback in July 1778 and spends five months riding through southern and central France inspecting every bookshop en route. In Marseille he spends 10 sols on refurbishing his pistols since the next stage of the road is infested with bandits, in La Rochelle 26 livres for new breeches, his old ones having been ruined by friction in the saddle. At Poitiers he spends 8 louis d'or on a new horse as the old one keeps collapsing in the mud. Since the publisher he works for does considerable business in illegal and pirated books, he spends time negotiating with smugglers on both sides of the Swiss-French border. He arranges for "porters" (*porte-balles*) to carry sixty-pound backpacks of illegal books along tortuous mountain trails from Switzerland to France and to receive 25 sols for a successful crossing. He is familiar with the "marrying" of illegal books with legal ones, the larding of the leaves of prohibited works inside the leaves of inoffensive ones (*Fanny Hill*, for example, married to the Bible) to ensure their safe passage before the eyes of the inspecting customs officers. The essay closes with a glimpse of some of the eighteenth-century libraries for which these books may have been destined, and of the further struggles in which their librarians engaged to ensure that this sometimes daring material actually reached the shelves.

In " 'The Advantages of Literature': The Subscription Library in Georgian Britain," David Allan describes in more detail the libraries for which books like Favarger's were so eagerly bought. The fiercely respectable Georgian subscription library represented "the library" in its proud new role as a forger of urban culture, membership providing a useful marker of social position, respectability, and enlightened credentials. The "advantages of literature," state the *Rules for the Regulation of the Carlisle Library* in 1819, are obvious to all: these include the "advancement in morals, manners, and taste" that attend the habit of reading and reflection, and as a result the Carlisle Library can be placed high on the list of the "judicious and salutary improvements which . . . have been carried into effect in Carlisle, much to the comfort and convenience of its inhabitants." Setting themselves scrupulously apart from the scurrilous circulating libraries, with their supposed bias toward low-grade narrative fiction, these associational libraries existed to accrue a wider set of cultural benefits.

Yet like Edith Hall in her consideration of civilization's earliest libraries, Allan sees these Georgian libraries, too, as possibly ambiguous spaces. He notes two conflicting impulses at work: on the one hand there is the freedom subscription library members had to control the books their money bought; on the other there is the all-too-rigid order imposed on

the book stocks by notions of taste and propriety. Various types of literature were off-limits on the grounds that they might pose a threat to social
order—books associated with party politics, for example, and of course
narrative fiction that might sensationalize or whitewash unacceptable
behavior, and that might be dangerously attractive to vulnerable readers
such as women and children. With their uncompromising commitment
to "the advantages of literature," the book-selection subcommittees of
the Georgian subscription libraries held both their book collections and
readers in an ultimately damaging stranglehold.

John Sutherland's discussion "Literature and the Library in the Nineteenth Century" presents a further knot of paradoxes. He shows how
Victorian books proliferated and were consumed by an exponentially expanding community of readers. Themselves industrialized by new mecha-
nized processes of papermaking, printing, and bookbinding, books were
"a cheap luxury," and suddenly plentifully available to a demographic that
had benefited from two reforming acts of Parliament. The 1850 Public
Libraries Act had instigated a shift from costly circulation libraries to
free ones, and the 1870 Education Act built further on this to drive up
levels of literacy among ordinary people. Here was a society in which easily produced books abounded and could, via libraries, be passed without
difficulty from hand to hand and from one social stratum to another.

Working in contrast to this exuberant opening up of the book
world to the Victorian reader was, as Sutherland explains however, the
nineteenth-century library's drive to control. The famous Mudie's Select
Library, for example, dictated the three-volume format in which books
had to be produced. Sutherland describes as "Mudieitis" the trap in
which both book buyers and publishers were caught. Insisting on a tem-
plate that allowed three library readers to borrow one title at the same
time, Mudie provided a guaranteed market for publishers but locked
them into a production arrangement from which they were unable to
deviate for half a century.

Again, too, Sutherland says, readers could be seen as the victims of
a kind of benign mind control imposed by nineteenth-century librarians' choice of stock and arrangement of it on the shelves. Careful in
their selection of texts, public librarians functioned as teachers of taste,
moral improvement, and social behavior. Classification schemes that

determined juxtapositions of books on shelves, catalogues that structured readers' pathways from one book to another, indexes that directed the navigation of a book's actual content—all exerted a subtle but insistent control of reading behavior. Describing the monstrous metal fumigator in which nineteenth-century library books were habitually placed to be cleansed in fumes of sulphuric acid, Sutherland suggests that the unspoken mission of the Victorian public library was to "disinfect" both books and readers. The dreadful machine becomes a symbol of the library's subterranean but rigorous regulation of its readers.

A trio of essays in a new section entitled "The Library in Imagination" allow the reader to step aside at this stage from the chronological trajectory of the pieces so far, to consider the meanings of the library to writers of both fiction and poetry, and to the makers of film. A transition from "time" to "timelessness" and the realm of ideas permits contemplation of the importance of the library to creative practitioners, without whom libraries could after all have no purpose.

In "The Library in Fiction" Marina Warner again plays with a plurality of oppositions: she enjoys the tropes of dispersal and reassembly, forgetting and memorializing, losing and finding, abstract and concrete, microcosm and macrocosm. She is fascinated by the hero Gilgamesh's promise to engrave "the whole story" of his life's adventures on stone so that it will be preserved for ever, and by the unearthing and piecing together of that story in the "millions of scattered, battered, and chipped clay pages" on which it was found millennia later in the Assyrian Library of Ashurbanipal. She sees fiction as a fashioning of stories (*fingo*, she reminds us, means "I fashion"), an assembly of tales, and libraries as places where these stories are preserved. If fiction aspires to monumentality, the library "becomes an archive, enshrining those fugitive, mobile, airy webs of words that make up stories." She sees that "without the library to preserve its creations, the imagination is mortal, like its protagonists." She shares her excitement at the paradox of Shahrazad's library in *The Arabian Nights*, the source of the stories she tells: the fact that Shahrazad's retellings are themselves written down on the Sultan's orders at the very end of the book imposes a "dizzy circularity" on the *Nights*, since these will be copies of tales already inscribed and kept in a library.

Like the scholars of Alexandria, Warner loves the idea that the library might encompass everything, that it might be here that "the whole" truth about human experience will be assembled and understood. *The Arabian Nights* are, for her, a microcosm of that ultimate library:

> The thousand and one in the book's title hints at infinity, and indeed the stories keep multiplying, podding off into different new stories, as well as into multiple versions and translations. The utopian fantasy of the book includes the possibility that someone could act as the keeper of memories on this vast and labyrinthine scale.

Warner is persuasive, too, in her contention that both libraries and books have power. Shahrazad's telling of tales from her library saves her life, she points out, agreeing with Borges that the library can be "a labyrinth in which readers find themselves while they are getting lost." Libraries can make real things happen.

In "The Library in Poetry" Robert Crawford is again alert to oppositions in the library's many meanings. While it can be "a fine, meditative space," the library can be a site of "conflict and devastation" too; it "can be threatening as well as nurturing." His survey of poems about libraries shows us poets adoring libraries, and longing for their works to be drawn into them, but also in a strange way fearing them. The library can make a poet feel small, anxious that his work will be assigned a place only on the margins of literature, in the "tatter'd row" of "Wits, Bards, and Idlers" rather than with the august tomes of History, Science, and Philosophy. The book room becomes "a site of struggle," a place "of both challenge and confirmation." It can both spur and counter the imagination, provide both an inspiring gateway to knowledge and a sepulchral space in which thought is subdued. It can open up careers for eighteenth- and nineteenth-century women seeking employment, and trap them in roles in which there is little possibility of advancement. Crawford's essay draws together poems about libraries and librarians from the seventeenth to the twenty-first centuries and celebrates the multiple ambivalences—the "combined enjoyments and drabness"—that adhere to meanings of the library over time.

Laura Marcus's discussion, "The Library in Film," explores the op-position between order and confusion in the library and analyses the contrast between the apparent rationality of the library as a system and its actual spaces—often its underground stacks—in which unquantifi-able mysteries lurk. She shows us Alain Resnais's documentary film of the Bibliothèque nationale, *Toute la mémoire du monde*, in which the library is "the repository of knowledge at once secret and universal," a place in which each reader sits "working on his slice of universal mem-ory [to] lay the fragments of a single secret end to end—the secret of human happiness." For this film, as for the Alexandrian scholars, the li-brary is the place where we strive to collate and preserve all knowledge, shaping it into a coherent, curated whole. Other films (*The Name of the Rose, Ghostbusters, All the President's Men*) explore the metaphor of "the library as labyrinth," and others again (*Shadow of a Doubt, Chinatown*) offer libraries as places where mysteries are decoded. Scenes where char-acters search through newspapers or legal documents condense the pro-cess of research and investigation and come to stand for the film's wider hermeneutics. Students in *The Paper Chase* for example, adventuring in the dark stacks of the college library at night, discover wisdom of the past hidden in the shelves—here lecture notes taken by the intimidating Professor Kingsfield. The library's contents—the books themselves—are valorized in other films: Truffaut's *Fahrenheit 451* ends memorably with people walking in woodland, speaking the books they have learned by heart before their paper pages were destroyed by dystopian overlords. Marcus shows film loving the library's spaces and ideas, its auras of both order and mystery and the interactions between the two. Examining the library in film, she points to the complex relationship between literature and cinema, between book and film, and indicates meanings for the li-brary as a memory place, treasure-house and keeper of ideas.

At the start of a closing section, "The Library Now and in the Future," Stephen Enniss moves us into a busy, twentieth-century book world in which librarians' horizons open up and in which they respond to the ex-citing challenge of building their archive collections from a global pool. His title, " 'Casting and Gathering' " immediately establishes the tensions he wishes to explore—those involved in libraries' efforts to develop the modern literary archive. It summons Seamus Heaney's poem for Ted Hughes, in which two fishermen stand on opposite sides of a riverbank, one casting, sending "a green silk tapered cast / . . . whispering through the air," the other gathering line-lengths in off his reel with a "sharp ratcheting" sound "like a speeded-up corncrake." For Enniss the castings and gatherings are those of British writers dispersing their manuscripts for sale on the global market, and of United States libraries drawing them expensively into their archives. The library now means a place where the whole opus of a writer can be preserved, where the whole story of his creativity, from handwritten page to published book, can be told.

Enniss enjoys the tension, too, between theory and reality, between the massive, Alexandrian, library-driven impetus to amass writers' archives in their entirety, and the real-life scenarios that see those documents scattered widely and inconveniently.

> One hoping to consult the papers of W. B. Yeats, for example, will need to visit the National Library of Ireland, the Harry Ransom Center at the University of Texas, the New York Public Library, Emory, Boston College, and literally scores of other libraries and archives across the UK, Ireland, and America.

The ultimate conundrum presented by the digital world intrigues him also. While the digitization of paper documents does indeed ensure continued life for them in a new medium, *born digital* documents on the other hand might ultimately defeat the library's efforts to preserve them. Thinking of the torrent of digital ephemera now associated with the modern writer's work—e-mail archives, computer-generated drafts of texts, personal webpages, a multiplicity of storage devices—Enniss asks,

> What institution will have the capacity to invest in the costly and painstaking work required to retain and preserve this highly unstable digital resource? Perhaps more to the point, will future researchers care that drawers of obsolete diskettes of this or that writer have been passed down to us? What new uses will be made of these electronic files if they have managed to survive?

In "Meanings of the Library Today" John P. Wilkin is confident that the library in the twenty-first century is in a much less ambiguous space. His essay riffs on the theme *Plus ça change, plus c'est la même chose*, plays with ideas of constancy and change within the library as an enduring institution, and shows how digital technologies can now make libraries the prime movers of large-scale curation and publishing projects and position them at the heart of intellectual life. Curating, producing and facilitating the use of the cultural record in all its myriad forms, digital and ancient libraries share the same mission; both have "a commitment to sustaining culture despite, and perhaps because of, changes occurring all around." Formerly executive director of the vast HathiTrust Digital Library, Wilkin is well placed to point to the benefits of mass-book-digitization projects such as Google Books and the Internet Archive, and to argue that, in the digital age, libraries will need to find more effective ways of managing print. Attention to four focal "pillars" of activity—curation; engagement with research and learning; publishing; and the management of spaces for users and collections—will ensure the library's relevance in the digital age. We must investigate networked curation, collaborative projects for maintaining print stock; we must become more enthusiastic and energetic *publishers* of content rather than simply minders of it; we must think large scale and collectively and concentrate on the ultimate goal of disseminating scholarly ideas rather than simply cataloguing and shelving the books in which they are expressed.

The collection ends with Librarian of Congress James H. Billington's wise consideration, in his essay "The Modern Library and Global Democracy," of why we continue to go to libraries, why we like them, and what they are basically for. They are, he says, "places for the pursuit of truth." They are where we need to go to allow "the ripening of acquired knowledge into practical wisdom," where we connect with the sum of understanding accumulated by human minds and, in an information-glutted world, discover more than mere data. Libraries facilitate a widening out of thought. They are, he says, "antidotes to fanaticism. They are temples of pluralism, where books that contradict one another sit peacefully side by side on the shelves just as intellectual antagonists work peacefully next to each other in reading rooms." Libraries are for everyone, inclusive in both their membership and holdings.

Exhilaratingly, Billington closes with a clarion call for reading itself.

Books are our guardians of memory, tutors in language, pathways
to reason, and our golden gate to the royal road of imagination. . . .
They are oases of coherence where things are put together rather
than just taken apart.

His conclusion on coherence is heartening and reassuring. The library's
endeavor toward wholeness may indeed be, as Manguel so limpidly puts
it, "doomed to failure," but we continue doggedly to go to libraries, to
read their books and enjoy their spaces, to build new ones, physical and
digital, and to campaign angrily against the closure of others. We remain
delighted by Terry Pratchett's *Discworld* concept of "all libraries everywhere" being connected, and stubbornly enjoy the idea of his infinite
"L-space" (library space) which is the place where our reading of books
takes us.[7] We empathize with others who have known themselves nurtured by libraries ("I have always been happy in libraries," says Alan Bennett; "libraries are about freedom. Freedom to read, freedom of ideas,
freedom of communication," writes Neil Gaiman; "A great library is
anything and everything," affirms Penelope Lively).[8]
    We know there is a paradox about what libraries are and what they are
trying to do, but we defy the contradiction and carry right on.
    We go to libraries perhaps because we love telling ourselves sto-
ries and are drawn to the places where these stories are held. What we
find in libraries helps us to shape things and make life seem coherent.
"However great the confusion of our times and of the information in
our minds, things can still come together in a book," says James H. Billington. Shaped and ordered by their shelves and catalogues, libraries,
like the books they contain, offer the order we crave and into which we
retreat for comfort, confirmation, and the reassurance that somewhere
there is meaning to it all. We like their silence signs, their solid shelves,
their serried rows of reading matter, their comfortable seats—their coffee shops if they have them. In St. Andrews we love the panelled oak
walls and high, shuttered shelves of our historic King James Library and
enjoy seeing new generations of students finding fresh pleasure in it each
year.

These essays look at many libraries and offer many meanings for them over many times. Perhaps after all, however, the simplest definition may be best. "Whatever else you do in life," says the Librarian of Congress, "do not fail to experience the simple pleasure of being alone with a good book on a rainy day."

"A place to read" may be meaning enough for any library.

NOTES

1. Press release from the Chartered Institute of Public Finance and Accountancy December 10, 2012. Online at http://www.cipfa.org/about-cipfa/press-office/latest-press-releases/national-survey-shows-that-library-cuts-have-begun-to-bite. (Reported in Alison Flood, "UK Lost More Than 200 Libraries in 2012." Theguardian.com, December 10, 2012. Online at http://www.theguardian.com/books/2012/dec/10/uk-lost-200-libraries-2012.) Epigraph: Alberto Manguel, *The Library at Night* (New Haven, CT: Yale University Press, 2008), 3.

2. Speak Up for Libraries http://www.speakupforlibraries.org/whoweare.asp; Voices for the Library http://voicesforthelibrary.org.uk/; Library Campaign http://www.librarycampaign.com/; Shout about School Libraries http://www.schoollibraries.org/.

3. James Boswell, *The Life of Samuel Johnson . . . Including a Journal of a Tour to the Hebrides. With Numerous Additions and Notes by John Wilson Croker* (London: John Murray, 1831), vol. 2, 299; Margaret Oliphant, "The Library Window: A Story of the Seen and the Unseen," *Blackwood's Magazine* 159 (January 1896): 1–30.

4. Peter Hoare, ed., *The Cambridge History of Libraries in Britain and Ireland* (Cambridge: Cambridge University Press, 2006); James W. P. Campbell, *The Library: A World History* (London: Thames and Hudson, 2013).

5. Michael H. Harris, *History of Libraries in the Western World* (Metuchen, NJ: Scarecrow Press, 1995); M. Lowell, *Enrichment: A History of the Public Library in the United States in the Twentieth Century* (Metuchen, NJ: Scarecrow Press, 1998); Matthew Battles, *Library: An Unquiet History* (London: Heinemann, 2003); Lucien X. Polastron, *Books on Fire: The Tumultuous Story of the World's Great Libraries* (London: Thames and Hudson, 2007); Stuart Murray, *The Library: An Illustrated History* (New York: Skyhorse; Chicago: ALA Editions, 2009).

6. K. Staikos, *A History of the Library in Western Civilization* (New Castle, DE: Oak Knoll Press, 2004–12); Simon Eliot and Jonathan Rose, eds., *A Companion to the History of the Book* (Malden, MA: Blackwell, 2007).

7. "All libraries everywhere are connected in L-space. All libraries. Everywhere." Terry Pratchett, *Guards! Guards!* (London: Corgi Books, 1989), 223.

8. Alan Bennett, "Baffled at a Bookcase," *London Review of Books* 33.15 (July 28, 2011): 3–7; Neil Gaiman, "Why Our Future Depends on Libraries, Reading and Daydreaming," theguardian.com, October 15, 2013. Online at http://www.theguardian.com/books/2013/oct/15/neil-gaiman-future-libraries-reading-daydreaming. Edited version of Reading Agency Annual Lecture, October 14, 2013; Penelope Lively, *Ammonites and Leaping Fish* (London: Fig Tree, 2013), 190.

PART 1

THE LIBRARY THROUGH TIME

CHAPTER 1

Adventures in Ancient Greek and Roman Libraries

Edith Hall

Libraries are commonly regarded as serious, even austere environments, so it may come as a surprise that it is in a comedy, indeed our earliest surviving and rather raucous Aristophanic comedy, that the first certain literary response to a library occurs. The library belongs to Euripides, one of the three great tragedians of Athens, and the play is Aristophanes's *Acharnians*, first performed in Athens in the late winter of 425 B.C. Athens and Sparta have been fighting the Peloponnesian War for six long years. The hero of the comedy, like many in his audience, is a peasant farmer who has suffered intensely as a result. His name is Dikaiopolis, which roughly translates as "the right way to run a city-state," and he wants to put the case that the Athenians need to make immediate peace with Sparta. He has decided that the most rhetorically effective outfit in which to address his fellow citizens and appeal to their pity consists of a poor man's rags. Since the famous dramatist Euripides was well known for writing tragedies in which royal heroes suffered from straitened circumstances and appeared in rags, Dikaiopolis's first port of call is the house of this tragic poet.

He knocks on the door and asks Euripides's slave—who turns out to be phenomenally intellectual—where his master is. The poet is apparently upstairs, hard at work writing a play. With the aid of some kind of stage machinery, Euripides, sitting elevated in his study, is "rolled out" into view and appears seated in the upper storey of his house. It is time for Dikaiopolis to make his request. But what he actually asks for is not a stage costume as such, but "the tatters of some old drama" (μοι ῥάκιόν τι τοῦ παλαιοῦ δράματος); as he says to Euripides, "I have to treat the chorus to a long oration (ῥῆσιν μακράν), and if I do it badly it will mean death for me" (415–17).

The comic action that ensues plays on the double meaning of the word for "tatters" here, *rhakion*, which alludes both to scraps of papyrus and to ragged old theatrical costumes.[1] Euripides seems to be sitting in a paper jungle constituted by papyri containing his own plays and tells his slave to get the "strips" (*spargana*, 431) of the play featuring the most ragged hero of them all, his famous (and alas, lost) *Telephus*: they are to be found, he says, close to the scraps of two other plays, "on top of the tatters of Thyestes, mixed up with those of Ino" (432–4). While Dikaipolis does collect a hat and other theatrical props from Euripides, the scene only makes sense if he also departs with a papyrus roll containing a famous speech from the tragedy *Telephus*. It is a comic and topicalized subversion of this oration that he shortly performs before the Athenian people.

In this wonderful theatrical episode we can see the invention of the type of Western comedy that creates laughter at the expense of tragedy. We can also see the very birth of the comic image of the library as a place inhabited by cerebral individuals who seem inherently funny to ordinary people of common sense. But the scene also demonstrates how the very *idea* of book assemblage could stimulate artistic inventiveness: the notoriously bookish Euripides's papyrus collection inspires a dazzling scene of comic metatheater. This scene may actually be the ultimate source of the ancient tradition, recorded in Euripides's Hellenistic biography, that he was the first recorded owner of a large personal library, and that this informed the very nature of his plots and poetry (see also Aristophanes's *Frogs* 943, 1049). In this tradition, we can see that the ancient Greeks were aware that the invention of book collections inevitably affected the contents of books, at least where dramatic poetry was concerned.

Since I am a scholar who has specialized in literature, my discussion in this essay will mainly address the relationship between the ancient library and ancient poetry rather than ancient geography, science, or philosophy. Unlike many accounts of ancient libraries, it will not be addressing the nuts and bolts—although they are inherently fascinating—of the cataloguing systems that the poet and librarian Callimachus pioneered more than two millennia before Melvil Dewey created decimal classification. I will not be discussing explicitly the parallels between the ancient library and modern digital projects such as Google Books and Europeana, although excellent examples of such discussions, by classical scholars, are available.[2] It is the *idea* of the library, which we inherit more or less directly from the ancient Mediterranean and near Eastern worlds, that constitutes my primary concern. I would have liked to write about the depiction of libraries in ancient Greek and Roman drama, poetry and fiction, along the lines of Debra Castillo's *The Translated World: A Postmodern Tour of Libraries in Literature* (1984), but there are, sadly, few enough libraries actually evoked or even described in surviving ancient literature.[3] But the dearth of literary representations of ancient book collections is out of all proportion to the vast amount of factual information we possess about them. The finds at Qumran alone have revealed far too much about the physical, material realities of the painstaking ancient process of book reproduction to discuss in a single essay—not just in the Dead Sea Scrolls themselves, but in the ink wells and even the plaster coverings of the desks at which the scribes labored.[4] The subject matter is enormous, even if we focus exclusively on the libraries of the pagan Greeks and Romans, to the exclusion of the Babylonians and Assyrians from whose library organization systems they learned, or of the Phoenicians, Egyptians, and Jews, let alone the early Christians, who inherited their basic library building plan from their pagan precursors.[5]

One man in antiquity was brave enough to attempt to write a comprehensive three-volume treatise on libraries. This was the erudite Varro, an Italian from the venerable Sabine settlement at Reate in central Italy, who in the mid-first century B.C. compiled his study *de Bibliothecis*. Varro's book must have been very substantial, at least to judge from his surviving three-volume work on agriculture. Varro was an encyclopedist, whom Julius Caesar appointed public librarian in Rome in 47 B.C. He was the only known ancient author to be granted the privilege of having a bust in his likeness installed in one of the main Roman libraries while he was still alive (Pliny, *HN* 7.30.115). His treatise may have been commissioned as an ideological accompaniment to Caesar's quest to expand the incipient Roman realm, "to connect world-literature with the world-empire."[6] The uneasy relationship between libraries and imperialism, indeed, will be a recurring theme in this essay, closely tied up with the relationship between libraries and cultural creativity. But first it is important to underline the sheer scale of the topic of the library in the ancient Greek and Roman worlds. Even as early as the first century B.C., before the great surge in library-building that was to occur under the high Empire, notably under the Emperor Trajan in the early second century A.D., Varro's project in compiling a universal historical treatise on libraries would have daunted anyone but him. And the history of great pagan libraries was to continue for several centuries thereafter, until 543 A.D., when the Emperor Justinian finally closed down the temple of Isis at Philae in Egypt, built under the same Ptolemies who built the library at Alexandria. Behind the massive colonnade of the Philae temple at least one massive room had functioned as a library.

The papyrus on which most ancient Greek and Latin books were recorded, as an organic material, was extremely vulnerable to rotting and wear and tear. Aristotle bequeathed his personal library to his student Theophrastus, but two generations later the collection of rolls ended up in the hands of some "ordinary people" of Scepsis in Asia Minor, who did not know how to store its precious contents (Strabo 13.1.54). When they realized that the books were actually extremely valuable, they hid them from the book collectors sent out by the rich Attalid dynasty at nearby Pergamum, who wanted to build up the collection in their library. Unfortunately, the uneducated owners of the books decided to conceal them as if they were gold or coins, in a dug-out trench. They were damaged dreadfully by both moisture and moths. When they were finally purchased, it was by a man who loved to collect books rather than by a philosopher, and he "restored" the texts in such an amateurish way that, when they were eventually published, they were found to be full of mistakes.

On the other hand, forgers sometimes stained brand new papyri to make them look like authentic ancient texts, perhaps those actually written by one of the famous canonical writers, in order to increase their monetary value. The ancients were very clear that there was a difference between the materialistic bibliophile who collected books as commodities, and the cultured person who actually understood their contents. The nouveau riche Trimalchio whose banquet is described by Petronius boasts that his libraries rivalled those of the emperor.[7] Some rich men did indeed use banquets as opportunities to display books that they had never studied (Seneca, *Dial.* 9.9.4). Lucian wrote a diatribe attacking a Syrian, *Against the Ignorant Book-Collector*. This rich man buys shiploads of books, is never seen without one in his hand, and endlessly glues and trims them, applying cedar oil and saffron, and keeping them in purple silk and leather cases. But he is deluding himself because "he thinks that by the multitude of books" he can rectify his "deficient education."

Libraries held many different kinds of collections. Some of the most important to advances in ancient intellectual life were the specialist libraries that mainly or exclusively collected the writings of members of a particular philosophical school, such as the Stoics, whose center of learning was on the island of Rhodes. There the great Stoic polymath scholar Posidonius, usually called "the Rhodian" but actually a native of Apamea in Syria, practiced during the first half of the first century B.C. Pompey, Caesar, Cicero, and Brutus all studied there. Rhodes was also renowned as a center of astronomical studies, a particular interest of the bookworm Emperor Tiberius, who spent several years on the island.[8] Other archives might house a special collection of, for example, theater scripts. The most famous of these was the depository in Athens, organized by the theater-loving orator and statesman Lycurgus, ruler of Athens from 336 until 324 B.C. It was probably housed in the old Athenian Metröon in the marketplace (originally a council house rather than a collection of papers), along with other documents related to the history and activities of the state. Lycurgus probably began the collection of plays because there were so many emendations being made by contemporary actors to the authentic texts of the plays of the great three tragedians of the previous century—Aeschylus and Sophocles as well as Euripides. Some of these plays were very popular in the performance repertoire, and thus vulnerable to creative adaptation.[9]

Libraries varied massively in scale as well as contents. On the one hand there were small book collections that could be carried around in handy containers, like the portable *scrinium* or *cista* on a Roman mosaic in Tunis shown in figure 1.1. It is probably to be imagined as holding the "parts" or whole plays in which the actor portrayed here specialized, or that had been written or enjoyed by the seated man, depending on

Fig. 1.1. Portable *scrinium* or *cista* on a Roman mosaic in Tunis. Reproduced by kind permission of the Musée archéologique de Sousse, Tunisia.

whether he represents an author who has collaborated with the actor or, more likely, his patron.[10] At the other end of the scale, there were vast libraries containing hundreds of thousands of papyrus rolls, housed in magnificent, purpose-built architectural edifices. In between these extremes there were private libraries in which solitary misanthropes hid from the world, like that of the tragedian Euripides; Xenophon remarks on the unparalleled size of the book collection amassed by the philosopher Euthydemus (*Mem.* 4.2.8). Other private libraries were large enough to accommodate the leading lights of a whole philosophical school comfortably, such as the "Villa of the Papyri" found in 1752 at Herculaneum. This was the vacation villa of no less a figure than Julius Caesar's father-in-law, Calpurnius Piso, where the famous philosopher

Philodemos of Gadara supervised his patron's magnificent collection of Epicurean texts.[11] The modern technology of multispectral imaging has allowed the remains of some of them, burnt by the same volcanic eruption that destroyed Pompeii in 79 A.D., to be deciphered and published by modern scholars.

The first public library of all may have been established by Clearchus, tyrant of Heraclea on the south coast of the Black Sea, who died in 353 B.C.[12] This Pontic despot had been educated at Athens by the two leading intellectuals of the time, Plato and Isocrates, and the tradition that he built a library is connected with the ancient perception that the Greeks of the Black Sea were anxious to avoid the accusation that they lived in a cultural backwater. But it was the people of the first two generations after Alexander the Great who saw the establishment of the first libraries that can be described as "public" in the modern sense, even though scholars disagree on the nature and degree of public access, especially given that literacy rates in many ancient cities may not have exceeded 10 to 20 percent of the population. Moreover, we are not in a position to tell whether most public libraries allowed borrowing of books at all, even to respected and trusted members: an inscription believed to have belonged to the library that Trajan built at Athens in 132 A.D. specifies its opening hours and proclaims, "No book shall be taken out. We have sworn it!"[13] The first great public libraries were set up in the kingdoms established by Alexander's successors, notably the Ptolemies' near-legendary library in the Egyptian Greek city of Alexandria. The city had been founded by the Macedonian conqueror himself in 331 B.C. He had been instructed on the precise location by the shade of Homer, who visited him in a dream (Plutarch, *Life of Alexander* ch. 26).

The Alexandrian library was said to have been designed with the assistance of the Athenian Peripatetic philosopher Demetrius of Phaleron, who brought with him to Egypt authentic Aristotelian intellectual credentials, having been taught by Aristotle's student Theophrastus. The library was either adjacent to or (at least originally) constituted part of the Alexandrian "Museum" (*Mouseion* or "temple of the Muses"); other book collections, of all sizes, were often attached to or housed within temples. Indeed, in the late fourth century, Demetrius had educated himself by reading Aristotle's own books, assembled in another *Mouseion* at Athens. Some libraries could be housed in public baths, which served as the ancient equivalent of a "leisure center," where social and sexual transactions could be made with ease in a pleasant environment; Caracalla's imposing baths, built at Rome in the second decade of the third century A.D., contained one room of texts in Greek and another one in Latin. Some libraries also served as public records offices, as bookshops, restaurants, and scientific laboratories. The library of Pantainos at Athens seems to have supported itself by renting out shops within the building complex, including one to a marble mason.[14] Libraries under Augustus could host meetings of the Roman Senate; large ones with a colonnade often provided a place to take quite a lengthy stroll. Libraries penetrated the unconscious mind to feature in people's dreams: Tiberius dreamt about the vast and beautiful statue of Apollo Temenites, which he brought from Syracuse to adorn the library of the New Temple (Suetonius, *Life of Tiberius* 74). You could build a library to serve as a sepulchre for your eminent family or forebears. Celsus buried his father, who had been governor of the province (Roman Asia), in a lead coffin, encased within a marble sarcophagus that he had set into a vaulted recess of the Ephesus library;[15] Dio Chrysostom interred his wife and child in the courtyard of the library at Prusa in northwestern Turkey. Libraries could even be used in courtship rituals: in his attempt to impress Cleopatra, Mark Antony made her a present of the great library of Pergamum, all two hundred thousand volumes of it, collected by the ancestral rivals of Cleopatra's Ptolemy family—the Attalids.

The evidence for these heterogeneous libraries of ancient Greece and Rome is equivalently diverse. We have dug up large library buildings with no books left, like the beautiful Roman provincial library excavated in the grid-city at Timgad in Algeria by the French in the early twentieth century. This quickly became the colonial set for avant-garde Modernist actresses from the Comédie Française, such as Mme. Silvaine, who performed a version of Sophocles's *Electra* there in 1907. We have dug up a rubbish dump containing whole libraries, but not a single brick, at the site of the ancient Greek town of Oxyrhynchus on a branch of the Nile in Upper Egypt. The "Oxyrhynchus papyri" include some of the contents of at least one impressive Oxyrhynchite private book collection, which contained copies of esteemed poetic works such as Euripides's *Hypsipyle*,

Pindar's *Paeans* and an extensive collection of prose writers. On the other hand, we know about some fascinating libraries even though they have disappeared altogether, along with their entire contents, because they were discussed as institutions in surviving written sources. One example is of course the Library of Alexandria, but another, later, and more typical instance is the library that Pliny the Younger funded lavishly at Comum (now Como) in northern Italy, north of Milan, in about 97 A.D.

The reason we know about Pliny's library is because there survives an inscription recording his benefactions to the town (*Corpus Inscriptionum Latinarum* 5.5262), along with a letter to a friend about it (*Epistle* 1.8, to Pompeius Saturninus), which accompanied a copy of the speech he delivered to some of the town magistrates at its inauguration. The speech itself does not survive, but the letter does.[16] Now this Pliny was a rich and well-regarded imperial administrator and senator. His quandary in the letter is whether he should publish the speech, given that in it he fulsomely praises the munificence of his ancestors. He fears that this praise of his own forebears, if circulated outside Comum, will offend against canons of modesty. He also describes some of the other themes the missing oration addressed: the presence of the library would itself encourage his townsmen in virtuous studies; his own contempt of riches and freedom from the chains of avarice; the commendation his benefaction deserved because it was the result not of a passing fancy but of deliberate resolution; his decision to bestow on his townsmen a library rather than shows or gladiators. This last point is particularly interesting, because another inscription shows that a city's populace might have reason to hope that the sort of benefactor who gave them a library might also donate gladiators: one such euergetist capped a gift of a library to his grateful public with no fewer than twelve pairs of these violent public entertainers (*Corpus Inscriptionum Latinarum* 3.1.607).

Regardless of whether the citizens of Comum would have preferred a benefactor more focussed on live spectacle, Pliny's gift is important in the history of ancient libraries. It seems to have been the first library ever donated by a private individual to a town in the Roman Empire, but it preceded "a spate of library-building throughout."[17] In libraries like that bestowed on Comum by Pliny, the benefaction signalled the importance of an individual statesman, from a particular landowning senatorial

family, and his role in fostering the maturity and cultural prestige of what
was (in the case of Comum) still a relatively new *colonia* of the Roman
Empire. The selection of the books within it might be assumed fundamentally to reinforce, rather than question or undermine, the values, self-
definition and self-framing through historiography of that individual, his
family, and the imperial regime he served. The selection or *de*selection of
books for inclusion in a library's collection was already acknowledged by
historians in antiquity to have been a charged political issue. Suetonius
tells us that if the Emperor Caligula had been allowed to have his way,
Homer, Virgil, and Livy, whom he loathed, would have been expelled,
both their works and their images, "*ex omnibus bibliothecis*" ("from all
libraries," Suetonius, *Life of Caligula*, 34):

> He even considered destroying the poems of Homer, demanding to
> know why he should not be allowed the same right as Plato, who
> excluded Homer from his ideal republic. Moreover, he very nearly
> took away the texts and statues of Vergil and of Livy from all the
> libraries, for he criticised Vergil as being a writer devoid of literary
> skill and erudition, and Livy as a wordy and inaccurate historian.

On the other hand, we may have so much of the historian Tacitus solely
because his namesake, the third-century Emperor Marcus Claudius Tacitus (who was actually no relation), ordered all the libraries to make comprehensive collections of his works (*Historia Augusta*, "Tacitus" 10.3).

The social and political role of the ancient library, however, was not
just a matter of whose written versions of history, reality, and experience
were made available to the grateful public. Of far more lasting significance, it seems to me, is the actual concept of the library as an institution
where the whole resource constitutes something infinitely greater than
the sum of the parts. The parts are the individual records left by individual writers; the whole is something far more ambitious: an instrument
designed to preserve intact the memory of humankind. The scholars at
the library of Alexandria undoubtedly undertook the Herculean task
of preserving the entire literary output of the Greeks, which is why they
went to such extreme lengths to obtain a copy of every known work, even
placing all books that arrived in the port of their city under embargo

until copies could be made. By conceiving this idea, the ancient Greeks also had to have conceived the opposite idea, that such a memory could be lost—a new, literate version of the universal myth of the fall or of the apocalypse. That is, the ancient experiment in the creation of collections of texts that could even *attempt* to include everything that had ever been written in the history of the world changed our mental landscape forever, and so did the idea that the entire memory of the human race was vulnerable to complete erasure. And because there really were attempts in the library at Alexandria to include at least Greek translations of the great works of other cultures and religions, notably the great books of the Jews, it has become possible, at least by our twenty-first century, for libraries to fulfill a new sociopolitical role as symbolizing a cosmopolitan and tolerant ideal.

This is an ideal represented by the ancient library of Alexandria in, for example, the Spanish movie *Agora* (2009). The thoughtful actress Rachel Weisz leapt at the role of Hypatia, an Egyptian Greek scholar in the fourth century A.D. Hypatia was the daughter of the Euclidean mathematician Theon, alongside whom she worked at the library of Alexandria. In the film she attempts—in vain—to save the library's unique collections from destruction when the Roman administration allows angry Christians to destroy the institutions symbolizing what they regarded as abominable pagan lore. But in this twenty-first century reading, Hypatia virtually personifies the library, as representative of an admirable, questioning, science-based, intellectual culture failing to withstand the arrival of an ignorant and fundamentalist strain of Christian religion. Weisz has said that she was attracted to the role because the science and philosophy physically embodied in Hypatia as she worked at the library represent at least the possibility of a tolerant multicultural future for humankind. Weisz claims that the film is "about today," because the conflict it portrays is analogous to the struggle in America of "Christian fundamentalism vs. science." Hypatia stands for "teaching Darwinian evolutionary theory or stem cell research." She is "trying to come to grips with our place in the universe and she's thinking not existentially of herself, she's thinking of the planet Earth . . . it's a humanist film."[18]

I do not know whether Weisz, any more than the scriptwriter Mateo Gil Rodríguez and the film's director, Alejandro Amenábar (who also collaborated on the script), is aware of Hypatia's cultural lineage. Their female intellectual lead is a direct descendant of the heroine of Charles Kingsley's *Hypatia* of 1853, a novel that first put her on the map of popular culture as a romantic figure.[19] Paradoxically, for Kingsley, Hypatia and her library did not so much represent Greek humanism as his own brand of highly adversarial and combative theology; he reassures us that his pagan Hypatia does indeed convert to an esoteric brand of Christianity before she is destroyed. But Kingsley's "muscular Christianity," although embracing science and celebrating sex, was anything but tolerant toward other denominations and religions. The novel was a strident polemic against Roman Catholicism and High-Church Anglicanism, the "New Foes with an Old Face" of its alternative title.

Kingsley's novel was enormously popular and produced several spin-offs in the Victorian theater, including a famous stage adaptation performed at the Theatre Royal, Haymarket, in 1893 (see figure 1.2).

The novel, the plays, and the recent movie all describe the Library of Alexandria and the woman who represents it in very similar terms. The fall of the library is epitomized by the sadistic assault on Hypatia's inevitably beautiful, fragile, papyrus-like white body, finally narrated in Kingsley's chapter 29. But readers have first met her in chapter 2, evocatively entitled "A Dying World," which finds the heroine at work in "that famous library," which "towered up, the wonder of the world, its white roof bright against the rainless blue; and beyond it, among the ridges and pediments of noble buildings, a broad glimpse of the bright blue sea." Hypatia is as beautiful as her environment:

> Her features, arms, and hands were of the severest and grandest type of old Greek beauty, at once showing everywhere the high development of the bones, and covering them with that firm, round, ripe outline, and waxy morbidezza of skin, which the old Greeks owed to their continual use not only of the bath and muscular exercise, but also of daily unguents. There might have seemed to us too much sadness in that clear gray eye; too much self-conscious restraint in those sharp curved lips; too much affectation in the studied severity of her posture as she read, copied, as it seemed, from some old vase or bas-relief. But the glorious grace and beauty of every line

HYPATIA—MISS JULIA NEILSON
ORESTES—MR. WALLER.   ISSACHAR—MR. TREE

Fig. 1.2. Hypatia on stage. Photograph by Alfred Ellis in theater program for *Hypatia*, by G. Stuart Ogilvie, produced by the Theatre Royal, Haymarket, Monday, January 2, 1893.

of face and figure would have excused, even hidden those defects, and we should have only recognised the marked resemblance to the ideal portraits of Athene which adorned every panel of the walls.[20]

When we hear Hypatia's thoughts in this section of Kingsley's novel (and its later imitations), she is contemplating the destruction of the library that she now fears is imminent: she visualizes in her mind the smashing of the statues: "The libraries are plundered. The alcoves are silent." She pledges to "struggle to the last against the new and vulgar superstitions of a rotting age, for the faith of my forefathers, for the old gods, the old heroes, the old sages who gauged the mysteries of heaven and earth."[21]

Of course Hypatia herself, as a Greek-speaker, did not call the library a "library," but a *bibliothēkē*, a "place to put rolls made out of papyrus (*byblos*)." This Greek word itself was not the sole contender: we might instead have inherited the word *bibliophylakion*, used in Greek of the royal archives in Egypt, which as a place to *guard* papyri rather than just *put* them might have been preferred by a certain stereotype of the possessive librarian. The Greek word that came to be universally used in antiquity, however, is preferred in German (*Bibliothek*), Russian (библиотека), French, Spanish, Italian and many others. The English word has different resonances: its root is *liber*, the ancient term for the skin, bark, or rind of plants. It was used to designate the thin rind of the ancient Egyptian papyrus,[22] and eventually, much as the term for tree trunk *caudex* was adopted in the word for a codex, the bark itself, the *liber* (with a short "i") became the book. But our idea of the library in English-speaking lands is ultimately if unconsciously affected by our adoption of a word from another semantic root than the factual, descriptive *bibliothēkē*.

There has been considerable confusion between the idea of books and the foliage-related Roman god Līber Pater, whose name was connected with the root *līber* where the "i" is long, an adjective that means "free": Līber Pater, associated with adult rights to free speech, was a favorite of the plebeian class and the recipient of the great festival of the Līberalia on March 17. But the false etymology, disguised by the variation in length of that vowel "i," seems already to have been causing problems in antiquity, since Līber Pater is often depicted with accoutrements that remind the viewer of botanical bark. A fine example comes from Dacia in modern Romania, the last province to be added to the Roman Empire and one of the first to leave it. The capital of Dacia was Apulum, where a major sanctuary and statue of the Roman god Līber Pater has been discovered: his *thyrsus* is clearly decorated with bark.[23] And in English-speaking lands, the visual rather than aural similarity between the words *library*, *liberty*, *liberalism*, and *liberal arts* has been one of the most ideologically potent results that can be imagined of a completely false etymology. I speak as a regular user of the online and alliteratively entitled *Library of Liberty*.[24]

We have already noted the possibility that Julius Caesar saw the potential of libraries as a tool or at least adornment of empire. But he is also one of the several putative villains in the long-standing and multiply authored mystery tale *Who Destroyed the Library of Alexandria?* (The other main suspects are anti-intellectual Christian bishops in the years after the death of Hypatia and the Arabs in the seventh century A.D.)[25] Caesar has therefore sometimes been seen in a more philistine light. In act 2 of Bernard Shaw's *Caesar and Cleopatra*, there is a dialogue in the royal palace of Alexandria between Julius Caesar and Theodotus of Chios, a historical figure whom Shaw found in Plutarch's *Life of Brutus* 33.3 and the surviving summary of Livy book 112. Theodotus is characterized as an unscrupulous rhetorician and tutor to the young King Ptolemy; he is also one of the opportunist and brutal murderers of Pompey. Theodotus brings news to Julius Caesar that fire has spread from his ships and the "library of Alexandria is in flames." Caesar's response is simply, "Is that all?" Theodotus is incredulous, outraged: "All! Caesar: will you go down to posterity as a barbarous soldier too ignorant to know the value of books?" Caesar answers that although he is an author himself, "it is better that the Egyptians should live their lives than dream them away with the help of books." The dialogue continues:

THEODOTUS: What is burning there is the memory of mankind.
CAESAR: A shameful memory. Let it burn.
THEODOTUS (WILDLY): Will you destroy the past?
CAESAR: Ay, and build the future with its ruins. But harken,
    Theodotus, teacher of kings: you who valued Pompey's head
    no more than a shepherd values an onion, and who now kneel

to me, with tears in your old eyes, to plead for a few sheepskins scrawled with errors. I cannot spare you a man or a bucket of water just now; but you *shall* pass freely out of the palace.[26]

This tragicomic scene crystallizes the tensions surrounding the legend of the destruction of the great ancient library at Alexandria, and metonymically the idea of the library defined far more widely. Shaw here puts his finger on the psychological wounds that lie just beneath the charged symbolism of the lost library of Alexandria and of all lost libraries everywhere.

The context is imperialism—indeed, the advance into northeast Africa of the Roman Empire, destined to become the greatest empire the West had ever yet seen. Ethnicity is a crucial issue; Shaw has Caesar refer to the users of the library not as Ptolemaic or Macedonian Greeks but rather patronizingly as "Egyptians," a term that bore a particular meaning to an audience of Britons at the play's premiere in 1898; their armed forces had themselves bombarded and ruined Alexandria in 1882 and were currently occupying the country. But Shaw also sets up a series of antitheses that the idea of the library triggers in his ancient interlocutors' minds: memory versus action, the past versus the future, vicarious experience versus firsthand experience of life, dream versus reality, the rights to survival of living humans over the right to survival of the thoughts of dead humans, recorded on the skin of dead animals. Even the toxic issue of social class is lightly touched on: Theodotus suggests that Caesar, unlike cultured Greek teachers of rhetoric, is but an ignorant, barbarous soldier: Caesar retorts that Theodotus's cavalier attitude to Pompey's life reduces him to the status of a shepherd. Here the contrasting images also insinuate the conflict between war and peace, the man of action versus the passive recluse, the soldier's weapon and the shepherd's staff, between European war stories and European pastoral.

In this scene, the ancient library becomes a sign of infinitely more than a collection, however large, of papyrus rolls. The destruction of the library of Alexandria—whoever was really responsible—becomes overdetermined: it *must* vanish because the tensions it crystallized have never yet been resolved. It is evidence that time can never be reversed because the dead are divided by silence from the living, even as it transcends time in representing a form of dialogue between them. It takes on a quasi-metaphysical status. Just as the Sumerians called libraries "the ordainers of the universe,"[27] the Romans could even envisage the goddesses who determine human destiny, the Parcae or Fates, as librarians: in the fifth century A.D. the late pagan writer Martianus Capella described the Parcae as "librarians of the gods and the guardians of their archive, *utpote librariae Superum archivumque custodes*" (1.65).

The library as an idea does indeed unify opposites: like rhetoric, it has no immanent ethics, no immanent qualities of virtue or vice, but is a tool that can both liberate and oppress. Bernard Shaw had of course not read Michel Foucault's *The Archaeology of Knowledge* (1969), in which book collections or archives of any kind were subjected to their first major critique as institutions for the collation of knowledge, created by mechanisms of power, and further reinforcing the exercise of that power. Shaw did not know that by the late twentieth century there would emerge a powerful feminist and postcolonial suspicion of the universal, monolithic repository of knowledge. He did not know that people would claim the impossibility in any ideologically conflicted world, let alone a truly democratic one, of a single institution accommodating the inevitably antithetical subjectivities of its inhabitants. Nor had George Eliot read Foucault when in *Middlemarch* (1874) she made the library of the classical pedant Edward Casaubon stand for everything that prevented the flowering of real intellectual enquiry, let alone love, in the education-starved Dorothea's soul.

When he claimed that Alexandria was the cultural capital of the world by founding its library in the early third century B.C., Ptolemy I Soter had certainly not read Foucault any more than Eliot or Shaw. Ancient creators of libraries were always either very powerful (like Ptolemy or Trajan) or just rich (like Pliny): for equally obvious reasons, they always presented the creation of a library, whether public or private, as a self-evidently good thing. They would all have decried the destruction of the libraries of Alexandria or anywhere else in univocal chorus with Shaw's brutal hyperintellectual professor of rhetoric, Theodotus of Chios. Most of the voices we can hear from antiquity, almost by definition the voices of well-read men, talked about libraries only in ways that imply that they improved and refined the quality of their own literary outputs. The orator and philosopher Cicero greatly valued his own collection of books and regarded the library as the "mind" or "brain" of a household (*ad Atticum* IV.8). The famed rhetorical teacher and literary critic Longinus was described wholly flatteringly by Eunapius in his *Lives of the Sophists* (456 B) as a "living library (*bibliothēkē empsychos*) and a walking museum." So it is important to ask whether there were, in fact, voices in ancient Greek or Latin that ever foreshadowed Shaw's Caesar or Foucault in suggesting that there might be negative consequences for culture or civilization—politically, intellectually, or aesthetically negative—in the uncritical adulation of libraries. Did the ancients ever ask whether the existence of libraries might actually be detrimental to the kind of writing and scholarship that were produced by the culture that had created these collections, let alone detrimental to its emotional and spiritual health?

The answer is "yes, a few." When it comes to historiography, there is one early voice raised loudly against the use of libraries by the writer. It is the voice of Polybius, a Greek from Arcadia who rose to prominence at Rome at the time of the Republic in the second century B.C., and travelled incessantly. In his *Histories* he launched an assault on an earlier Greek historian, Timaeus of Sicily. Timaeus is said to have spent four decades in Athenian libraries writing a massive forty-book *Histories* of Greece from earliest times to the Punic Wars. Polybius has at least two axes to grind against Timaeus, one political and one more private and Oedipal, but even so, what he says about libraries reveals in the ancient discourse one strand to which we rarely have access:

> Nature has given us two instruments, as it were, by the aid of which we inform ourselves and inquire about everything. These are hearing and sight, and of the two sight is much more veracious. . . . Now, Timaeus enters on his inquiries by the pleasanter of the two roads, but the inferior one. For he entirely avoids employing his eyes and prefers to employ his ears. Now the knowledge derived from hearing being of two sorts, Timaeus diligently pursued the one, the reading of books, as I have above pointed out, but was very remiss in his use of the other, the interrogation of living witnesses. It is easy enough to perceive what caused him to make this choice. Inquiries from books may be made without any danger or hardship, provided

only that one takes care to have access to a town rich in documents or to have a library near at hand. After that one has only to pursue one's researches in perfect repose and compare the accounts of different writers without exposing oneself to any hardship. Personal inquiry, on the contrary, requires severe labour and great expense, but is exceedingly valuable and is the most important part of history. (Polybius 12.27).

Polybius certainly had a point: how many of us have had our perspectives altered on a poem or historical event by visiting a physical place related to it or talking to an eyewitness? The experimental although different ways in which the traveller Herodotus and the soldier Thucydides wrote history, in an era before libraries on any scale and with few predecessors in historiography, might have become severely compromised if they had stayed in Athens all their adult lives.

When it comes to poetry rather than prose, there were also a few who seem to have believed that libraries were not always beneficial to the artistic quality of new works produced. The most famous of all is the Sceptical Pyrrhonist and satirical poet Timon of Phlius (near Corinth), who spent time in Asia Minor and then Athens. He was a coeval of the famous poets associated with the early decades of the library in Alexandria under Ptolemy II: Theocritus (most famous for his pastoral *Idylls*), Apollonius (author of our only surviving Greek epic, albeit a short one, on the theme of Jason and the Argonauts), and Callimachus. The independent-minded Timon despised their great project of editing all the texts of the old poets, along with Zenodotus, the first librarian and "corrector" or critical editor (*diorthōtēs*) of Homer. When Timon was asked by Aratus how best to obtain the "pure" text of Homer, he replied that the only way would be "If we could find the old copies, and not those with modern emendations."

Timon, who was *not* financially supported at Alexandria, sarcastically expressed his views on its library in another famous quip. This is traditionally translated, "Many are feeding in populous Egypt, scribblers on papyrus, ceaselessly wrangling in the bird-cage of the Muses" (fr. 12 Diels, quoted in Athenaeus 1.22d). Timon's brilliant image was often understood as deriding this generation of versifiers as unimpressive poetasters who were salaried but caged, suggesting that they were somehow censored by the blue pencil of the autocratic Ptolemy family. It is true that these poets were very self-conscious about their craft, and discussed their disagreements within their poems. But Alan Cameron has argued that the famous image of the cage is a misleading translation of the *talaros* of the Muses, which means something plaited out of twigs or wicker, but usually in the shape of a dish, and therefore is more likely to suggest "nest" than "cage."[28] The image is, rather, of rivalrous chicks in a nest, trying to out-squawk each other to get the most feed. It may also be relevant that the term *talaros* is often used of women's workbaskets, especially those containing wool ready for weaving, thus implying that these dependent poets are or have become somehow effeminized. The possibly unmanly poets, who are being financially supported in Ptolemy's library and guzzling his food, are all scribbling on the papyri, but are also, of their own free will, *vying* for attention and stipends, perhaps in contrast to Timon's own far more independent and freely spoken satires. These, interestingly, did *not* survive for us to read in more than pitiful quotations. Perhaps not enough librarians believed that they were worth copying out for posterity.

Yet the most important question here is this: might we have enjoyed better poetry from these men if they had *not* been so immersed in the contents of the library, let alone so focussed on praising the monarchy that bankrolled it? The aesthetic and the political became entwined in early Alexandria in a wholly new way, completely different from the panegyric literature of earlier praise poets such as Pindar and Bacchylides, precisely because of the presence of all those old books. The weight of the past Hellenic literary tradition necessarily exerted an influence over the new poetry of the new political order. That first generation of Hellenistic poets certainly produced fascinating new mixtures of preexisting genres, and created new and sometimes striking aesthetic effects in the process. In the case of Theocritus, the dialogue-rich pastoral poem whose subject matter is actually poetics is perhaps the one truly original type of poetry to have emerged from the library. But almost as quickly as Ptolemy had brought the great poets of his new empire to its headquarters in Alexandria, innovation in Greek poetry ceased almost altogether; the only genre in which really experimental advances are subsequently perceptible is the epigram. The tonal variety of late epigram is indeed remarkable. In 1975, Tony Harrison published his translation of a selection of epigrams by Palladas, a fourth-century citizen of Alexandria, and one of the last pagan poets, whose uniquely cynical voice Harrison has described as "the authentic snarl of a man trapped physically in poverty and persecution, and metaphysically in a deep sense of the futile."[29] But this epigrammatic form itself was of course of great antiquity and had been first brought to one type of sonorous, melancholy perfection centuries before by Simonides of Ceos.

I must tread carefully here. While my own aesthetic taste has always run to larger-scale artistic projects of the archaic oral epic poets and the fifth-century democratic dramatists, there have always been admirers of Hellenistic Greek literature, with its self-consciousness, irony, allusiveness, erudition, and often challenging new juxtapositions of inherited literary tropes. There are many scholars who are not put off by its ideological project, which was to celebrate the new political order, and show how the old poetic forms and themes were adaptable to suit a monarchical society newly centered on the north coast of Africa. Indeed, interest in Hellenistic Greek poetry, much of which was produced at the Alexandrian library, has been massively increased over the last couple of decades, at least within Classical scholarship, for three particular reasons. First, there have been some undeniably exciting new finds on papyrus, especially the poetry book of Posidippus of Pella, which has given us 102 poems by this contemporary of Theocritus, Apollonius, and Callimachus, only two of which were known before. This amazing papyrus was not published until 2001: it had been sitting in Milan for many centuries, having been used to wrap an Egyptian mummy in Fayum in about 280 B.C. (Milan Papyrus P.Mil.Vogl. VIII 309). The second reason for the current high profile of Hellenistic poetry has been the current postcolonial fascination with hybridity, migration, and diasporas, which has renewed interest in the whole Ptolemaic project of creating a new Greek cultural metropolis in Egypt, with all the cultural syncretism in relation to indigenous Egyptian religion and ceremonial practices that that entailed. The third reason is more aesthetic—our own postmodern aesthetics are arguably far too welded to past forms of literature: at the cinema, we have entered a whole new age of nostalgia and remakes and pastiches of old movies and television programs, as if seams of truly new creativity have run dry.[30] Our current obsession with endless recycling of inherited artefacts inevitably makes us relate to the highly wrought, allusive pseudo-archaic *Hymns* of Callimachus, or the whimsical, precious response to the atavistic genre of dactylic hexameter epic in Apollonius's *Argonautica*.

The fourth reason for the increased recent interest in Alexandrian literature connected with the library is that it has become all too clear to scholars of Latin literature that many of their greatest poets, from Catullus and Virgil to Propertius, Horace, and Ovid, themselves were responding at every turn to the Hellenistic Greeks. Studying Callimachus and his coevals can therefore only enhance our understanding of the Augustans, who so admired them. What the Roman poets heard in the Alexandrians was an allusiveness, a sophisticated knowingness, a style, a grace, a literariness, the appeal of the miniature, of chiaroscuro, of studied asymmetry, and a delicate, refined sensibility. They yearned to make these qualities possible using the much smaller vocabulary, rougher consonants and more limited metrical precedents available in their Latin tongue. To do so, they needed books to fertilize their poetic imaginations and refine their literary sensibilities: Catullus implies that the personal library he needed to help him write poems contained a myriad of texts (68.36). In order to write satire, Horace felt he needed copies of Plato, Menander, Eupolis and Archilochus at hand, as well as creative energy (2.3.11–12). By the mid-first century B.C., Greek Literature had been in existence for at least seven centuries, but literature in Latin for not much more than two, and the simple quantitative difference between the outputs in the two languages must have become painfully obvious with the opening of the first public Roman libraries in the early Augustan era, especially as it was customary to shelve works in the two languages separately, often in quite different rooms. The Augustan poets consciously strove to fill up the "Latin" shelves erected for the desired new Latin canon with their new works. Their frequent claims to having deserved immortality, or to being heirs and descendants of the Alexandrian bards, underlines how much the existence of libraries was encouraging them to compose.[31]

In doing so, I can't help thinking that their achievement was far greater than that of the scribblers out-twittering and out-smarting one another in the financial safety of the Ptolemaic birds' nest. One day, moreover, those old mythical themes really would run out of steam, as Juvenal vituperates in the famous opening to the first of his *Satires*. He can't stand listening any more to all that old stuff about Theseus, Telephus, and Orestes, the grove of Mars and the cave of Vulcan, Aeacus, and the golden fleece: all the new poems on these themes, he snorts, are just so much wasted paper. But Juvenal may have put his finger on at least part of the reason why these themes proved so difficult to dislodge and replace—or at least supplement—with new ones. Under Ptolemaic monarchs or Roman emperors alike, the old stories were the safest: you don't have to worry about incurring the wrath of the mighty if you stick eternally, however inventively, with the heroic adventures of Aeneas or Achilles.

If I have come perilously close to claiming that the emergence of great libraries of literature had a hand in killing off innovation and experiment in Greek poetry, I need to stress that I am convinced that they were a crucial fertilizing agent for many genres of scholarly prose—geography, scientific treatises, biography, Lucianic dialogue. The third director of the Alexandrian Library, for example, and the successor of the poet Callimachus, was Eratosthenes of Cyrene, an incomparable geographer who succeeded in calculating the circumference of our planet to within fifty miles. It is almost inconceivable that Claudius Ptolemy could ever have made the advances in astronomy that resulted in his *Almagest* (more correctly known as his *Mathēmatikē Syntaxis*) without the earlier treatises on cosmology, trigonometry, and geometry that he could consult in the libraries of Roman Egypt. But I am also convinced that the libraries of the ancient Greek world, which may have stifled innovation in Greek poetry, were a crucial fertilizing agent for poetry in *Latin*. For by 30 B.C., the time of the deaths of the last Ptolemies on the Egyptian throne, Cleopatra VII and her son by Julius Caesar, Ptolemy Caesar or "Caesarion," the Romans were implementing "the most momentous cultural appropriation that has ever taken place anywhere in the world. They conducted the wholesale transfer of the major elements of Hellenic religion, myth, legend, philosophy, literature, manners, customs, and plastic arts to Roman setting and their translation into a Roman idiom, through which they have come down to us."[32]

In order to illustrate this conviction, I want to explore two poems by Ovid, written nearly three centuries later than Callimachus. When Ovid wrote them he had been sent into exile, as punishment for some misdemeanor closely connected with his love poetry, to Tomi, now Constanta in Romania. The idea of the library, for Ovid, had indeed become representative of civilization as a whole. The first and last poem of the third book of his *Tristia* could never have been written without the abstract *idea* of the library, as well as his memories of concrete libraries at Rome, although part of the bitter point Ovid is making is that in the Euxine he is desperately deprived of intellectual stimulus of any kind whatever.

The first poem of the book mostly takes the form of a speech by the book itself. The book, like Ovid, is homeless, and desperately seeking a library shelf on which to settle: it opens by addressing the reader as if s/he is a person in the street from whom the animate book is asking for directions (*Tristia* 3.1.1–4):

> "I'm a frightened new arrival in town, a book sent here by an exile;
>   Please lend me a gentle hand, dear reader: I'm exhausted.
> Don't cringe away from me, in case I bring shame upon you:
>   Not one verse on this paper teaches anything about love."

The book is shabby and lame, with one pace longer than the other, and begs to be excused: "perhaps it's my elegiac metre, or perhaps the length of my journey." But despite its tatty appearance and elegiac limp, the volume succeeds in finding one man who can point out the libraries of Rome. At this chronological moment there were three public libraries, and Ovid's poetry book visits each of them in turn. First it approaches the Palatine Hill, home of the Temple of Apollo, with its library that had been established by Augustus himself. This library refuses the book entrance. Then the book fails to be allowed into the Library at the Portico of Octavia, Augustus's sister. Third and last, the book is refused entrance to the oldest of the three, the library in the Atrium Libertatis, created by Gaius Asinius Pollio and opened no later than early in the year 28 B.C. Ovid's poem shows us a literary reflection of the truth that the great public libraries of Rome partly functioned, if obliquely, as instruments of censorship.[33]

The trope of the literary tour of central Rome was not itself Ovid's own poetic invention. The most famous of all examples comes in *Aeneid* 8, when Evander shows Aeneas and Ascanius round the site of the future Rome, the grove of Romulus, the wolf's cave, the Tarpeian rock and the capitol, "now all gold, but once bristling with wild thorns." Evander himself lives in poverty, surrounded by cattle lowing where the Roman Forum would later stand. What is so brilliant about Ovid's version, however, is that the tour is from the viewpoint of a book of poetry, and is focussed primarily on the libraries rather than the most imposing landmarks of Rome. The Romans loved to think about how their great city had transformed the simple rural environment: Ovid displaces that primitive poverty from the temporal past to his spatial place of exile, among the nearly bookless and completely library-less Getae. Yet the very simplicity of this poetry, its straightforward emotional voice and absence of dense mythological allusions, have perhaps only become *possible* in an environment where books are so scarce. Perhaps, just perhaps, the *idea* of the library is more generative for literature than the actual contents of the library itself.

To underline this intuition, I conclude with the final elegy of the same book by Ovid, *Tristia* 3.14. It is addressed to some kind of senior librarian, perhaps to be understood as working at one of those four libraries that Ovid's personified book itself had approached in the first poem of this cycle. Augustus died in 14 A.D., to be replaced by the Emperor Tiberius, and Ovid died about three years later: we do not know the exact date of *Tristia* 3. But we do happen to know the name of the man whom Tiberius appointed, at some point before 37 A.D., to the august office of commissioner of libraries as well as the less well-defined role of "adviser": Tiberius Iulius Pappus, a freeborn Roman citizen from the Greek East. This superlibrarian's tomb inscription survives, having been discovered east of Rome on the Via Praenestina.[34] It is just possible that the prestigious post may not have existed during Ovid's lifetime, but its creation soon after his death indicates the cultural power that the men in charge of the imperial book collections were already accumulating. Ovid's voice from the Pontus was addressed to a man or men just like Commissioner Pappus:

To the Keeper and Overseer of Learned Men:
    Sir, what have you done to help me as my friend?

You *used* to sing my praises when I was a "safe" poet;
    Do you *still* do anything to make sure I don't disappear alto-
        gether?
Do you do *anything* to obtain my poems (except for the ones about
    the "Arts"
    which did so much damage to their author)?
Actually, what I want to say is this: I *beg* you, as an enthusiast for new
    poets,
    To do *anything* in your power to keep my corpus of work in town.
I was sentenced to exile, but no exile sentence was passed on my books.
    They don't deserve to be punished along with their master.
Fathers are often enough deported to remote shores,
    But their children are still allowed to live in town.
Like Pallas Athene, my poems were born from me without a mother;
    They're of my family line; they're my descendants.
Into your hands I commend them: the longer they're deprived of
    their father,
    The heavier a burden they'll prove to you as their guardian.
Three of my children have been laid low by my infection:
    Make sure that the rest of the rabble are looked after by you *publicly*.
There are also fifteen volumes of metamorphosed forms,
    Songs seized from their master at his last rites.
That work might have gained a more secure reputation
    If I'd put the finishing touches to it before I met my end.
Now it has arrived on people's lips unrevised,
    —that is, if *anything* of mine is on their lips at all.
Add this little something to my books, as well:
    it is delivered to you from a distant world.
I don't know whether anyone will read it, but if anyone does,
    he needs to bear in mind when and where it was composed.
He'll be fair-minded about poems he realises were written
    during a period of exile in a barbarous place.
And he'll be astonished that in such adversity I produced any poem
    at all,
    trying to keep writing in my hand of sorrow.

My problems have destroyed my talent; it wasn't even that
 abundant before, and flowed only in a small trickle.
But whatever it was once, it's run away since nobody kept it working,
 and dried up completely in this far-flung place.
There are few books here to entice or nourish me;
 the sounds are made by bows and weaponry instead of books.
In this country, if I recite my poems, there's nobody around
 who can listen to them with any comprehension or discernment.
There's nowhere for me to be alone. The guards on the wall
 and the bolted gates keep out the restive Getae.
I often try to remember a word, a name, a place-name,
 but there's no one I can ask to check that I am right.
I often try to put something into words, but I'm ashamed to say
 that the words elude me; I have *un*-learned how to speak.
I'm virtually surrounded by the sound of the Thracian and Scythian
 languages;
 I'm convinced I could write in Getic metres.
Believe me, I'm scared that you'll read Pontic words in my writings,
 all mixed up with the Latin ones.
And so, please deem this little book, however mediocre, worthy of
 indulgence;
 excuse it on the ground of the fate which has befallen me.

This is a great poem in its own right. It is a clear, emotionally authentic, elegiac expression of cultural isolation, intellectual loneliness, and the poet's terror of his works falling into instant and permanent oblivion. It is written in concise, beautiful Latin, the plangent effect of which my humdrum translation fails to convey. But it is also, to my mind, the most profound statement of the importance of libraries to have survived from antiquity. In closing book 3 of his *Tristia* with this direct appeal to the "Keeper of Learned Men" back in Rome, while lamenting the problems of keeping his poetic creativity alive in the absence of the culture of the library, Ovid's voice speaks as none other from Mediterranean antiquity of the vital symbolic role that great book collections played in its imaginative life.[35]

NOTES

1. Colin MacLeod, "Euripides' Rags," *Zeitschrift für Papyrologie und Epigraphik* 15 (1974): 221–22, reprinted in his *Collected Essays* (Oxford: Clarendon Press, 1983), 47–48.

2. E.g., Monica Berti and Vergilio Costa, *La Biblioteca di Alessandria: Storia di un paradiso perduto*. [= *Ricerche di filologia, letteratura e storia* 10.] (Roma: Edizioni Tored, 2010), ch. 5.

3. Debra A. Castillo, *The Translated World: A Post-Modern Tour of Libraries in Literature* (Tallahassee: University of Florida Press, 1984).

4. See James A. Sanders, "The Dead Sea Scrolls: A Quarter Century of Study," *Biblical Archaeologist* 36.4 (1973): 109–48; Jodi Magness, *The Archaeology of Qumran and the Dead Sea Scrolls* (Grand Rapids, MI: William B. Eerdmans, 2002).

5. Janet Charlotte Smith, "The Side Chambers of San Giovanni Evangelista in Ravenna: Church Libraries of the Fifth Century," *Gesta* 29.1 (1990): 86–97.

6. Theodore W. Koch, "New Light on Old Libraries," *Library Quarterly* 4 (1934): 246.

7. *Sat.* 484; see Raymond J. Starr, "Trimalchio's Libraries," *Hermes* 115.2 (1987): 252–53.

8. George W. Houston, "Tiberius and the Libraries: Public Book Collections and Library Buildings in the Early Roman Empire," *Libraries and the Cultural Record* 43.3 (2008): 248.

9. Pseudo-Plutarch, *Lives of the Ten Orators*, "Lycurgus" 841F; see Edith Hall, *The Theatrical Cast of Athens* (Oxford: Oxford University Press, 2006), 51; and Johanna Hanink, *Lycurgan Athens and the Making of Classical Tragedy* (Cambridge: Cambridge University Press, 2014).

10. The image is also reproduced and discussed in greater detail in Edith Hall, "Tragic Theatre: Demetrios' Rolls and Dionysos' Other Women," in O. Taplin and R. Wyles, eds., *The Pronomos Vase and Its Context* (Oxford: Oxford University Press, 2010), 159–79.

11. See S. Sider, "Herculaneum's Library in 79 A.D.: The Villa of the Papyri," *Libraries and Culture* 25.4 (1990): 534–42.

12. Herodorus in *Die Fragmente der griechischen Historiker*, ed. F. Jacoby, 434, trans. A. Smith on *Attulus* website, section title "Memnon: History of Heracleia" at www.attalus.org/translate/memnon1.html.

13. Quoted in Michael H. Harris, *History of Libraries in the Western World* (Metuchen, NJ: Scarecrow Press, 1995), 63.

14. G. P Stevens, "A Doorsill from the Library of Pantainos," *Hesperia* 18 (1949): 269–74. On the many different functions served in antiquity by libraries, see especially Yun Lee Too, *The Idea of the Library in the Ancient World* (Oxford: Oxford University Press, 2010).

15. Wilhelm Wilberg, *Forschungen in Ephesos*, vol. 5.1, *Die Bibliothek* (Vienna: A. Holder, 1953).

16. See N. Sherwin-White, *The Letters of Pliny* (Oxford: Clarendon Press, 1966), 102–6.

17. T. Keith Dix, "Pliny's Library at Comum," *Libraries and Culture* 31.1 (1996): 85.

18. Ron Messer, interview with Rachel Weisz on *Collider* website, May 2010. Online at http://collider.com/rachel-weisz-interview-agora-face-value-the-invisible-x/29455/.

19. Kingsley was not, of course, the first to adopt Hypatia as a heroine and indeed mouthpiece in the wars between different religious groups, and between religious people and freethinkers, from the Enlightenment onward. In the wake of his novel, however, numerous plays that made Hypatia the center of a love interest were written, especially in German, by, e.g., the Gräfin Adele Bredow and the dramatist Arnold Beer (both 1878).

20. Charles Kingsley, *Hypatia* (London: Parker, 1853), 22–23.

21. Kingsley, 24.

22. See Pliny 13.11.21, § 69: *antea non fuisse chartarum usum. In palmarum foliis primo scriptitatum, dein quarundam arborum libris.*

23. I. Haynes, A. Diaconescu and A. Schafer, "Apulum: Romania," *Current World Archaeology* 10 (2005). Illustrated summary available online at http://www.world-archaeology.com/features/apulum-romania/.

24. The *Online Library of Liberty*, available at http://oll.libertyfund.org/.

25. On this long-standing scholarly conundrum, see the widely divergent views expressed in the highly readable study by Luciano Canfora, *The Vanished Library: A Wonder of the Ancient World*, trans. Martin Ryle (Berkeley: University of California Press, 1990); and in Bojana Mojsov, *Alexandria Lost: From the Advent of Christianity to the Arab Conquest* (London: Duckworth, 2010). For further discussion, see also Edith Hall, *Introducing the Ancient Greeks: From Bronze-Age Seafarers to Navigators of the Western Mind* (New York: Norton, 2014), 204–27.

26. George Bernard Shaw, *Caesar and Cleopatra* (New York: Brentano's, 1906), 49.

27. Steven Roger Fischer, *A History of Reading* (London: Reaktion, 2003), 25.

28. Alan Cameron,*Callimachus and His Critics* (Princeton, NJ: Princeton University Press, 1995), 32.

29. Tony Harrison, *Palladas: Poems* (London: Anvil Press, 1984), 10.

30. Frederic Jameson, *The Cultural Turn: Selected Writings on the Postmodern 1983–1998* (Brooklyn: Verso, 1998), 15–17.

31. Nicholas Horsfall, "Empty Shelves on the Palatine," *Greece and Rome*, 2nd ser., 40.1 (1993): 58–67.

32. John Rodenbeck, "Literary Alexandria," *Massachusetts Review* 42.4 (2001–2): 535.

33. Anthony J. Marshall, "Library Resources and Creative Writing at Rome," *Phoenix* 30.3 (1976): 262–63.

34. George W. Houston, "Tiberius and the Libraries: Public Book Collections and Library Buildings in the Early Roman Empire," *Libraries and the Cultural Record* 43.3 (2008): 250–58.

35. Since this essay was written, an outstanding collection of essays stressing the diversity of ancient libraries has been published by a team led by researchers in the School of Classics at the University of St. Andrews. See Jason König, Katerina Oikonomopoulou, and Greg Woolf, eds., *Ancient Libraries* (Cambridge: Cambridge University Press, 2013).

CHAPTER 2

The Image of the Medieval Library

Richard Gameson

Libraries, medieval and modern alike, are simultaneously collections of books, spaces in which books are kept, and concepts. They are a body of knowledge and also a means of organizing it—for the way in which books are classified, and with what they are juxtaposed (not to mention how easy it is to gain access to them), can be as important as their own content in defining how they are used and perceived.

Our sources for medieval libraries fall into several classes. There are book lists and catalogues of widely differing degrees of detail and sophistication.[1] If the fullest, most heavily annotated examples offer vistas of libraries developing through time, most by their nature show but part of a particular collection at a specific moment. Then, of course, there are the extant manuscripts and printed books (ideally, still bearing shelfmarks and ex libris inscriptions) that can be linked with a particular individual or institution.[2] These reveal what were really on the shelves, and from whence they came; some also preserve evidence of the ways in which the books were used, and how systematically they were cared for. Needless to say, where the catalogues for a particular foundation are relatively wide-ranging and its surviving manuscripts comparatively numerous, the picture is altogether fuller: here one can often perceive collections within collections, each with its own character, purpose, and even space. Complementarily, monastic custumals, university library regulations, and other such documents may permit us to glimpse something of the day-to-day operation of the facilities in question.[3] Next, there is archaeological, architectural, and other artifactual evidence for the spaces in which books were kept and for the means used to store them: surviving book recesses, library rooms, and (occasionally) fittings of one sort or another provide insight into the practicalities—sometimes, one is tempted to say, the impracticalities—of storage and consultation.[4] And, offering an entirely different perspective, there are literary references to medieval libraries, physical and conceptual. At one extreme stand vague evocations such as Chaucer's mention of the shelf of books at the head of the bed of a rakish Oxford scholar, or the indirect allusion to his own collection of sixty unidentified titles.[5] At the other, there are those authors, extending from Cassiodorus in the sixth century to Aeneas Silvius Piccolomini in the fifteenth, who drew up long lists of authors and titles that institutions should own and that individuals ought to read (simultaneously advertising their own cultivation and concerns).[6]

All these sources have been mined for generations, and, while their rich "seams" are far from exhausted, the basic value of each is clear. There is, however, a further class of evidence that has been used rather less, and certainly less critically: namely depictions of libraries by medieval and early Renaissance artists. If these are, naturally, uninformative about the details of what was held in a given collection (they almost never identify specific titles), they nevertheless cast a broad complementary light across the field as a whole.

In point of fact, while medieval and early Renaissance art includes countless depictions of books—clutched by manifold saints, on desks in front of writers, and presented by one figure to another[7]—images of libraries as such are comparatively rare. Indeed, if one were to discount the private book collections that appear as part of the setting for many authors and scribes in the later Middle Ages, the number would be negligible. When relevant pictures have been discussed, it has generally been for other reasons—in connection with the "school" or style of their artwork, for example, or as a small part of an illustrative cycle mainly concerned with other matters.[8] If the depicted libraries were indeed the focus of attention, they were often treated as faute de mieux renderings of technical details—fittings and fixtures—that are principally known from other sources (actual survivals and documentary records). Here, however, we shall consider such depictions in their own right. Proceeding broadly in chronological order, we shall survey most of the scarce early examples and a representative cross-section of the more plentiful but often-repetitive later ones, considering them in relation to other sources as appropriate. We shall conclude by airing the general points that, as a group, they raise.

❦

If we take the Fall of Rome (410) as our starting point, we encounter our first image of a library a generation later, in the second quarter of the fifth century. It appears in the so-called Mausoleum of Galla Placidia at Ravenna.[9] The mosaic in the lunette of the south arm of this cruci-form structure shows a saint (most probably Lawrence), a gridiron, and a book cupboard. This *scrinium* or *armarium* is a robust structure, raised up on four legs, and capped with a triangular pediment surmounted by a cross (plate 1). The panelled doors are open to reveal two shelves, each supporting a pair of hefty codices that lie flat on their back-boards, fore-edges outward, their identity as the four gospels signalled by bold in-scriptions (or fictive titles) on their front-boards. Given the scale of the cupboard in relation to the saint, the volumes are implausibly large for individual gospels; however, they are admirably visible in their architec-tural setting, and this was doubtless the aim. Viewed through the open doors of the cupboard, they function as a revelation of the gospel mes-sage (echoing the four evangelist symbols in the pendentives of the main vault above) and hence, by extension, of Christ—the reason for which a saint might go to martyrdom, and because of whom suffering and death are not the end.

At the opposite end of Europe over 150 years later a similar but larger book cupboard was included in Codex Amiatinus, the third of three pan-dects made at Wearmouth-Jarrow in Northumbria by 716 (plate 2).[10] This armarium has a solid base (possibly containing further storage space) rather than legs, and four shelves (plus the floor of the main cavity) as opposed to two; it boasts more elaborate decoration on the frontage,[11] and some sort of pole or ratchet at the end of one of the doors (presuma-bly a fastening mechanism). Nevertheless, it is essentially the same piece of furniture as that shown at Ravenna. Generally believed to reflect a Cassiodoran exemplar painted in the later sixth century, this image raises unanswerable questions about the relationship between "art" and real life—issues that will reappear in different guises throughout this study. If such book cupboards were used at Vivarium in southern Italy in the sixth century (where the presumed but lost visual model was created), were they also constructed at Wearmouth-Jarrow in the early eighth (where the image that has come down to us was certainly painted)? The heroic efforts made at that Anglo-Saxon foundation to imitate "Roman" culture across fields as varied as stone building, glassworking, chanting, and script forms—and in the last case with spectacular success—incline one to think that they probably were, though this is ultimately speculation.

The page is commonly known as the "Ezra portrait" after its writing figure, who is identified thus in the inscription above the picture. By dint of its size and centrality, however, the book cupboard is at least as important as the scribe and is inseparable from his significance. The nine large books that it so blatantly displays lie flat, identified by the titles that were once visible on their spines as the individual parts of a nine-volume Bible—arguably Cassiodorus's *novem codices*. The restoration, preservation, and transmission of scripture—by Ezra (and perhaps also by the community of Wearmouth-Jarrow)—is the real subject here, as the titulus implies.[12] This image thus embraces three senses of the word *bibliotheca*—as bookcase, library, and Bible.[13]

The word *bibliotheca* was the subject of a chapter in the encyclopedia (*De rerum naturis*) that was compiled late in life by the Carolingian author Hrabanus Maurus of Fulda and Mainz (d. 856).[14] Heavily indebted throughout this section to his venerable predecessor in the genre, Isidore of Seville (d. 636), Hrabanus began by informing the reader that *bibliotheca* was a Greek word and that it denoted the place where books were stored. Then he observed that Ezra restored the Bibliotheca of the Old Testament, namely its texts, going on to survey the great libraries of the Greeks.[15] Remarkably for such a work, *De rerum naturis* appears to have been supplied with illustrations at an early date—though no illustrated copy older than the eleventh century has come down to us, and only two extant witnesses preserve a complete cycle of over three hundred images.[16] The earliest of these two fully illustrated copies was made at Monte Cassino at some point between 1022 and 1035.[17] The image therein for this chapter is dominated by a book cupboard (plate 3).

About the height of a man, this armarium is (like the example at Ravenna: plate 1) essentially rectilinear and raised up on four legs, being decorated (akin to that in Codex Amiatinus: plate 2) with birds on the front. Yet how exactly it opens is unclear—as is where the librarian's left hand has gone (he "reaches" toward the top of the façade, but no arm projects from the sleeve in question). The large size of the item and the tripartite façade hint that it is front-opening; however, it is difficult to see how the three panels could give satisfactory access to the shelves inside,[18] while the apparent void between the façade and the top (into which the librarian's left hand has presumably disappeared, and across which runs a prop or a clasp) implies a lifting lid. One way to make sense of these contradictory indications is to hypothesize an underlying visual model similar to the Ravenna cupboard, but interpreted by an artist who was personally more familiar with book chests. Although the librarian is receiving volumes from (or issuing them to) a couple of readers or helpers, the emphasis is principally on the item of furniture: underlining the first rather than the second phrase of Hrabanus's text, this bibliotheca is less the collection of books than the object in which they are stored.

The other copy of Hrabanus's *Encyclopedia* that has a full set of illustrations was made in Germany, probably for Elector Ludwig III, in 1425—so almost exactly four centuries after the Monte Cassino manuscript, and nearly six centuries after the text itself was composed (plate 4).[19] Though utterly different in style, the essential content of the late Gothic illustration for the chapter on bibliotheca is the same as that drawn at Monte Cassino. We see two figures on the left, one to the right, of a massive rectangular piece of furniture that is raised up on a substantial pediment resting on four legs linked by rounded arches; small shelves or cupboards set within the main body support four books; while, most curiously, its flat top appears to rise from left to right at a modest angle. This fifteenth-century storage unit is even more difficult to understand than its eleventh-century predecessor—until one realizes that it is ultimately the same object (a substantial cupboard) interpreted in the light, not of a book chest this time but of the lectern desks with shelves below them that were standard pieces of library furniture in the late Middle Ages (images of which will be considered in due course: plate 23).

The closeness of the relationship between the illustrations in these two copies of Hrabanus's *Encyclopedia*, the exact date of the ultimate archetype, and whether *that* in turn was based on an illustrated Isidore or was a compilation from a range of sources, are all matters of debate. There is little doubt, however, that the extant copies ultimately reflect a common archetype dating from the ninth century that was itself indebted to antique and late antique models. If the interpretations advanced above are correct, however, these eleventh- and fifteenth-century bibliothecae not only warn against assuming that such images show real-world practices from the periods in which they were produced, but also caution against regarding them as reliable guides to those of the time of the archetype.

Images of book chests that are broadly contemporary with the compilation of Hrabanus's *Encyclopedia* appear in the so-called Vivian Bible, a volume made at Tours between 845 and 846 for presentation to King Charles the Bald.[20] The scenes from the life of St. Jerome that form the frontispiece to the Old Testament include, as the lowest register, a depiction of that scholar distributing copies of his Vulgate from a stock stored in two chests at his feet (plate 5). These are solid square objects with fastening lids. The books in the chest on the left (from the viewer's point of view) are stacked upright; those in that on the right might be arranged likewise, or are possibly lying flat on their backs. Though various earlier depictions of *capsae* containing scrolls are known,[21] this is seemingly the oldest representation of chests holding codices. A similar Jerome cycle in the Reimsian San Paolo Bible, made a generation later (c. 870), is believed to descend from a lost Touronian exemplar akin to the Vivian Bible; here the corresponding vignette features a single book chest.[22]

The status of the relevant image in the Vivian Bible itself—Carolingian creation, copy of a late Antique model, or something in between—has been much discussed. The current orthodoxy is that it was essentially a Carolingian creation that drew extensively for its many late Antique elements on the "Vatican Vergil," a manuscript dating from c. 400 which is known to have been at Tours when the Vivian Bible was being made there.[23] No image of a book container survives in the "Vatican Vergil"; however that volume is now incomplete, and we can be confident that if it formerly had one (as an element within an author portrait, for instance), then this would have featured a *capsa* containing scrolls (as is the case in the slightly younger "Roman Vergil" manuscript).[24] In show-ing book chests with codices, the artists of the Vivian Bible were thus substituting—or simply introducing—objects from their own time. By accident rather than design one suspects, these items were in fact correct for Jerome's world of the fifth century (as opposed to Vergil's of the first century B.C.).

The so-called *Chronique majeure* of Saint-Wandrille in Normandy, a mid-eleventh-century compilation of historical and hagiographical texts relating to that abbey, includes a depiction of a book chest that, though cruder and more stylized than that in the Vivian Bible, nevertheless dis-plays otherwise unrepresented details (plate 6).[25] Prefixed to the *Vita* of Ansbert (the third abbot of Saint-Wandrille then archbishop of Rouen, who died after c. 690) is a miniature of that saint, a monk at his feet. Beside the latter figure, under a separate arch evoking a room or clois-ter, appears a chest containing three books. Although rather higgledy-piggledy, the volumes are seemingly all arranged with their spines down and clasped fore-edges up. What is of particular interest here, however, is the delineation of a mechanism for holding open the lid of the chest, an eminently practical convenience. There would seem to be a hinge at one side and, at the other, a ratchet pole, permitting several resting points. While the inclusion of the book chest is conceivably a reference to St. Ansbert's assiduous spiritual reading celebrated in the *Vita* that fol-lows,[26] it is more probably a device for underlining the spiritual resources of the community—fortified by a patron saint in heaven and by its books on earth. (Certainly, similar ideas had been articulated a generation ear-lier in the manuscripts of the Flemish abbeys of Saint-Bertin and Saint-Vaast via inscriptions and images of different sorts.[27])

Comparable concepts also underlie an image that was produced at Monte Cassino a generation later (c. 1075). Heading a luxurious lec-tionary is a picture of Abbot Desiderius (1058–87) offering the material resources of the community, including a body of books, to its patron saint, Benedict.[28] Here interestingly, the volumes are not in any sort of recepta-cle but are seemingly spread out on the ground between the two figures. This is plainly a schematic presentation, the books paralleling the basilica and chapels above and the lake and the landscape dotted with buildings below, as complementary symbols of the vigor of the community. The two-part verse inscription under Desiderius, articulating his imprecation to the saint, highlights all these resources and what he hopes to obtain in return: "Along with the buildings, O Father, receive the many wonderful books. Fields, lakes I show; be a grantor of heaven to me."[29] As a visual model for a heap of books, one may point to that which appears in the above-mentioned copy of Hrabanus Maurus's *Encyclopedia* made at Monte Cassino a generation earlier, where it forms part of the illustration for the entry on the authors of the Old and New Testaments.[30] The pile in the lectionary might conceivably evoke the laying out of books that was part of the annual Lenten distribution of reading matter in certain communities at the time: the contemporary *Constitutions* of Lanfranc (c. 1077), echoing the custumal of Cluny and elaborating the prescription in the *Rule of St. Benedict* itself, describes the communal book stock (or some portion of it) being set out on a carpet in the chapter house, to which last year's borrowings were returned and from which a new distribution was made.[31] Yet whether or not it evoked a similar ceremony, the Desiderian image certainly articulates the idea of a monastic library as a collection of books pure and simple (rather than in terms of a particular container or room). It is equally a useful caution—if one were necessary—against regarding a picture as a source for the quantity of books that were held or acquired by a medieval monastery, or an individual abbot, at a given time. Eight manuscripts are shown, yet we know that Monte Cassino's collection grew by nearly a hundred volumes in Desiderius's time; and even though this particular image was produced around the midpoint of his abbacy, it is still a minimalist evocation, not in any sense a true representation, of the size of the library in his day. The number of books is no more realistic than is the size of the buildings. A preference for symbolic as opposed to naturalistic depiction is another feature common to much of our corpus, as we shall see.

The frontispiece to a Cologne lectionary of c. 1130 brings us back to book chests, a pair of which flank the figure of Frederick I of Schwarzenburg, the archbishop of that see from 1100–31 (plate 7).[32] Cursorarily delineated, the objects themselves have neither fittings nor lids. By contrast, the six books that each contains (hence a neat apostolic total of twelve altogether) are clearly distinguished by color, and are all shown to be stored upright. Framed by cardinal virtues, prophets, and apostles, and seated immediately below—indeed echoing—Christ, Frederick is the model Christian leader, daily meditating on holy law. Christ's scroll exhorts: "Anyone who loves me will heed my word, then my Father will love him and we shall come to him and make our dwelling with him" (John 14:23). Frederick's scroll answers (in the words of Psalm 118:97): "O how I have loved your law, O Lord; it is my meditation all the day," a point that the book chests underline. Whether or not they are supposed to evoke an archiepiscopal library as such, they certainly demonstrate that Frederick is attentive to, and learned in, the word of God. The volumes in these chests are a channel for, indeed an earthly embodiment of, the prophets, apostles, and virtues, not to mention Christ himself.

This is by no means the last image of a book chest (later examples range from the crudely drawn one that dominates the background of the picture of Abbot Simon in a collection of historical texts compiled at St. Albans at the end of the fourteenth century,[33] to the carefully rendered one in the foreground of Jerome's study as depicted in the *Très Belles Heures de Notre Dame*, dating from the early fifteenth century[34]); however, hereafter they become rarer. In point of fact, depictions of libraries are in generally short supply during the later twelfth century and throughout the thirteenth. The circumstance that the period in question postdates the golden age of the monastic library yet pre-dates the heyday of princely and university ones is surely part of the explanation for this.[35] The related mismatch between the preexisting traditions of imagery (as just surveyed) and the new types of patrons and libraries that were emerging may have been another restraining factor. Certainly, the relevant images from the thirteenth century appear profoundly conservative: three of them are in the late thirteenth-century "codice rico" of the Cantigas of Sancta Maria,[36] where a bishop, a monk, and a cleric are each shown in front of a substantial book cupboard. The *armaria* themselves are versions of the furniture seen at Ravenna in the fifth century (plate 1), while the use of them as a motif to evoke the spiritual erudition of writing figures stands in the tradition that we first encountered with the Ezra image from Wearmouth-Jarrow (plate 2).

The new directions in the patronage of books and book collections are then signalled by the fact that two of the most striking images of libraries produced in the fourteenth century appear in the context of secular rather than sacred texts. The first is the enormous book cupboard that features in a couple of copies of Benoît of Sainte-Maure's *Roman de Troie* that were made in northern Italy during the second quarter of the century (plate 8).[37] The object renders in visual form the *aumaire* that is mentioned in the prologue, in a passage that purports to establish the authority of the work as a whole: one day while rummaging for grammar books at his school in Athens, Cornelius Nepos finds an account of the destruction of Troy written by the supposed eyewitness Darius the Phrygian.[38] The large wooden cupboard, both taller and wider than the height of a man, is subdivided by five shelves (or four plus an elevated base). The books lie flat, fore-edges outward, three on the bottom two shelves, four on the upper pair—a realistic touch since common sense recommends, and numerous medieval library catalogues confirm, that lower shelves would typically hold smaller numbers of larger volumes, and upper ones larger numbers of smaller ones. A compact top cupboard contains a single tome.[39] While the door of the latter appears to consist of a simple panel (or lattice) hinged at one side, those of the main cupboard are evidently of folding construction, seemingly in three sections. This is plausible, at least in the abstract, given the size of the opening that they have to cover.[40]

The second particularly striking image is the famous depiction of Charles V of France that heads the dedicatory copy of the French translation of John of Salisbury's *Policraticus* that that king himself commissioned in 1372.[41] Charles is portrayed in a panelled study or carrel beside a three-tier book stand (plate 9). The base, resting on an anchoring platform-cum-footrest, contains cupboards (or at least spaces in which to store books); it also provides a surface on which to stack them. The middle has a circular plate, supporting volumes at eye level for a seated reader. The top is crowned with a double-sided lectern, its books at an appropriate height for perusal while standing. Wheel desks, sometimes with a screw spindle, permitting the height of the plate to be adjusted, are reasonably well known from other late medieval depictions.[42] This one is unusual on account of its three tiers and—self-evidently related—for the number of volumes that it holds. Wheel desks are often shown with three or four volumes, sometimes with five or six.[43] This one, by contrast, boasts ten and is clearly meant to suggest a substantial book collection—

and, by implication, the considerable learning of its user. As the inventories of the Louvre library in 1380 itemize 917 volumes (and there were other royal books elsewhere), the king's holdings were indeed remarkably large; moreover, the documentation relating to the installation of the collection in a tower of the Louvre a decade earlier reveals that the fittings included two book wheels.[44] The depicted Charles is reading the start of the prologue of the work in which the illumination appears; this pointedly declares, "*Beatus uir*[45] *qui inuenit sapientiam*" ("Blessed is the man who finds wisdom") and the king's wisdom is underlined visually by the number of books that he has to hand, ready for perusal. Correspondingly, because Charles manifestly *inuenit sapientiam*, he is shown (by the presence of the hand of God) to be *beatus*. The point is underlined by the illustration that appears a few folios later where, under the blessing person of Christ, the king contemplates Fathers of the Church along with ancient philosophers (Plato and Aristotle), figures whose learning is embodied in the books and scrolls in the basket in front of them; while, below a procession of courtiers, a group of kneeling commoners prayerfully declaims: "*benedicta terra cuius rex sapiens*" ("blessed is the land whose king is a wise man").[46]

A generation later a more typical reading wheel appears among the furniture of a private study that is so full of books that it is clearly meant to evoke an outstanding personal scholarly library and by extension the exceptional erudition and literary pursuits of its owner—none other than Francesco Petrarca (d. 1374: plate 10).[47] Though sadly damaged, the image delineates the form and operation of one such wheel with greater clarity, showing open books propped up against a central, multangular rest, as well as lying flat on the plate. Further books rest on Petrarch's writing desk, and on (and doubtless within) a chest behind it; they are stacked flat in deep cupboards within a wooden bureau against the far wall and lean against its base. In total at least thirty-six volumes (not to mention his dog, Zabot) are shown in this study—a substantial number for such a context.

The image—in an illustrated manuscript of Petrarch's *De uiris illustribus*—appears to be a fairly faithful copy of a much grander version that was painted in the *Sala uirorum illustrium* in the Reggia (palace) of the Carrara family at Padua.[48] The "original," though not entirely lost, has been extensively repainted—an open view to a mountainous landscape replaced the book cupboard, for instance. Nevertheless, it seems highly unlikely that this, any more than the manuscript version, showed the true proportions of Petrarch's remarkable library.[49] On the contrary, the artist merely added a few extra volumes to a fairly standard image of a study—the iconography of learning—as had been the case with the representation of Charles V. No attempt was made to depict collections comprising hundreds of volumes, as we know to have been the reality; and subsequent versions of the image of Petrarch reduce the number of books still further.[50]

If the previous examples were artistically distinguished yet limited by convention as to what they show, a remarkable vignette in a mid-fourteenth-century cartulary is, by contrast, technically poor yet seemingly more "documentary" in terms of what it portrays.[51] One of a suite of sketches illustrating the statutes of the Parisian college of Hubant or "Ave Maria," it represents a type of library that we have not hitherto seen (plate 11). To the right of the drawing is a line of six figures, the first of whom gives a book to (or conceivably receives it from) a seventh figure standing to the left who, with his other hand, is adding another book to (or taking it from) a pile of them on the floor behind him. Ave Maria College was established by John of Hubant for six students aged between eight and sixteen (plus six *beneficiarii* who could be up to twenty years old). Perhaps on account of the immaturity of many of the boys, the rules for the library prescribed a particularly rigorous regime of weekly inspection. Every Saturday the officer of the week was to go through all the books, chained and unchained, with the next week's officer, pointing out any damage; the master and the chaplain were also to inspect them. If any volume was lost or damaged and the culprit identifiable, he was to be flogged; if his identity was unascertainable, then all the boys would be beaten; their parents were to be responsible for making good any loss. That the vignette depicts some part of the inspection is made clear by its caption—"*commant li semeniers doit le semadi rendre compte de touz les livres de la chapele et de autres livres*" ("how the weekly officers must account on Saturdays for all the books of the chapel, and other books")—though who exactly is performing it (weekly officers, master, or chaplain) is unclear. Given the imperative to preserve the books in good condition, it is ironic that the (mediocre) artist does not suggest that they were put anywhere in particular, or even stacked with much care, during this process.

A different type of institutional library and its security were illustrated in the illuminated statutes of the Collegium Sapientiae at Freiburg, which was founded in 1497 by John Kerer, a former master of that university, ultimately suffragan bishop of Augsburg.[52] Typically for such an institution, the regulations say nothing about the acquisition of books and little about their organization (except that any member of the house could have access to them *congruis horis*, at appropriate times), but two chapters are devoted to the need to keep them safe. The first of these treats "whether the books set out, or which ought to be set out in the library of our house can be moved therefrom," including to an individual's quarters—to which the answer is predictably "no," unless every other member agrees and the borrower deposits a more valuable volume or equivalent pledge as security.[53] The second concerns the key to the library, which was to be entrusted to a particularly reliable and careful member of the community who should permit entry at the "appropriate times," but must be vigilant that no book be removed nor any outsider, whatever his status, enter—other than with the permission of the president.[54]

Concordant with the injunctions, the illustration for the second of these sections shows the key bearer outside a robust stone or brick-built chamber, its windows protected by grilles, and the portentious inscription "alpha et o" over the wooden door, the handle of which he grasps (plate 12). The illustration to the previous section—while still emphasizing the solid walls, the wooden door defended by a massive lock, and the fortified windows (this time protected by bars)—affords a slightly clearer view of the interior: well-lit with generous window apertures, the facility contains nine rows of lectern desks entirely covered with books (a visible total of about twenty-five: plate 13). In striking contrast to the other miniatures in the volume that teem with people, but echoing the tone of the statutes in relation to the library, nobody is within—this is about safeguarding, more than the transmission of, knowledge.

The library is depicted again at the end of the document in connection with the regulation that a copy of the statutes written on parchment be positioned in a secure place within it, fixed to a lectern.[55] The main differences between this image and the first depiction are that there is a step running along the outside wall of the structure, and that the bars on the windows take a different form yet again. Contrary to the prescriptions in the accompanying text, the book of statutes, though chained, is shown lodged on a window ledge without rather than within the library room itself.

Complementing these rare views inside a college library is the glimpse of the interior of a conventual biblioteca afforded by a predella panel from the altarpiece that was painted by Stefano di Giovanni (known as Sassetta) in 1423–24 for the Arte della Lana (guild of wool merchants) in Siena (plate 14).[56] Within an oratory-like space are five rows of lecterns, open and closed books resting on, rather than chained to, them. Clearly shown (at the bottom of the nearest lectern) is the sill or lip that prevents the books from sliding off. Seating is provided in the form of freestanding stools (as opposed to long benches joined to the desks). The altarpiece (regrettably dismembered in 1777) was commissioned for the annual celebration of the feast of Corpus Christi. The lost central panel boasted a monstrance upheld by angels, while the side panels showed Anthony Abbot and Thomas Aquinas. Two of the seven extant predella scenes also concerned Aquinas.[57] The second apparently depicts the miraculous commendation of his writings by a speaking crucifix. The first shows Thomas Aquinas at prayer before an altar, set against a background comprising, to the left, a cloistered garden (complete with fountain) and, to the right, the library. This panel thus illustrates the sources of orthodox Christian knowledge—prayer, secluded contemplation, and spiritual reading. The presentation of the library room in this context, with architecture that evokes a church, and juxtaposed with the cloister garden, invites the viewer to understand its books as a wellspring of knowledge in parallel to the fount of life symbolized by the fountain.

These last two examples took us into the fifteenth century, by which time the corpus of images relevant to our topic as a whole had multiplied dramatically. A good number of them portray libraries in broadly similar terms, albeit with differences of detail, and more or less artistic license. In a late fifteenth-century copy of the popular *Livre de bonnes meurs* of Jacques le Grand (d. 1415x18), for instance, the section *"comment on doibt etudier, aprandre et especialement la saincte escripture*" ("how one must study and learn, especially the holy scriptures") was illustrated with an image of a small, brick, barrel-vaulted reading room equipped with a single lectern-desk, to which a couple of volumes are chained (plate 15).[58] The chains run from the underside of the desk to the top of the front-board of one book and to the head of the spine of the other. A pair of readers, side-by-side, indicate how "cosy" might be the conditions if two individuals wanted to consult volumes that were chained to the same desk (and the inconvenience that readers might get in each other's way does feature among the contemporary complaints recorded in relation to such facilities).[59] A shelf on the wall behind them displays four further volumes, propped upright, back covers outward. The image would seem to be a mélange of plausibility and approximation. One may doubt that a communal reading room will ever have had but a single desk; yet the fact that that desk is positioned at right angles to a window, maximizing the fall of light on the pages to be read, is precisely what one would expect. The circumstance that the chains start from the underside of the desk, rather than from a rod along its ridge, while not the norm, is not unknown; however, the fact that one chain runs to the top of the front-board, the other to the spine of their respective books is decidedly odd. The rising angle of the wall shelf, by contrast, is not a side effect of errant perspective but rather a plausible reflection of the real-world use of forward-projecting, L-shaped, wall-mounted shelving.[60]

If the library room in the *Livre de bonnes meurs* seemed underfurnished, the chamber shown in a copy of Jean de Meung's translation of the *Consolation of Philosophy* illuminated in the circle of Jean Colombe in 1476 seems overequipped and is evidently modelled on a library rather than a private study (plate 16).[61] The facility boasts three long double-sided lecterns (only one of which is realistically aligned in relation to a window, however), on which are a couple of open books and several closed ones, the latter all arranged with their back-board outward. A similar mixture of the plausible and implausible characterizes the furniture used in a copy of an English translation of Guillaume de Digulleville's *Pilgrimage of the Life of Man* to illustrate the scene where Hagiography shows Pilgrim and Lady Lesson her "*queynte marchaundyse*" (plate 17).[62] Four open and two shut books are laid out on a pair of lecterns. Though reasonably aligned at right-angles to the many windows, these each sport two equal-sized angled desks, a most unusual feature. An impractical adaptation of the well-attested lecterns that had a smaller shelf tucked in below the main desk's surface (cf. plate 22), this design is surely an exercise in artistic license concocted to make the point that literary merchandise is being displayed to Pilgrim—as also to the reader. Given the apparently hybrid character of the lecterns, not to mention the use of the word "*marchaundyse*," it is hardly surprising that the room has occasionally been described as a bookshop as opposed to a library.[63]

Many of these diverse furnishings are reprised in the woodcuts of *La Mer des hystoires*, a translation of *Rudimentum novitiorum* (a universal chronicle compiled in 1470–74 by an anonymous cleric of Lübeck) that was printed in Paris in 1488–89. Three of its many woodcuts (all multiply reused) show studies or reading rooms equipped with book wheels, lecterns, bureaus, and/or wall shelves.[64] The third of these to appear depicts a corner of a room entirely furnished with angled wall shelves on which books—some stored with back cover outward, others front cover out—are consulted as well as kept (plate 18). Further volumes are stacked on the floor, leaning up against the wall, or precariously balanced on top of the upper edge of the volumes that are on the shelves.[65] Whatever the plausibility of such an arrangement, it is an effective reminder of the fact that any and every storage solution was sooner or later going to be surpassed by continuing acquisitions or disrupted by human carelessness. Versions of this particular image, which evokes both a wealth of book learning and a reader's engagement with it, were to reappear in printed books for at least another half century.[66]

Iconographically quite distinct is the book collection featured as one of three miniatures in the manuscript of the *Roman de Jean d'Avesnes* that was transcribed by Jean du Chesne for Philippe de Croÿ shortly before 1473, but then this avowedly depicts the personal study of a nobleman (plate 19).[67] Illustrating the compiler's account of discovering the Latin exemplar for the work while browsing old tomes in a private collection he happened to visit, the grisaille miniature shows a moderate-sized chamber with two low shelves running along one wall under a window, and three higher ones on another (filling the alcove beside the fireplace), all of them covered with books; in the center of the room is a substantial chest on whose flat top lie two books, one closed, the other open, the latter being consulted by the compiler. In total, at least thirty-five volumes are shown. Dominated by a central fireplace, in front of which is a settle complete with cushion, and beside which is a bureau (on which are propped two further books), this room admirably conveys the idea of a comfortable "retreat" for leisure reading. A comparably commodious private study-library is shown as the setting in which the scribe-printer-scholar Colard Mansion prepares the *Dialogue des créatures* (1482) that this manuscript contains: he sits on a long, draped settle, working at a large wheel lectern beside a window, a substantial fireplace behind him; three angled wall shelves, supporting eight large books, dominate the back wall, above a comfortable chair complete with a cushion; the presence of two frolicking dogs adds to the domesticity of the chamber.[68] This text, the miniature declares, carries the authority of a prosperous, professional, and studious man of letters.

A feature of private or scholars' libraries that, though not in the images we have just considered, does appear in a range of late medieval examples is the provision of curtains to screen off the shelves from the rest of the chamber.[69] Such is the case, for instance, for the collection of a van Eyckian Jerome of c. 1442, whose books are stored flat, but otherwise anyhow, on the shelf in question, which is shielded by a pelmet as well as a curtain (plate 20);[70] as also for that of Vincent de Beauvais in a copy of the *Miroir historiale* (the French version of his *Speculum historiale*) that was made in Bruges around 1478–80 for King Edward IV of England (plate 21).[71] Vincent's books, all substantial, are propped up (some with their front-board, others with their back-board forward) on two angled shelves that run round two sides of the room. The function of such curtains was surely less to conceal the books than to give them modest protection against light and, above all, dust—a far from negligible concern in chambers heated by open fires (examples of which, it will be remembered, feature prominently in the domestic book rooms considered above: plate 19).[72] Angled, L-shaped wall shelving, likewise widely depicted, was particularly relevant in an era whose library culture was based on lecterns and whose books might accordingly have titles inscribed on the front- or the back-boards. Indeed these shelves are, in effect, single-sided lecterns hanging on the wall.

Our final image, a fresco in the Ospedale di Santo Spirito in Rome, presents a public facility of a different scale from those considered earlier.[73] The hospital was rebuilt by Sixtus IV (r. 1471–84) and one of its ground-floor halls was decorated (after 1482) with frescoes showing the improvements that that learned but worldly pope worked on the city of Rome. These included, alongside the eponymous Sistine Chapel, the realization of the Vatican library that had been initiated under Nicholas V (r. 1447–55). Preliminary plans for a completely new library building were rapidly abandoned in favor of refurbishing the former storeroom in which Nicholas V's books were kept: it was adapted to comprise four separate reading rooms—the Biblioteca Latina and the Biblioteca Graeca (together forming the public library), plus the Bibliotecae Segreta and Pontificia (which were not open to the general reader).

The hospital fresco, a work of fairly modest quality, shows a somber chamber with four pairs of long desks separated by a central gangway (plate 22). All the desks have a subsidiary shelf in addition to their main surface; and if the former appear to be empty, the latter are entirely covered with books, those to the left of the gangway placed front-cover up, those to the right back-cover up. The close similarity of the main figures at the back of the room to those that appear in the imposing fresco by Melozzo da Forli that once adorned the Biblioteca Latina itself suggests that alongside the pope stand his nephews plus Platina, the librarian.[74] In contrast to the locked and unpopulated facility shown in the statutes of Sapientia College, Freiburg (plates 12 and 13), in this part of the Vatican library there are three readers—all apparently so engrossed in their books as to be oblivious of the papal delegation. The presence of the readers implies that this is part of the communal library, and the image is presumably meant to evoke its grandest chamber, the Biblioteca Latina. Assuming this to be so, we can see that it bears some resemblance to reality for the Latin Library was indeed divided into two parts and its desks were indeed equipped with two shelves. On the other hand, the books are clearly not chained, yet we know that in reality they were; only four sets of desks are shown to both left and right, yet we know that there were nine or ten and seven respectively; and no attempt has been made to suggest the décor of a room whose walls were frescoed with twelve figures of ancient philosophers, the father and doctors of the church by the Ghirlandaio workshop, plus the image of Sixtus IV by Melozzo da Forli.[75] While some simplification was inevitable, it is sobering to reflect that this depiction of a specific library, painted at the height of the Italian Renaissance in the same town as the facility in question to commemorate its benefactor and his work, is not especially accurate as an historical record.

❦

What then are the general issues raised by the images that we have surveyed? We should start with their limitations, before moving on to their potential. If the most obvious restriction is the paucity of examples prior to the fifteenth century, the most prevalent, mercurial and insidious problem is artistic tradition itself. Fundamental to the use for library history of any of this material must be a keen awareness of the norms and patterns that conditioned it—moreover, this applies not just to the earlier depictions that are obviously stylized, but also to those of fifteenth-century date that appear to be altogether more realistic. One must be circumspect about how far one accepts any such image as a factual record of particular library practices. The point might seem unnecessary—were it not for the circumstance that this is precisely how some of them have been deployed in certain modern discussions.

As the reasons for the visual limitations are multiple and their implications varied, they are worth spelling out.

The most obvious factors are stylistic conventions: the illuminations from Saint-Wandrille (plate 6) and Monte Cassino were presumably by monks who had firsthand acquaintance with the libraries they were portraying; yet the nonrealist artistic idioms of their day imposed strict limits on the extent to which their lines could embody their knowledge. Then, some were patently the work of mediocre artists: the Saint-Wandrille image once again, the illustrations in the statutes of Sapientia (plates 12 and 13) and, above all, those of Ave Maria College are cases in point (plate 11). The modest talents responsible cannot be relied on to have conveyed with particular precision the reality of those facilities, even if they knew them.

Conversely, a great artist, endowed with finer skills and superior aesthetic sensitivity, need not necessarily have been any more accurate at the level of "documentary" detail, since he was just as, if not more likely to manipulate individual elements in the service of iconographic purpose or overall design. The Ravenna book cupboard is a competent example of semirepresentational late antique art; however, its proportions were clearly defined as much by the need to fit the available space in the lunette, to match the saint, and to showcase books that would be big enough to be seen, and their *tituli* read, from some distance, as by contemporary reality (plate 1). The plate of a wheel-desk that, with blatant disregard for foreshortening, is rendered as an implausibly large, perfect circle at the very center of the first image in an early fifteenth-century copy of *Le livres des propriétés des choses* does relate to some real-world library furniture; however, the way this example is presented was conditioned by the artist's wish to use it to suggest the orb of the earth, in a miniature that was designed to evoke both the divine Creation and human investigation of the resulting world.[76] Again, the van Eyckian Jerome gives an impression of the almost-photographic realism that one associates with that supremely talented Netherlandish master (plate 20). Yet in common with other works of the same school, while individual elements are uncannily realistic, the overall design is a construct. Here the shelf packed with books is as much an attribute as is the lion, which in the composition it neatly parallels. Moreover, the former existence of a matching composition—complete with closely similar shelf of books, curtain, and pelmet—used for Thomas Aquinas in the destroyed Turin-Milan hours, and the imitations of the design in Bruges illuminations of the mid-fifteenth century, alert us to the dependence of many such images on pictorial, as opposed to real-world, models.[77]

This leads directly to the next aspect of the limitations, namely that much of the imagery was defined, at least in part, by artistic models or iconographic tradition. Such was most evidently the case in relation to Hrabanus Maurus's *Encyclopedia*—the "library" shown in a fifteenth-century copy being related in outline to an eleventh-century one, both of which probably reflected a ninth-century archetype (plates 3 and 4)—but equally applies to more naturalistic-seeming portrayals (such as the van Eyckian Jerome) and even to apparently idiosyncratic ones. Ezra's cupboard in Codex Amiatinus arguably echoes a lost archetype drawn at Vivarium 150 years earlier (plate 2), and similar debts to late antiquity may reasonably be suspected to underlie the book cupboards and chests that appear in Carolingian art and (indirectly via the influence of Carolingian exemplars) in the Romanesque period (plates 5, 6, and 7). This does not mean that the depicted objects might not also reflect a contemporary reality; however, it makes it more difficult to assess the extent to which they may do so.

If debts to chronologically distant models might be less of a problem in relation to the images of later medieval libraries, these are still likely to be products of artistic convention as much as, if not more than, of observation of reality. The multiplication of examples led to the emergence of an iconography of scholars, scholarship, and learning, of which books and library furniture formed an integral part. It may be doubted that many fifteenth-century artists sketched actual libraries and their fittings to guide them, as opposed to copying or confecting from other images. The interrelated Jerome and Aquinas images with curtained shelving have just been remarked (plate 20). The odd chaining we noted in one depiction of a library (plate 15), the strange double-level desks in another (plate 17), and the inconsistent arrangement of books on lecterns in various images suggest that most artists were not overly concerned with the accuracy of minutiae—meaning that the historian of libraries must judge every aspect of each case on its own merits. Even in the custom-designed statutes of Sapientia College, the discrepancies between the three images of the same facility—one with grilles over the windows (plate 12), two with bars of different forms (plate 13)—warn against affording much credit to any particular detail. Visual conventions probably dominate even those portrayals that are superficially individualistic or idiosyncratic: no attempt was made to represent the actual size of the libraries of Charles V and Petrarch, it will be remembered—the particularly grand, multilayered reading desk and the accumulation of library furniture that distinguish these images respectively are arguably just intensifications of the conventions for private studies, in order to convey the general idea of a superabundance of books (plates 9 and 10).[78]

In effect, a relatively modest number of books became the iconography for a major library. The point is underlined by the famous images of the foolish bibliophile who heads Sebastian Brant's *Das Narrenschiff* (*The Ship of Fools*) first published in 1494 and much reprinted, translated, and reworked at an early date (plates 23 and 24).[79] While the text stressed that this ignoramus amassed a vast hoard of unread books ("*congestis libellis*," "*multitudine librorum*," "*librorum multitudine*," to cite from the Latin translation of Jacobus Locher), the original artist evoked the idea with some sixteen books and with wall shelves that frankly look rather empty; an imitator for the Nuremberg "pocket" edition of the same year, halved the number of books to eight, and some later versions reduced it still further (plate 24).[80] Conversely, these images (like other later medieval ones) do illustrate two further aspects of contemporary libraries that were, in general terms, authentic: first, the coexistence of different types of storage—desks or lecterns, shelves, chests and cupboards—and second, the likelihood that books were not invariably stacked or shelved neatly therein or thereon.

The overarching point here, of course, is that all our depictions, however realistic (or otherwise) they may appear, were designed less to represent the reality of a library than to convey its essence, to show what it stood for, rather than the banalities of how it operated. Accordingly, it was largely irrelevant whether one depicted the windows at Sapientia College fortified with bars or with grilles—both were equally effective for underlining the treasured status of the collection and the care with which it was to be safeguarded. The depictions of libraries of educational institutions, whatever their limitations, unmistakably broadcast the concern for the security and preservation of the books that indeed characterized such bodies. Equally, the corpus of illustrations, restricted though it is, does document in its stylized way the diachronistic evolution of library facilities from chests and cupboards to desks and shelves, simultaneously reflecting the slow but steady growth in the size of collections—with a handful of titles in the earlier images, two or three times as many in the later ones. No attempt is made to show real numbers; however, by the fifteenth century thirty volumes rather than ten are typically deployed to suggest a substantial library, a three-fold rise. This phenomenon was noted in relation to the images of Charles V and Petrarch (plates 9 and 10), and it is equally true for the fresco of the Vatican library (plate 22). With two to three thousand titles, that collection as a whole was exceptionally large; although only about fifty books are included in the Ospedale fresco, this is still, appropriately, the highest total in any of our depictions.

The relationship of our images to reality is thus at best impressionistic. Yet while the pictures tell us little or nothing about particular titles held by specific libraries, they do make important points about medieval intellectual life and culture in general. They reveal a world in which libraries were valued, and a society that pondered the purpose of book collections and how they should be used. Thus if their deficit of documentary detail is at one level a weakness, at another it is perhaps a strength: for the depictions shed light on much wider issues—the nature and function of a library in medieval times. More than any other source, these images illuminate "the library as a concept" and give us visual pointers to how its role in nourishing the mind, not to mention the soul, was understood. It is here that we reach their real potential.

The corpus of depictions embraces a broad range of library types—ecclesiastical, royal, private leisure, individual scholarly, institutional scholastic—with different furnishings, corresponding in different degrees to objective reality; yet almost all the depictions, in their divers ways, portray the library as an emblem of wisdom and learning. The imagery thus corresponds to the laudatory views expressed in writing by such commentators as the celebrated bibliophile Richard de Bury (d. 1345), who declared, "That the treasure of wisdom is chiefly contained in books,"[81] and the learned teacher Pier Paolo Vergerio (d. 1444), who considered that they were "the communal repository of all things knowable."[82]

Furthermore, our images overtly transfer these favorable characteristics to the users of libraries, be they Jerome and Aquinas, Vincent de Beauvais and Petrarch, or unidentified savants. A figure in a study that was lined with weighty tomes was self-evidently a man of letters whose ownership of a collection of books indicated metaphysical as well as physical possession of the learning that they contained. When, in a manuscript of rhetorical treatises that belonged to Raphael de Mercatalis (d. 1508), Cicero is shown as a medieval scholar teaching students in a room lined with books, this is less to suggest that instruction might happen in a library than to evoke a milieu of education and scholarship and, more particularly, the learning of Cicero himself (whose elevated throne-like chair, all the books flank).[83] The point that books represent wisdom was spelled out in the image of Charles V, who, it will be remembered, is actually shown reading the words, "*Beatus uir qui inuenit sapientiam*" (plate 9); and it is underlined at Sapientia College by the "Alpha and o" over the library door (plate 12)—the library in principle embraced everything, as Vergerio said.[84] The photographic portrait of the modern academic humanities author, posed in front of bookshelves, makes the same point (and it will be interesting to see, in the current age of "information technology," when or if this iconography is replaced by an image of the scholar surrounded by computer screens). Correspondingly, the misguided bibliomaniac of *Das Narrenschiff* had to be portrayed with a brush or fly-whisk and a jester's hood to signal the fact that, though in a private library (a potent symbol of wisdom), he was nevertheless a fool concerned with the external appearance rather than the internal content of books (plates 23 and 24).

Whereas in the Romanesque images, reflecting the monastic culture of slow ruminative reading, a glimpse of a few volumes in a chest or cupboard was sufficient to evoke appropriate engagement, in later centuries, with changing patterns of book use, the volumes were shown to be available on shelves or desks. Though chests and storerooms were still current, it was the "open-shelf ready-reference" aspect of the facilities that was generally stressed. We must leave for another occasion consideration of the thorny issue of whether neatly stacked closed books, or a chaos of open ones better conveyed the idea of knowledge—if the former might evoke systematic study and orderly learning, the latter could suggest an inspired frenzy of literary labor. (That both could be applied to the same elevated subject is exemplified by the contrasting portrayals of Jerome's study on the panel by Antonello da Messina of c. 1475,[85] and in the Bible of the Hieronymites at Lisbon, illuminated in Florence by Attavante delgi Attavanti between 1494 and 1497.[86])

If the setting of a library "flattered" the figure working in it, reciprocally that person could add dynamism to the library, indicating use and transmission, as opposed to mere accumulation, of wisdom. The various figures of Jerome in a book-filled study are manifestly at work (plate 20); and in the Vivian Bible Jerome's book chests are part of a scene of the distribution of his intellectual labors (plate 5). The point is particularly relevant to compilers such as Vincent de Beauvais and, to a lesser extent, translators such as Colard Mansion, who were thereby presented as the means through which the content of a library (or some part of it) was synthesized or otherwise made more accessible for a new audience (plate 21). Particularly voracious consumption (and distillation) of book learning is conveyed in one fourteenth-century image of Vincent de Beauvais at work in his study by the inclusion, in front of the wall shelves and a table or lectern adorned with books, of two men staggering in with armfuls of further weighty tomes for him to use.[87]

In a development of this theme, Sixtus IV, whose new library is populated with readers engrossed in their studies, is immortalized in the role of one who freely spreads wisdom (plate 22). This is the visual equivalent of the verbal praise heaped first by Poggio Bracciolini (d. 1454) then by Vespasiano da Bisticci (d. 1498) on Niccolò Niccoli (d. 1437) for endeavoring to turn his substantial personal book collection into a public resource (as it eventually became in the form of the library at San Marco, Florence), and for creating a public library at Santo Spirito for the books of Boccaccio that had hitherto languished there in chests.[88] It is no coincidence, however, that this broader humanistic concept of bibliographical munificence—the library as a vehicle for spreading knowledge freely for its own sake—is only represented in imagery at the very end of our period in an example from Italy.

A further and equally weighty symbolism of the library, represented throughout much of our corpus, was as a vehicle of spirituality. Generally implicit, this is sometimes explicit: the open book cupboard at Ravenna is a revelation of the gospels (plate 1); the value of Frederick of Cologne's episcopal book collection is externalized by the allegorical, biblical, and divine figures around him (plate 7); the worth of that of King Charles V is evoked by the words he is reading, with their scriptural overtones (plate 9);[89] while the spiritual potency of Aquinas's library, as interpreted by Sassetta, is expressed by its church-like setting and the juxtaposition with a (highly symbolic) fountain (plate 14). A Modenese painting of the 1460s or 1470s provides a complementary example, illustrating how when Aquinas studied in a library, he benefitted from the miraculous presence of SS. Peter and Paul, ready to explain a passage in Isaiah.[90] The shelves of books that dominate images of particular monastic cells function in the same way, demonstrating that their occupant is perpetually in the presence of, and communing with, the word of God and his saints.[91]

To foster wisdom and holiness: this was the purpose of a medieval library, however it was constituted and arranged. Almost all our images, whatever they do or do not record about cupboards, chests, chains, desks, and lending procedures, admirably convey this point. Whether by accident or design, many of the images also communicate an intimately related idea, namely that the actual number of books is less important than using them properly. When the fount of all truly worthwhile knowledge was contained between the covers of a single volume (the Bible), when education was based around the detailed study of selected key texts, when the essential material for even so complex a subject as law was embodied in but nine tomes,[92] and when the continual expansion of knowledge and commentary was balanced by regular syntheses of it—be they Hrabanus's *De rerum naturis* or Vincent de Beauvais's *Speculum maius* (plates 3, 4, and 21)—true wisdom was grounded more in depth than in breadth of reading. Pictures showing chests, cupboards, shelves, or lecterns with limited numbers of substantial tomes conveyed precisely this idea. Collecting, preserving, and using the right texts in the right way—which often meant slowly and contemplatively—was far more valuable than just accumulating different titles (as is underlined by *Das Narrenschiff*'s satirization of the fool who loves books per se rather than the wisdom they contain: plates 23 and 24). That is a lesson which—in a society obsessed with making ever vaster quantities of information instantly available, yet permitting less and less time in which to digest it—we could usefully relearn today.

Abbreviations

BAV: Biblioteca Apóstolica Vaticana, Vatican City
BL: British Library, London
BnF: Bibliothèque nationale de France, Paris
ÖNB: Österreichische Nationalbibliothek, Vienna

Notes

1. General overview: A. Derolez, *Les Catalogues de bibliothèques* (Turnhout: Brepols, 1979). A repertory of French examples: A.-M. Genevois, J.-F. Genest,

A. Chalandon, *Bibliothèques de manuscrits médiévaux en France* (Paris: Editions du CNRS, 1987). Italian ones are listed in the series: *Repertorio di Inventari e Cataloghi di Biblioteche Medievali* (Florence: International Society for the Study of Medieval Latin Culture, 2009–). Editions of Belgian ones, A. Derolez et al., *Corpus Catalogorum Belgii* (Bruxelles: Paleis der Academiën, 1994–); of German and Swiss ones, *Mittelalterliche Bibliothekskataloge Deutschlands und der Schweiz* (Munich: Bayerische Akademie der Wissenschaften, 1918–); of English and Scottish ones, Corpus of British Medieval Library Catalogues (London: British Library-British Academy, 1990–).

   2. N. R. Ker, *Medieval Libraries of Great Britain*, 2nd ed. (London: Royal Historical Society, 1964) with *Supplement*, ed. A. G. Watson (London: Royal Historical Society, 1987); S. Krämer, *Mittelalterliche Kataloge Deutschlands und der Schweiz, Ergänzungsband, Handschriftenerbe des deutschen Mittelalters*, 2 vols. (Munich: Bayerische Akademie der Wissenschaften, 1989).

   3. E.g., *The Monastic Constitutions of Lanfranc*, ed. D. Knowles and C.N.L. Brooke (Oxford: Oxford University Press, 2002); *The Observances in the Augustinian Priory of Barnwell, Cambridgeshire*, ed. J. W. Clark (Cambridge: Macmillan and Bowes, 1897); R. Sharpe, "Monastic Reading at Thorney Abbey (1323–1347)," *Traditio* 60 (2005): 243–78. For a college library and a university library see below, notes 51–52.

   4. Overviews: J. W. Clark, *The Care of Books* (Cambridge: Cambridge University Press, 1901); B. H. Streeter, *The Chained Library: A Survey of Four Centuries in the Evolution of the English Library* (London: Macmillan, 1931); J.-F. Genest, "Le mobilier des bibliothèques d'après les inventaires médiévaux," *Vocabulaire du livre et de l'écriture au moyen âge, Actes de la table ronde, Paris 24–26 septembre 1987*, ed. O. Weijers (Turnhout: Brepols, 1989), 136–54; R. Gameson, "The Medieval Library (to c. 1450)," *The Cambridge History of Libraries in Britain and Ireland I*, ed. E. Leedham-Green and T. Webber (Cambridge: Cambridge University Press, 2006), 13–50.

   5. "The Miller's Tale," ll. 3208–12: *The Riverside Chaucer*, ed. L. D. Benson, 3rd ed. (Oxford: Oxford University Press, 1987), 68. Chaucer categorizes his own library—with what accuracy is irrecoverable—as "sixty bokes olde and newe" ("The Legend of Good Women," G273–74: *Riverside Chaucer*, 597). For an overview of Chaucer's reading (not, of course, identical to the books that he actually owned) as inferred from his writings, see D. Gray, ed., *The Oxford Companion to Chaucer* (Oxford: Oxford University Press, 2003), 86–89. Equally, in his prologue to *Eneydos* (c. 1490), William Caxton describes himself "sittyng in my studye where as laye many diverse paunflettis and bookys": N. F. Blake, *Caxton's Own Prose* (London: Andre Deutsch, 1973), 78.

6. *Cassiodori Senatoris Institutiones*, ed. R.A.B. Mynors (Oxford: Clarendon Press, 1937). Aeneas Siluius Piccolominaeus, "De liberorum educatione," in *Humanist Educational Treatises*, ed. C. W. Kallendorf (Cambridge, MA: Harvard University Press, 2002), 126–259.

7. Two examples from many in which books are particularly abundant: Hubert and Jan van Eyck, "The Adoration of the Mystic Lamb" (completed 1432), Gent, St. Bavo's Cathedral: P. Coremans and A. Janssens de Bisthoven, *Van Eyck, L'Adoration de l'Agneau Mystique*, Les Primitifs Flamands 1 (Antwerp: De Nederlandsche Boekhandel, 1948); E. Dhanens, *Hubert and Jan van Eyck* (New York: Tabard, 1980), 72–121 and 373–81); and Benozzo Gozzoli, "The Triumph of St. Thomas Aquinas" (1471; formerly in Pisa Cathedral; now Paris, Musée du Louvre): D. Cole Ahl, *Benozzo Gozzoli* (New Haven, CT: Yale University Press, 1996), cat. 50; M. Opitz, *Benozzo Gozzoli* (Cologne: Konemann, 1998), ill. 99.

8. A rare and important exception: C. Rabel, "L'estude d'un tres noble seigneur garny a planté du pluiseurs beaulx livres. L'iconographie des bibliothèques médiévales dans les manuscrits enluminés," *Le Goût du lecteur à la fin du moyen âge*, ed. D. Bohler (Paris: Editions du Léopard d'or, 2006), 245–89.

9. D. M. Deliyannis, *Ravenna in late Antiquity* (Cambridge: Cambridge University Press, 2010), 74–84. General view, as seen from the entrance: G. Bovini, *Ravenna* (New York: Abrams, 1971), pl. 7. Colour: C. Bertelli, *The Art of Mosaics* (London: Cassell, 1989), 66–67.

10. Florence, Biblioteca Medicea Laurenziana, Amiatino 1: R. Marsden, *The Text of the Old Testament in Anglo-Saxon England* (Cambridge: Cambridge University Press, 1995), 76–139, esp. 119–22 and 134–39; L. Alidori et al., *Bibbie Miniate della Biblioteca Medicea Laurenziana di Firenze* (Florence: SISMEL, Edizioni del Galluzzo, 2003), 3–58, esp. 9–10. Color image of the full page including titulus inscription: K. Weitzmann, *Late Antique and Early Christian Book Illumination* (London: Chatto and Windus, 1977), pl. 48.

11. Interpreted by J. Ramirez, "Sub culmine gazas: The Iconography of the Armarium on the Ezra Page of the Codex Amiatinus," *Gesta* 48.1 (2009), 3–18.

12. Codicibus sacris hostili clade perustis / Esdra deo fervens hoc reparauit opus ("The sacred books having been consumed by fire through enemy aggression, Ezra zealous for God restored this work"; trans. from Marsden, *Text of the Old Testament*, 120). See further P. Meyvaert, *The Art of Words: Bede and Theodulf* (Aldershot: Ashgate, 2008), nos. V–VII, with his subsequent reflections, x–xiv (where the corresponding figure in the model is presumed to have been Cassiodorus).

13. Compare *Digesta Iustiniani Augustini*, ed. Th. Mommsen, 2 vols. (Berlin: Weidmann 1952–3), 32.52.7, where "biblioteca" is understood to embrace "locus," "armarium," and "libri."

14. *Patrologia Latina*, ed. J.-P. Migne, 221 vols. (Paris: Garnier, 1844–64), vol. 111, cols. 9–614 at cols. 121–22.

15. Cf. Isidore, *Etymologiae*, VI.iii: *Isidori Hispalensis Episcopi Etymologiarum sive originum libri XX*, ed. W. M. Lindsay, 2 vols. (Oxford: Clarendon Press, 1911), I (no pagination).

16. There are, in addition, three imperfect illustrated copies: Berlin, Preussische Staatsbibliothek, Cod. fol. lat. 930 + New York, Columbia University, Plimpton 128 (Catalonia; *s*. xiv; many miniatures excised); Paris, BnF, lat. 17177 (Germany; *s*. xii/xiii; a couple of folios including four pictures); and Vatican City, BAV, Reg. lat. 391 (Italy; *s*. xv; only eight miniatures executed; the spaces reserved for the rest remained unfilled).

17. Monte Cassino, Archivio della Badia, 132, 96: M. Reuter, *Text und Bild im Codex 132 der Bibliothek von Montecassino, "Liber Rabani de originibus rerum"* (Munich: Arbeo-Gesellschaft, 1984), 96–97, ill. 25, pl. xiii; F. Newton, *The Scriptorium and Library at Monte Cassino 1058–1105* (Cambridge: Cambridge University Press, 1999), ch. 6, fig. 25; G. Orofino, *I Codice Decorati dell'Archivio di Montecassino* II.2: *I codici preteobaldiani e teobaldiani* (Rome: Istituto Poligrafico e Zecca dello Stato, 2000), 50–86, ills. X–LXV, esp. XVI(b).

18. Although it is theoretically possible that the central panel was joined to one of its neighbors by hinges, and that both opened together concertina fashion (compare Cornelius's book cupboard in BnF, fr. 782 [see note 37] and a Macrobius in Oxford [see note 40]), it seems more probable that the artist was not overly concerned by the practical operation (or otherwise) of his cupboard.

19. Vatican City, BAV, Pal. lat. 291: E. Mittler, ed., *Bibliotheca Palatina*, 2 vols. (Heidelberg: Braus, 1986), I, cat. C8.1. The bibliotheca (on fol. 43r) is reproduced in color in R.M.W. Stammberger, *Scriptor und Scriptorium. Das Buch im Spiegel mittelalterlicher Handschriften* (Graz: Akademische Druck-und Verlagsanstalt, 2003), no. 22.

20. W. Koehler, *Die karolingischen Miniaturen I: Die Schule von Tours*, 3 vols. (Berlin: Deutscher Verein fur Kunstwissenschaft, 1933), II, 50–53 and 321–23; III, pl. 69; H. L. Kessler, *The Illustrated Bibles from Tours* (Princeton, NJ: Princeton University Press, 1977), 84–95; F. Mütherich and J. E. Gaehde, *Carolingian Painting* (New York: Braziller, 1977), pl. 21. See further P. Dutton and H. Kessler, *Poetry and Painting in the First Bible of Charles the Bald* (Ann Arbor: University of Michigan Press, 1997), 59–60; D. Ganz, "The Vatican

Vergil and the Jerome Page in the First Bible of Charles the Bald," *Under the Influence: The Concept of Influence and the Study of Illuminated Manuscripts*, ed. J. Lowden and A. Bovey (Turnhout: Brepols, 2007), 45–50; and H. L. Kessler, "Jerome and Vergil in Carolingian Frontispieces and the Uses of Translation," *Les Manuscrits carolingiens. Actes du colloque de Paris, Bibliothèque nationale de France, le 4 mai 2007*, ed. J.-P. Caillent and M.-P. Laffitte, Bibliologia 27 (Turnhout: Brepols, 2009), 121–40, esp. 125–32.

21. E.g., the *saec.* v "Roman Vergil" (BAV, Vat. lat. 3867), fols. 3v, 9r, and 14r: D. H. Wright, *The Roman Vergil and the Origins of Medieval Book Design* (London: British Library, 2001), 16, 18, and 20.

22. Rome, San Paolo Fuori le Mura, s.n., fol. 3v: V. Jemolo and M. Morelli, *La Bibbia di S. Paolo fuori le Mura* (Rome: De Luca Editore, 1981), pl. III; W. Koehler and F. Mütherich, *Die karolingischen Miniaturen* VI: *Die Schule von Reims. Zweiter Teil: von der Mitte bis zum Ende des 9. Jahrhunderts*, 2 vols. (Berlin: Gebr. Mann Verlag, 1999), I,109–74, esp. 127–29; II, pl. 224. It, too, was made for Charles the Bald. See further J. Gaehde, "The Touronian Sources of the Bible of San Paolo fuori le Mura in Rome," *Frühmittelalterliche Studien* 5 (1971), 359–400; and Kessler, "Jerome and Vergil in Carolingian Frontispieces." Book chests (or *capsae*) accompany all four evangelists both on the *maiestas* page (259v) and in the individual portraits preceding each gospel in the San Paolo Bible (260v, 270r, 277r, 287r): Jemolo and Morello, *La Bibbia*, pls. XVIII–XXII.

23. BAV, Vat. lat. 3225. D. H. Wright, "When the Vatican Vergil Was in Tours," *Studien zur mittelalterlichen Kunst 800–1250: Festschrift für Florentine Mütherich*, ed. K. Bierbrauer, P. Klein and W. Sauerländer (Munich: Prestel, 1985), 53–66.

24. See note 21.

25. Le Havre, Bibliothèque municipale, 332 (A.34), fol. 41v: H. Omont, *Catalogue général des manuscrits des bibliothèques publiques de France: Départements* II (Paris, 1888), 332–5; F. Avril, *Manuscrits normands XI–XIIème siècles* (Rouen: Musée des beaux-arts, 1975), no. 55 (with photograph of the relevant page, but so cropped as to remove most of the book chest); M.-C. Garand, G. Grand and D. Muzerelle, *Catalogue des manuscrits en écriture latine portant des indications de date, de lieu ou de copiste VII: Ouest de la France et Pays de Loire*, 2 vols. (Paris: Centre national de la recherche scientifique, 1984), I, 157. Full page reproduced: A. Vernet, ed., *Les bibliothèques médiévales: Du VIe siècle à 1530*, Histoire des bibliothèques françaises 1 (Paris: Promodis / Cercle de la librairie, 1989), 364. Color: P. Plagnieux, ed., *L'art du moyen âge en France* (Paris: Citadelles and Mazenod, 2010), 216.

26. Principally c. 6, but also c. 13 (*Passiones Vitaeque Sanctorum Aevi Mero-vingici*, ed. B. Krusch and W. Levison, Monumenta Germaniae Historica, Scriptorum Rerum Merovingicarum V (Hannover and Leipzig: Hahn, 1910), 613–41 at 622–23 and 627 respectively).

27. R. Gameson, " 'Signed' Manuscripts from Early Romanesque Flanders," *Pen in Hand: Medieval Scribal Portraits, Colophons and Tools*, ed. M. Gullick (Walkern: Red Gull Press, 2006), 31–73.

28. Vatican City, BAV, Vat. lat. 1202, fol. iir. Facsimile: *The Codex Benedictus: an Eleventh-Century Illustrated Lectionary*, ed. P. Meyvaert (New York: Johnson Reprint Corp., Harcourt Brace Jovanovich, 1982). B. Brenk, *Das Lektionar des Desiderius von Montecassino: ein Meisterwerk italienischer Buchmalerei des 11. Jahrhunderts* (Zürich: Belser, 1987), esp. 27–39, with pl. 2; M. Siponta de Salvia, *The Vatican Library: Its History and Treasures* (New York: Belser, 1989), pl. XX-VIII; Newton, *Scriptorium and Library at Monte Cassino*, 65–67 and 291–307.

29. Cum domibus miros plures pater accipe libros. / Rura lacus presto. Caeli michi prestitor esto.

30. Monte Cassino, Archivio della Badia, 132, p. 82: Newton, *Scriptorium and Library at Monte Cassino*, 301 (with fig. 8), where the comparison is made.

31. *Monastic Constitutions of Lanfranc*, cc. 20–22, ed. Knowles and Brooke, 30–32. *Consuetudines Cluniacensium Antiquiores*, ed. K. Hallinger, Corpus Consuetudinem Monasticarum VII.2 (Siegburg: Schmitt, 1983), no. 34, p. 54.

32. Cologne, Dombibliothek, 59: A. Legner, ed., *Rhein und Maas: Kunst und Kultur 800–1400* (Köln: Schnürgen-Museum, 1972), cat. J.41; J. M. Plotzek, *Glaube und Wissen im Mittelalter* (Köln: Hirmer, 1998), no. 30 with color reproduction of the page in question on p. 14.

33. BL, Cotton Claudius E. iv, part I, fol. 124r (Clark, *Care of Books*, 293, fig. 134). The *Gesta abbatum S. Albani* includes (rudimentary) images of each abbot, many of whom are shown reading—or at least holding—a book; Symon alone has a book chest. The account of Symon begins by stressing how he labored to improve the library, mentioning volumes *in almario* near the tomb of Roger the hermit. Whether or not the chest is supposed to represent that almarium in particular, it clearly evokes a bibliophile abbot and the book collection that he built up (further on which see R. M. Thomson, *Manuscripts from St. Albans Abbey 1066–1235*, 2 vols. (Woodbridge: Brewer, 1982), I, 48–62). Notwithstanding the limited skill of the artist, the chest is unmistakably meant to be of wood with decorative metal braces, its top fastened by two locks; it holds three books and one scroll.

34. This part of the MS (also known as the "Turin Prayerbook") was destroyed in 1904 and is now known only from black-and-white photographs

taken before the fire: reproduced, F. Boespflug and E. König, *Les Très Belles Heures* (Paris: Editions du Cerf, 1998), 149.

35. Images of universities tend to show instruction or disputation in "schoolroom" contexts (each participant equipped with a book), not libraries as such: it is thus, for instance, on the famous Bolognese tombs (e.g. G. C. Cavalli, *Introduzione al Museo Civico Medievale* [Bologna: Comune di Bologna, 1985], nos. 19–21 and 24–25) and in many legal MSS (e.g., Lyon, Bibliothèque municipale, MS 374, fol. 1r: Cino da Pistoia, *Commentary on the Code*: S. Cassagnes-Brouquet, *La Passion du livre au Moyen Age* [Rennes: Ouest-France, 2003], 60; or Oxford, Bodleian Library, Canon. Misc. 416: Azzo, *Summa*: O. Pächt and J.J.G. Alexander, *Illuminated Manuscripts in the Bodleian Library, Oxford 2: Italian School* [Oxford: Clarendon Press, 1970], no. 107, pl. X). Correspondingly, "disputation" iconography could be borrowed for other contexts, such as to illustrate the tale of the seven philosophers in the late medieval Italian compilation, BL, Add. 15685 (fol. 83r). Here the emperor's son is shown amazing the philosophers by his precocious learning in a chamber equipped with a long C-shaped desk around which the learned elders sit, each clutching or pointing to a book, a couple of extra tomes on the desk and seven further ones in recesses in its front; but contrary to the way it is sometimes described, this is not a "library." For miniatures of "schoolrooms" in which shelves of books are particularly prominent see notes 72 and 83.

36. El Escorial, Real Biblioteca, T.j.1, illustrations for cantigas II (a square, flat-topped unit raised on legs, containing two shelves—bearing a total of six books, spines down—closed by a single pair of folding doors), LVI (a narrower cupboard raised on legs, with an elaborate pediment and a domed top; two shelves both closed by a pair of doors—a total of seven books, spines down) and CLVI (a tall cupboard with a pediment, its lower portions concealed by the writing figure; the visible section is closed by a pair of doors, the books stacked spine down). Facsimile: *Alfonso X el Sabio, Cantigas de Santa Maria: Edición facsimile del Codice T.I.i de la Biblioteca de San Lorenzo el Real de El Escorial, siglo XIII* (Madrid: Edilán, 1979). See also J. Guerrero Lovillo, *Las Cántigas. Estudio Arqueológico de sus Miniaturas* (Madrid: Consejo Superior de Investigaciones Científicas, 1949), pls. 4, 63, and 171, with discussion (and line drawings) of the *armaria* on pp. 301–3.

37. BnF, fr. 782, fol. 2v (the relevant detail is reproduced in colour in Cassagnes-Brouquet, *La Passion du livre au moyen âge*, p. 19, and (grossly enlarged) in J. Glenisson, *Le Livre au Moyen Age* (Paris: CNRS, 1988), 4–5; and Vienna, ÖNB, 2571, fol. 2r (miniature described: H. J. Hermann, *Die italienischen Handschriften des Dugento und Trecento 2: Oberitalienische Handschrif-*

ten der zweiten Hälfte des 14. Jahrhunderts [Leipzig: Karl W. Hiersemann, 1929],139). See further M.-R. Jung, *La légende de Troie en France au moyen âge*, Romanica Helvetica 114 (Basel and Tübingen: Francke, 1996), esp. 177–80 and 297–306.

38. Lines 87–92: *Le Roman de Troie par Benoît de Sainte-Maure*, ed. L. Constans, Société des anciens textes français, 6 vols. (Paris: Firmin Didot, 1904–12), I, 6.

39. One might compare, e.g., the "*theca* above the door" that features among the cases or cupboards inventoried in the Meaux library catalogue of 1396: *The Libraries of the Cistercians, Gilbertines and Premonstratensians*, ed. D. N. Bell, *Corpus of British Medieval Library Catalogues* 3 (London: British Library-British Academy, 1992), list Z14, nos. 50–51.

40. Two-part folding doors are clearly shown, for example, in the *Cantigas of Santa Maria* (see note 36) and on Macrobius's book cupboard in Oxford, Bodleian Library, Canon. Lat. class. 257, made at Bologna in 1383 (Macrobius, *De somnio Scipionis*: Pächt and Alexander, *Illuminated Manuscripts 2*, no. 128). This last cupboard itself—with five inserted shelves plus the base of the cabinet, the whole raised up on four legs—is similar to those at Ravenna and in the Codex Amiatinus.

41. BnF, Fr. 24287, fol. 2r. F. Avril and J. Lafaurie, *La librarie de Charles V* (Paris: Bibliothèque nationale, 1968), no. 28; M.-H. Tesnière, *Trésors de la Bibliothèque nationale de France I: Mémoires et merveilles VIIIᵉ-XVIIIᵉ siècles* (Paris: Bibliothèque nationale, 1996), no. 28. For the translation: *Le Policratique de Jean de Salisbury (1372), Livres I-III*, trad. Denis Foulechat, ed. C. Bruckner (Geneva: Droz,1994).

42. Discussed by Clark, *Care of Books*, 293–96; and J. Vezin, "Le mobilier des bibliothèques," *Histoire des bibliothèques françaises*, ed. Vernet, 364–71 at 70. For documentary evidence see M. Beck, "Rota, roe = pluteus versatilis," *Zentralblatt für Bibliothekswesen* 62 (1948), 291–304, and Genest, "Mobilier des Bibliothèques," 149–50. On an early example described in the *Life* of St. Eloi (d. 660) written by St. Ouen (d. 686) see M. and R. Rouse, "Eloi's Books and their Bookcase," *Manuscripta* 55 (2011): 170–92, esp. 188–91.

43. The double level wheel desk with multangular plates at which Charles V is shown in a MS of Nicolas Oresme and Pèlerin de Prusse (Oxford, St. John's College, 164, fol. 33r), has two books; another image in the same volume (fol. 1r) depicts a version with a single multangular plate supporting four books: C. R. Sherman, *Imaging Aristotle: Verbal and Visual Representation in Fourteenth-Century France* (Berkeley and Los Angeles: University of California Press, 1995), figs. 2 and 4; R. Hanna, *A Descriptive Catalogue of the Western*

Medieval Manuscripts of St. John's College, Oxford (Oxford: Oxford University Press, 2002), 227–30. An example having a single round plate with a raised lip appears in London, Lambeth Palace Library, MS 326 (Guillaume de Digulleville trans. Jean Galopes, *Pèlerinage de l'âme*; ?Paris; c. 1427: R. Palmer and M. P. Brown, *Lambeth Palace Library: Treasures from the Collection of the Archbishops of Canterbury* [London: Scala, 2010], no. 13, with ills. on pp. 60 and 62); it holds four books. For further, typical examples see Clark, *Care of Books* figs. 135 (BL, Royal 14 E. v: a generous multangular lectern on a screw stem, holding three books), 142 (BL, Yates Thompson 3; a multangular tray; two books shown); 150 (unidentified; a round plate, a two-sided lectern above; four books shown); and 151 (Oxford, Bodleian Library, Douce 381; two books shown). Other exceptionally laden cases include Chantilly, Musée Condé, MS 291 ("Fleurs de toutes vertues"; *s.* xv: F. Vergne, *La Bibliothèque du Prince. Chateau de Chantilly, Les manuscrits* [Paris: Editions Editerra, 1995], 221; two wheels holding twelve volumes) and BnF, Fr. 380, fol. 27v (*Roman de la Rose*; *s.* xiv^ex: M.-H. Tesnière, "Manuscrits enluminés du *Roman de la Rose* au début du XVe siècle," *Art de l'enluminure* 42 (2012): 2–57, ill., 41; an enormous wheel with two plates holding seventeen volumes).

44. In 1367–68: Delisles, *Recherches* I, 85–8, 263–4. Text printed: Clark, *Care of Books*, 292, n. 1.

45. "Homo" in the main text below.

46. Fol. 12r: Tesnière, *Trésors*, 27 (ill. 5). Compare Ecclesiasties 10:17; there is also, of course, an echo of Psalm 1:1. See more generally C. R. Sherman, "Representations of Charles V as a Wise Ruler," *Medievalia et Humanistica*, new series, 2 (1971): 83–96.

47. Darmstadt, Universitäts- und Landesbibliothek, MS 101, fol. 1v (Donato degli Albanzani's vernacular version of Petrarch's *De uiris illustribus*; 1397 or later): G. B. Molli, G. C. Mariani and F. Toniolo, *La Miniatura a Padova dal Medioevo al Settecento* (Padua: Panini, 1999), no. 64; M. Krenn and C. Winterer, *Mit Pinsel und Federkiel: Geschichte der mittelalterlichen Buchmalerei* (Darmstadt: Primus, 2009), ill. 71.

48. Now the Sala dei Giganti: Th. Mommsen, "Petrarch and the Decoration of the Sala uirorum illustrium in Padua," *Art Bulletin* 34 (1952): 96–116; D. Norman, "Splendid Models and Examples from the Past: Carrara Patronage of Art," *Siena, Florence and Padua: Art, Society and Religion 1280–1400*, ed. D. Norman, 2 vols. (New Haven, CT: Yale University Press, 1995), I, 154–75, esp. 164–69 with pl. 175.

49. Th. Mommsen, *Petrarch's Testament* (Ithaca, NY: Cornell University Press, 1957), esp. 43–50; G. Billanovich, "Nella Biblioteca del Petrarca," *Ita-*

lia medioevale e umanistica 3 (1960): 1–58; and A. Petrucci, *La scrittura di Francesco Petrarca* (Vatican City: Biblioteca Apostolica Vaticana, 1967), esp. 115–29. For a convenient list of identified books see M. Feo, ed., *Petrarca nel tempo* (Arezzo: Comitato Nazionale per le celebrazioni del VII centenario della nascita di Francesco Petrarca, 2003), 461–96; with the further comments of N. Mann, "Petrarcha Philobiblon: The Author and His Books," *Literary Cultures and the Material Book*, ed. S. Eliot, A. Nash, and I. Wilson (London: British Library, 2007), 159–73.

50. Thus Florence, Biblioteca Medicea Laurenziana, Strozzi 172, fol. Iv; and Florence, Biblioteca Nazionale Centrale, Palatino 184, fol. Iv: M. Feo, ed., *Codici Latini del Petrarca nelle Biblioteche Fiorentine* (Florence: Le Lettere,1991), pls. X and XVI. Equally, the iconographically distinct tradition of Petrarch in his study as represented by Francesco d'Antonio del Chierico's image in a fine Florentine copy of the *Rime e Trionfi* of the 1470s (Milan, Biblioteca Trivulziana, MS 905, fol. 1v: C. Santoro, *I Codici Miniati della Biblioteca Trivulziana* [Milan: Commune di Milano, 1958], pl. LXIX; G. Bologna, *Miniature Italiane della Biblioteca Trivulziana* [Milan: Commune Ripartizione cultura, 1974], 97), although it features an imposing set of shelves rising to the ceiling above Petrarch's writing desk, nevertheless shows them sparingly furnished with but fifteen books.

51. Paris, Archives nationales, MM406, fol. 10v (image number 26): A. L. Gabriel, *Student Life in Ave Maria College, Mediaeval Paris: History and Chartulary of the College* (Notre Dame, IN.: University of Notre Dame Press, 1955), 3–7 and 166–70 with pl. XXI. Clearer reproduction: Vernet, ed., *Bibliothèques françaises*, 103.

52. Freiburg-im-Breisgau, University Archives, MS A. Facsimile: Johannes Kerer, *Statuta Collegii Sapientiae*, ed. J. H. Beckmann, 2 vols. (Lindau and Konstanz: Jan Thorbecke, 1957).

53. Fol. 44r.

54. Fol. 44v.

55. Fol. 53v.

56. Budapest, Szépmüvészeti Múzeum, n. 32: K. Christiansen, L. B. Kantor and C. B. Strehlke, ed., *Painting in Renaissance Siena 1420–1500* (New York: Metropolitan Museum of Art, 1988), cat. 1(b); M. Seidel et al., *Da Jacopo della Quercia a Donatello: Le Arti a Siena nel Primo Rinascimento* (Siena: Frederico Motta, 2010), cat. C.17(e).

57. Digital reconstruction incorporating all the surviving panels: Seidel, ed., *Da Jacopo della Quercia*, 222.

58. Chantilly, Musée Condé, MS 297, fol. 71v (heading the final chapter of Part I): Vergne, *La Bibliothèque du Prince*, 224; also (cropped and greatly

enlarged) on the dust wrapper of Vernet, ed., *Bibliothèques médiévales*. Text: *Archiloge Sophie. Livre de Bonnes Meurs*, ed. E. Beltran, Bibliothèque du XVᵉ siècle 49 (Paris: Slatkine, 1986).

59. E.g., for such problems at the old university library room in Oxford (the upper chamber of the annex attached to the University Church of St. Mary's) see Oxford University Archives, Registrum F, fols. 71v–72r.

60. Clearer representations of such angled wall shelves in a more realistic perspectival idiom appear in, e.g., Carpaccio's "The Vision of Augustine" of 1502x8, Venice, Scuola di San Giorgio degli Schiavoni: J. Lauts, *Carpaccio, Paintings and Drawings: Complete Edition* (London: Phaidon, 1962), no. 14, with pls. 102, 104 and 105; D. Thornton, *The Scholar in His Study: Ownership and Experience in Renaissance Italy* (New Haven, CT, and London: Yale University Press, 1997), ill. 27: they are shown to be sprung forward at the bottom and supported there by metal arms. Another version from many appears behind St. Luke in a Book of Hours of c. 1495 associated with Jean Bourdichon, BAV, Vat. lat. 3781, fol. 12v (facsimile: *Das vatikanische Stunden-Buch Jean Bourdichons*, ed. E. König [Zurich: Belser, 1984]).

61. BL, Harley 4335, fol. 1r. Reproduced in colour as the frontispiece to *Boethius, Consolation of Philosophy*, trans. V. E. Watts, preface by B. Keenan (London: Folio Society, 1998).

62. BL, Cotton Tiberius A. vii, fol. 91v: K. L. Scott, *Later Gothic Manuscripts 1390–1490*, 2 vols. (London: Harvey Miller, 1996), II, no. 89, with illustration of this picture in vol. I, p. 64; also reproduced in colour on the dust wrapper of A. Gillespie and D. Wakelin, ed., *The Production of Books in England 1350–1500* (Cambridge: Cambridge University Press, 2011). Text: *The Pilgrimage of the Life of Man, englisht by John Lydgate, A.D. 1426*, ed. F. J. Furnivall and K. B. Locock, EETS 77, 83, 92 (1899–1904). On the authorship of the translation: R. Firth Green, "Lydgate and Deguilville Once More," *Notes and Queries* 223 (1978): 105–6.

63. Thus L. H. Loomis, "The Auchinleck Manuscript and a Possible London Bookshop of 1330–1340," *Proceedings of the Modern Language Association* 57 (1942): 595–627.

64. Printed by Pierre le Rouge for Vincent Commin (copy consulted: Manchester, John Rylands University Library, Inc. 26. A.6–7 [19932]). The first image type shows a figure writing at a desk supported on a wheel pedestal; further books appear in the back of his chair, on wall shelves, on a wheel lectern in the background, and on the floor. This picture was first used in vol. I, fol. ii r (St. Augustine on monsters), being redeployed twenty times thereafter. The second type has a seated figure writing on a support propped on the base stand of a

book wheel, on and around which are shown twelve volumes. This first appears in vol. I, fol. iiii v (On false Gods—citing Cicero, Augustine, Plato, etc.), being reused a further ten times thereafter. The third type is first seen in vol. I, fol. hh 7v (Periander), reappearing a further eight times thereafter.

65. The colored example from the deluxe copy on vellum that was offered to King Charles VIII of France (BnF, Imprimés, Rés Vélins 676–77) is reproduced in U. Baurmeister and M.-P. Laffitte, *Des livres et des rois, La Bibliothèque royale de Blois* (Paris: Bibliothèque nationale, 1992), no. 17, p. 27 (hand-painted variants being shown on pp. 28–29). Further on this particular copy see *Bibliothèque nationale, Catalogue des Incunables* II (Paris: Bibliothèque nationale, 1981–5), no. R-221; and Tesnière, *Trésors de la Bibliothèque nationale de France I*, no. 53.

66. Appearing, for example, in the 1538 edition of Boccaccio, *Des nobles maleureux* (Paris: Nicolas Couteau for Jean Petit): *Index Aureliensis. Catalogus librorum sedecimo saeculo impressorum* (Geneva, 1965–), 120.270.

67. Paris, Bibliothèque de l'Arsénal, MS 5208, fol. 1r: B. Bousmanne and Th. Delcourt, ed., *Miniatures flamandes 1404–1482* (Paris-Bruxelles: Bibliothèque nationale, 2011), no. 24 (with col. ill. of this picture on p. 194). Text: *L'istoire de tres vaillans princez monsegneur Jehan d'Avennes*, ed. D. Quéruel, Textes et perspectives. Bibliothèque des Seigneurs du Nord (Villeneuve d'Ascq: Septenrion Presses Universitaires, 1997), the relevant passage reading: "je m'estoire trouvé dans l'estude d'un tres noble seigneur garny a planté de plusieurs beaux livres desquels m'aprouchay en encommenchay lire." The corresponding image in the slightly earlier copy of the work that ended up in the collection of Duke Philip the Good of Burgundy (Paris, BnF, Fr. 12572, fol. 1r: Bousmanne and Delcourt, *Miniatures flamandes*, no. 98, col. ill. on p. 362) only featured four books; but then its illustrations were by the Wavrin Master, an artist celebrated for his sketchy yet vivid style and his gift for evoking subject matter and narrative with a minimum of elements.

68. Vienna, ÖNB, MS 2572, fol. 1r: F. Unterkircher, *Bibliothèque nationale d'Autriche: Manuscrits et livres imprimés concernant l'histoire des Pays-Bas 1475–1600* (Bruxelles: Bibliothèque royale de Belgique, 1962), no. 47, pl. 10; also Vernet, ed., *Bibliothèques médiévales*, p. 253. The text: *Le Dialogue des créatures*, ed. P. Ruelle (Bruxelles: Palais des Académies, 1985).

69. In Alexander Barclay's *The Shyp of Folys* (London: Richard Pynson, 1509), an English version of *Das Narrenschiff* (for which see note 79), the bookfool declares, "But if it fortune that any learned men / Within my house fall to disputacion / I drawe the curtyns to shew my bokes then / That they of my cunnynge sholde make probacion."

70. Detroit, Institute of Arts, Inv 25.4: M. W. Ainsworth, ed., *Petrus Christus: Renaissance Master of Bruges* (New York: Metropolitan Museum of Art, 1994), no. 1; B. Heller and L. Stodulski, "Recent Scientific Investigation of the Detroit Saint Jérôme," *Petrus Christus in Renaissance Bruges: An Interdisciplinary Approach*, ed. M. W. Ainsworth (New York and Turnhout: Brepols, 1995), 131–42; T.-H. Borchert, ed., *Le Siècle de van Eyck* (Gent: Ludion, 2002), no. 30 with ill. 113; T.-H. Borchert, *Van Eyck* (Köln: Taschen, 2008), 78. Thirteen books and one scroll are visible on a single shelf.

71. BL, Royal 14. E. i, vol. I, fol. 3r: col. pl.: J. Clegg, *The Medieval Church in Manuscripts* (London: British Library, 2003), ill. 48; S. McKendrick, J. Lowden and K. Doyle, eds., *Royal Manuscripts. The Genius of Illumination* (London: British Library, 2011), no. 57. Other examples include: BnF, Fr. 6275, fol. 1r (Vincent de Beauvais, trans. Miélot, *Miroir de la salvation humaine*: Vernet, ed., *Histoire des bibliothèques françaises,* 241); BL, Royal 14 E. v (Boccaccio, trans. Laurens du Premierfait, *Livre des cas des malheureux nobles hommes et femmes*: Clark, *Care of Books*, fig. 135); and Bruxelles, Bibliothèque royale, 9242, I, fol. 2r (Chroniques de Hainault: P. Cockshaw and C. Van den Bergen-Pantens, ed., *Les Chroniques de Hainault ou les Ambitions d'un Prince Bourguignon* [Bruxelles-Turnhout: Brepols, 2000], col. pl. on p. 258).

72. An "institutional" example appears in the frontispiece to the *s.* xv² Netherlandish copy of Nicolas Oresmes, *Les Ethiques d'Aristote*, BL, Egerton 737, fol. 1r: the setting for this scene of instruction includes desks, angled wall shelving, and an armarium unit set very high up the wall (three shelves supporting twenty-three books, all lying flat), its front covered not by doors but by a single curtain.

73. Reproduced in color: Siponta de Salvia, *Vatican Library*, 21. For the building itself: Clark, *Care of Books*, 207–33; J. Ruysschaert, "La Bibliothèque Vaticane dans les dix premières années du pontificat de Sixte IV," *Archivium historiae pontificae* 24 (1986): 71–90.

74. N. Clark, *Melozzo da Forlì, pictor papalis* (London: Sotheby's, 1990), 27–41, pl. VII.

75. Apparently not the extant version: J. Ruysschaert, "Platina et l'aménagement des locaux de la Vaticane sous Sixtus IV (1471–1475–1481)," *Bartolomeo Sacchi, Il Platina: Medioevo e Umanesimo* 62 (Padua: Antenore, 1985), 145–52; Clark, *Melozzo da Forli*, 27–29.

76. Glasgow University Library, Hunter 8 (Bartholomew the Englishman translated by Jean Corbichon), fol. 10r: N. Thorp, *The Glory of the Page: Medieval and Renaissance Illuminated Manuscripts from Glasgow University Library* (Glasgow and London: Harvey Miller, 1987), no. 51 with illustration on p. 105.

77. Olim Torino, Biblioteca Universitaria, K.IV.29, fol. 73v: Boespflug and König, *Les Très Belles Heures*, p. 142. Baltimore, Walters Art Museum, W 721, fol. 277v: M. Smeyers, "A Mid-Fifteenth-Century Book of Hours from Bruges in the Walters Art Gallery (MS 721) and Its Relation to the Turin-Milan Hours," *Journal of the Walters Art Gallery* 46 (1988): 55–76. Also Paris, BnF, n.a.l. 3110, fol. 163v; and San Marino, Huntington Library, MS HM 1087, fol. 135r (C. W. Dutschke, *Guide to Medieval and Renaissance Manuscripts in the Huntington Library*, 2 vols. [San Marino: University of California Press, 1989], II, ill. 98).

78. Correspondingly, the personification of Prudentia in an Italian tract on the Cardinal Virtues (BL, Add. 15685, fol. 69v) is shown enthroned on a bench with a lectern to either side, an open book on each; books, open and shut, lie on the bench and platform below. Although the total number of volumes at her disposal is a mere nine, the presence of not one but two lecterns was evidently felt to be a powerful device for conveying the idea that she was supremely—or at least doubly—wise.

79. Basel: Johan Bergmann. The woodcut in question is ascribed to the "Master of the Haintz-Nar." D. Wuttke, ed., *Sebastian Brant: Das Narrenschiff; Faksimile der Erst-ausgabe Basel 1494* (Baden-Baden: Koerner, 1994). The images in, for example, the Latin editions of Godridus de Marnes (Paris, 1498) and the French edition of Guillaume Ualfarin (Lyon, 1498) preserve fifteen or sixteen books.

80. Nuremberg: Peter Wagner, 1 July 1494, fol. A5r. This type reappears, for example, in Johan Bergman de Olpe's pocket edition of 1497 (Basel) and in Johann Schönsperger's pocket Latin and grander German versions of April 1497 and May 1498 respectively. The cut in the Strassburg (Johann Reinhard Grüninger) edition of 1497 (fol. 9r) features eleven books, on one of which sits a fly. The reversed version in the Lübeck edition of 1497 (fol. ix r) features ten books (one on a rear shelf, the rest on or in a lectern desk) but two flies, which, by giving direct purpose to the fool's flail, slightly subvert the implement's initial role as an emblem of vacuity and vanity.

81. "Quod thesaurus sapientiae potissime sit in libris:" Richard de Bury, *Philobiblon*, ed. E. C. Thomas, rev. by M. Maclagan (Oxford: Basil Blackwell, 1960),14.

82. "De ingenuis moribus et liberalibus adulescentiae studiis liber," § 38: *Humanist Educational Treatises*, ed. and trans. Kallendorf, 47.

83. Gent University Library, MS 10, fol. 37v: A. Derolez, *The Library of Raphael de Marcatellis* (Gent: E. Story-Scientia, 1979), no. 24, 141–45; this image reproduced in color on p. 82. The books are propped upright on narrow wall shelves. Compare BL, Egerton 737, fol. 1r (see note 72).

84. One might also note the exceptional images of the annunciate Virgin Mary where the standard motif of her reading a book is expanded to suggest that she is doing so in a private study—for example, on Master Bertram's 1379–83 altarpiece for St. Peter's, Hamburg (Hamburg Kunsthalle, Inv. 500), where she is surrounded by three separate lecterns, a book on each, with a further couple stacked under the lowest of them (M. Sitt and S. Hauschild, *Der Petri-Altar von Meister Bertram* [Hamburg: ConferencePoint Verlag, 2008], ill. 3); and in the s. xv missal, Paris, Bibliothèque Mazarine, MS 412, fol. 8r, lower register, where her prie-dieu is placed beside an angled wall shelf supporting a run of books (G. de la Batut, *Les Principaux manuscrits à peintures conservés à la Bibliothèque Mazarine de Paris*, Bulletin de la Société Française de reproductions de manuscrits à peintures, 16ᵉ année (Paris, 1933), 47–48, pl. XIX).

85. London, National Gallery, NG 1418: G. Barbera, *Antonello da Messina* (Milan: Electa, 1998), no. 29, 102–3.

86. Lisbon, Arquivos Nacionais, Torre do Tombo 161: J.J.G. Alexander, ed., *The Painted Page: Italian Renaissance Book Illumination 1450–1550* (London: Royal Academy of Arts, 1994), no. 1. Col. pl. of relevant page: A. P. Cardoso, "La Bible des Hiéronymites," *FMR* nouvelle série 10 (2006): 43–71 at 45. Further on Jerome's study: Rabel, "L'iconographie des bibliothèques médiévales," 263–71, contrasting the disorder shown in Flemish depictions with the orderliness in Italian ones.

87. Vatican City, BAV, Reg. lat. 538, fol. 1r. Reproduced in color: M. Puhe, ed., *Aufbruch in die Gotik. Der Magdeburger Dom und die späte Stauferzeit*, 2 vols. (Mainz: Philipp von Zabern, 2009), I, 449.

88. Poggio Bracciolini, *Opera Omnia* I (Turin: Bottega d'Erasmo, 1964), 276–77. *The Vespasiano Memoirs: Lives of Illustrious Men of the XVth Century by Vespasiano da Bisticci, Bookseller*, trans. W. George and E. Waters (London: Routledge,1926), 401–2. See further B. L. Ullmann and P. A. Stadter, *The Public Library of Renaissance Florence: Niccolò Niccolai, Cosimo de' Medici and the Library of San Marco* (Padua: Antenore, 1972).

89. See note 46.

90. By Bartolommeo degli Erri (d. after 1479): New York, Metropolitan Museum of Art, acc. no. 23.140: F. Zeri with E. E. Gardner, *Italian Paintings: A Catalogue of the Collection of the Metropolitan Museum of Art; North Italian School* (New York: Metropolitan Museum of Art, 1986), 15–17 with pl. 12. From the St. Thomas altarpieces of San Domenico, Modena—one of a set of narrative scenes that formerly surrounded a grand central image of Aquinas.

91. For example those of Vincent Ferrer in a panel painting attributed to Colantonio (d. c. 1470) in Naples (Museo di Capodimonte: M. Lucco, ed.,

Antonello da Messina: L'opera completa (Milan: Silvana, 2006), 298–99), and of Jerome by the "Master of the *De civitate Dei* di Cesena," in an incunable copy of his letters (Venice: Antonio di Bartolomeo Miscomini, 1476) now in Rimini (Biblioteca Gambalunghiana, 4.P.II.6: G. M. Canova, P. Meldini and S. Nicolini, *I Codici miniati della Gambalunghiana di Rimini* (Rimini: Cassa di risparmio di Rimini, 1988), 23.

92. S. Chodorow, *Law Libraries and the Formation of the Legal Profession in the Late Middle Ages* (Austin: University of Texas Press, 2007), 7–8.

❦

CHAPTER 3

The Renaissance Library and the Challenge of Print

Andrew Pettegree

·

Gian Vincenzo Pinelli, of Padua, in northern Italy, was one of the great book collectors of the sixteenth century. As he approached the end of his life in 1601 he made plans for his magnificent library to become a permanent monument to his taste and erudition.[1] The ten thousand volumes he had accumulated were to be transported to his family home near Naples, where a library was to be constructed on the family estate for the public to share, and admire, his majestic books. Such aspirations were not unusual in the sixteenth-century scholarly world. But the actual fate of his collection provides a cautionary tale of the dangers facing any scholar seeking to build a legacy. First of all the Venetian government intervened to remove certain manuscripts they regarded as politically sensitive. A servant stole some of the books. The collection was eventually loaded onto three ships for transportation through the Adriatic, but one was intercepted by pirates. When they discovered the cases of freight contained nothing but books they threw several overboard. The abandoned ship was washed ashore and plundered by local fishermen. Of the thirty-three cases of books left on board the authorities could recover only twenty-two. The valuable volumes taken by the locals were dismembered and used to mend boats or provide primitive window coverings. The stiff parchment pages of the most valuable manuscripts, which included a phenomenal and world famous collection of Greek texts, proved to be excellent draught excluders.

Barely had the remains of the collection made its way to Naples when Pinelli's nephew died. The idea of a permanent collection died with him. After prolonged litigation the collection was purchased at auction by Cardinal Borromeo for his new library in Milan (the Biblioteca Ambrosiana).[2] Borromeo's agents now made a careful selection for the long journey back to northern Italy, discarding those damaged by water or rodents, and books of less interest to their new owner. The following year what remained of the manuscripts and a selection of printed texts finally reached their new home.

The unfortunate history of Pinelli's library is perhaps more colorful than most. The majority of books published during the Renaissance fell victim to more mundane dangers: rats and mice, birds and moths, worms or damp. Fire, neglect, and use all took their toll. But it does illustrate vividly the great gulf between the rhetoric of the humanist book world, and the practical experience of those who sought to build a library. It might have been thought that the invention of printing in the fifteenth century, and the huge increase of the availability of books, would usher in a great new age of library building. In fact the opposite was the case. Many of the great Renaissance collections were broken up, the victim of predators, politics, or neglect. In the sixteenth century the library, as a public and private institution, as a focus of wealth and display, took a backward step.

In the following pages I will try to explain why this should be: why the invention of printing so celebrated by fifteenth-century scholars and intellectuals, posed such a testing challenge to the Renaissance library.[3] I will then go on to explain how, with the technologies of the twenty-first century, we can do something to repair the damage done by time—and pirates—to the Renaissance library; and how much of this work is taking place in St. Andrews.

We should begin, as do most discussions of the Renaissance library, with the great collections of the fifteenth century, the era before the invention of printing. Printing, of course, did not invent the book. Mediaeval Europe was full of books, all carefully crafted by hand.[4] Some were objects of great beauty, others more utilitarian, for study and use. Most owners possessed no more than a handful of books, but in the fifteenth century a few privileged individuals began to draw together collections of considerable size. Some were scholars, who made books their life's work. But most were princes, rulers of Europe's city-states and emergent monarchies, for whom a library was a symbol of both wealth and cultural aspiration. Their collection building was encouraged and assisted by exponents of the new humanist scholarship. Scholars provided both the intellectual agenda for collecting and more practical services: advice on which books to buy, how to obtain desired texts, and introductions to capable scribes to make the copies.[5]

Facilitated by this harmonious partnership, the rulers of Europe began to amass libraries of considerable size. The kings of France and Dukes of Burgundy both had collections of over a thousand books by 1450.[6] But the biggest collections were in Italy. The papal library grew to several thousand volumes; the Medicis of Florence also spent a fortune on manuscripts. None could match the ambition of a new collector, the king of Hungary, Matthias Corvinus.[7] When the vagaries of politics brought this obscure nobleman to the throne in 1458, Corvinus decided to bring to Budapest the best of Italian culture. Over four thousand manuscripts were commissioned in Florence and carted over the Alps. Several hundred were still in production when Matthias died in 1490.

The interesting point here is that Matthias's enormous collection of manuscripts was still being assembled in the last decade of the fifteenth century, a full forty years after the invention of printing. Contrary to what is often supposed, the invention of printing did not immediately destroy the manuscript trade. On the contrary, the two modes of book production coexisted happily for at least two generations.

What scholars and collectors wanted was texts. It was the huge demand for texts that had helped fuel the search for a new means of mechanical reproduction. The traditional purchasers of manuscripts were among the greatest enthusiasts for the new experimental printed books. It was said of the Duke of Urbino that his taste was so select he did not have a single printed item in his library, but most fifteenth-century purchasers were not so particular: they collected manuscripts and printed items indifferently, and often bound them together in the same volume.[8] The extent of this bundling has been disguised by the interventions of nineteenth-century librarians, who often carefully disbound these collections to send the manuscripts and early printed items to different reading rooms: a well-meaning vandalism that has considerably distorted our understanding of early reading practice.[9]

Some manuscripts were actually copied from printed books—a counterintuitive reversal of what we think of as the normal chronology. Collectors' acceptance of the new printed books was assisted by the fact that the first printers consciously modelled their work on manuscripts: the type was designed to look like contemporary handwriting, and the printed page often copiously decorated. Sometimes, indeed, it is quite difficult to tell whether we are looking at a manuscript or a printed item. In the sixteenth century all of this began to change. The printed text completed its evolution to an independent artifact, less and less like its manuscript forebear. Rather than hand the text over, half-finished, to an illuminator, printers devised decorative features that could be incorporated directly into the text, using woodcut blocks and initial letters. The highly painted pseudo-manuscript of Gutenberg's day became a more utilitarian object: black text on white paper.

Mostly, though, it was the sheer profusion of books that doomed the Renaissance library. Before print, the creation of a library was the work of a lifetime. Each text had to be tracked down, borrowed, and copied. But within fifty years of the invention of printing, the world was full of books. Something like nine million printed objects were in circulation before 1500.[10] And although many were still precious and expensive—a Gutenberg Bible would have cost more than a small town house in Mainz in 1460—many of these printed books were small and relatively cheap. After 1500 the pace of production accelerated further. Thanks to the work of scholars on the St. Andrews–based Universal Short Title Catalogue project (USTC), we are now in a position to offer for the first time a reliable estimate of this total book production.[11] Assessed country by country, the Europe-wide production of printed books amounted, by 1600, to some 345,000 separate editions: about 180 million printed items (see table 3.1).

Suddenly books were no longer an object of wonder, but an everyday aspect of life. For Europe's ruling elites the accumulation of a library lost its allure. If a middle-ranking official of the Paris Parlement like Antoine du Prat could by 1550 accumulate a collection of four thousand

Table 3.1. Summary of printed outputs throughout Europe, 1450–1600.
(Data from the Universal Short Title Catalogue)

	Vernacular	Scholarly	Total
France	40,500	35,000	75,500
Italy	48,400	39,600	88,000
Germany	37,600	56,400	94,000
Switzerland	2,530	8,470	11,000
The Low Countries	17,896	14,021	31,917
Subtotal	146,926	153,491	300,417
Percentage of Total	81.99%	92.48%	87.03%
England	13,463	1,664	15,127
Spain	12,960	5,040	18,000
Scandinavia	873	793	1,666
Eastern Europe	4,980	4,980	9,960
Subtotal	32,276	12,477	44,753
Percentage of Total	18.01%	7.52%	12.97%
Total	179,202	165,968	345,170

volumes, the size of one of the great Renaissance collections, then Europe's crowned heads had to look to other forms of conspicuous consumption to awe foreign visitors and their subjects.[12] Spending on sculpture, tapestry, paintings, palaces, and warships replaced the building of a library. Whereas Matthias Corvinus built his library next door to his throne room, we do not even know where Henry VIII kept his books: and Henry was a man who prided himself on his education.

As princes turned their fickle attention to other pursuits, the great Renaissance libraries suffered a rapid decline. Some are lost completely, like the library of Matthias Corvinus and his collecting rival Lorenzo de' Medici. Others declined through neglect. In the fourteenth century the City of Venice had promised the great humanist Petrarch a pension and a free home for the promise of his library after his death (a promise he contrived not to keep). But when two centuries later the great collector

Cardinal Bessarion left to Venice his priceless collection of Greek manuscripts, it would be one hundred years before the city fulfilled his stipulation that they be housed and conserved for public access.[13] For most of the intervening years they hung around in the Venice Council Chamber, packed into crates and getting in the way. The time of the public library had not yet come.

Many of the great princely collections went through similar travails. The Emperor Maximilian I had been one of the greatest princely collectors. The period of his reign coincided exactly with the transition from manuscript to print, and he provided generous patronage for artisans of both the new and the traditional art of the book. Among the works of art created specifically for Maximilian were the *Theuerdank*, an epic family chronicle in 188 chapters. But Maximilian also made innovative use of print as an instrument of government, sponsoring extensive use of broadsheet publications to promote his policies to the German people: some were composed by the famous German author Sebastian Brant, author of the *Ship of Fools*. Naturally Maximilian gathered a magnificent library, continued fitfully by his successors. But by the mid-sixteenth century this had fallen into irretrievable decay. When the Dutch Calvinist Hugo Blotius visited the imperial *Hofbibliothek* in Vienna in 1575 it was anything other than magnificent:

> How neglected and desolate everything looked! There was mouldiness and rot everywhere, the debris of moths and bookworms, and a thick covering of cobwebs. The windows had not been opened for months and not a ray of sunshine had penetrated through them to brighten the unfortunate books, which were slowly pining away: and when they were opened, what a cloud of noxious air streamed out.[14]

Blotius rolled up his sleeves, and after ten months' work he had discovered that the collection numbered 7,379 volumes—a century before this would have been a massive collection; now it was not enough to attract the emperor's attention.

The great collections of the Burgundian dukes had also passed into Habsburg hands, as rulers of the Low Countries. But these fared little better. The royal library in Brussels had, in 1559, 666 printed books and 960 manuscripts. Yet by 1683 there were 128 fewer items than a century before. When fire consumed the building in which the library was housed in 1731 five hundred of the most precious items were saved by being hurled out of a window.[15] Even Philip II's library in Spain, at his newly built monastery palace, El Escorial, was not immune. Philip envisaged his library as a private resource and repository of pious literature, not a place of meeting and conversation. In consequence the fabulous collection of manuscripts and printed books that the king accumulated was virtually unused for the three centuries after Philip's death.

In the new age of print you did not need to be one of Europe's major rulers to imagine a vast new library, and the opportunity it provided to gather together the world's learning. One of the new century's greatest collectors was Fernando Colón, son of Christopher Columbus, discoverer of the Americas. Fernando had no appetite to follow his father overseas. He eschewed the swamps and jungles of the newly discovered lands and gave himself to conquering another new world: the book world of sixteenth-century Europe. As an advisor to the Emperor Charles V he accompanied the emperor to many of Europe's leading centers of the book trade. His father's career in the New World had left him a wealthy man, and Fernando bought anything he could—first in person, and then through a network of agents. The books were shipped back from Lyon, Montpellier, Venice, Mainz, and London to the library he had built on the banks of the Guadalquivir—by his death it amounted to some fifteen thousand items.[16]

Colón's forty-four-page will was entirely directed to the preservation and augmentation of his library. Instead, it quickly suffered the depredations commonplace of this age. In 1577 Philip II removed the early manuscripts to the Escorial. Fourteen years later the collection came under the scrutiny of the Inquisition. Colón's carefully assembled collection of works by the Protestant reformers was all removed. In the centuries that followed the neglect was so profound that the underlibrarian's children used the books as toys: "the neglect was such that some volumes were drenched by leaking gutters and reduced to dust."[17] Now only about a third of the original collection survives. Happily what remains is the small pamphlets that Colón, very unusually for his day, gathered up in such numbers. No one else at the time thought them worth stealing—now they contain many unique and otherwise unknown items.[18]

What then of institutional libraries, like those of schools and universities? Here, as with the princely collections, the second century of print brought something of an existential crisis. In the manuscript era, men journeyed from England and Scotland to the great book production centers of Italy, France, and the Low Countries to buy books. William Gray, Bishop of Ely, gathered up over 150 manuscripts in Florence in the 1440s, all of them later donated to Balliol College, Oxford.[19] The magnificent gift of Duke Humphrey of Gloucester, more than 280 precious manuscripts, helped reestablish the library of Oxford University in the fifteenth century.

But in the sixteenth century these institutional collections also receded in importance. The simple reason is that collections of this size, eye-catching in the manuscript age, were now commonplace. By the middle of the sixteenth century a junior scholar at Oxford or Cambridge might have a sizeable collection of books, perhaps as many as one hundred.[20] This was the size of a decent college collection one hundred years before. A professor or senior fellow often amassed a far more substantial collection. When John Bateman, a fellow of Gonville and Caius College, Cambridge, died in 1559, the contents of his four-room chambers were valued at £48. His study housed a collection of five hundred books. This was a remarkable scholarly collection. Without repairing to the university or college library Bateman would have been able to consult a virtually complete range of standard editions of the church fathers. He had no fewer than twelve Latin Bibles, two in Greek, and six in Hebrew. He owned numerous grammars. This represented a revolution in learning. Bateman had collected assiduously more recent controversial literature, and a fairly conventional sprinkling of the classics. There was also room in this busy life for recreation. The library included at least thirty books in English, including Chaucer, Gower, and Lydgate, together with translations of Guevara and Quintus Curtius.[21]

Furthermore, these personal collections had the advantage that, bought on the contemporary market, they often contained the most recent and up-to-date scholarship. Institutional collections, accumulated by donation, were obliged to accept books no longer relevant to the syllabus, or duplicates of books they already owned. The religious and educational controversies of the Reformation era posed a further challenge to institutional libraries, which could now be characterized, unhelpfully, as repositories of the despised Scholasticism. The conflicts between Catholics and evangelicals also spilled into the libraries, as the prevailing power insisted that the shelves be searched for anything forbidden or heretical.

These then were testing times for institutional collections. In the middle of the sixteenth century the university library closed in both Oxford and Cambridge. Oxford University disposed of the books and even the furniture from its library. It was only in the early seventeenth century that the university library found its role in the new age of print. Encouraged by royal patrons such as James VI, or alumni such as Sir Thomas Bodley, the founder of Oxford's Bodleian library, universities began to accumulate serious collections of books: by donation, and by volume purchasing in the international book market. Bodley began his project in 1598.[22] He had hoped that if he provided the funds for the building and equipment of the shelves, other scholars would donate the books. When these hopes were not initially realized, he began to buy books himself. Although Bodley had employed a highly capable librarian, Thomas James, he was not a hands-off patron. His views on how the shelves should be stocked, and how their use should be regulated, occupied a stream of testy letters to the long-suffering James. By the time James published his second printed catalogue in 1620 the library had assembled a collection of around sixteen thousand items, and the Bodleian library was, as Bodley had hoped, a magnet for visitors from all over Europe—though most of the overseas visitors in fact came to consult rare manuscripts, rather than the large theological tomes that stocked the shelves. This was hardly surprising, since most of the books had been imported from continental Europe and would have been available far closer to home. Bodley was also responsible for drafting the first version of the Bodleian oath, which new readers were required to read out loud before inscribing their names as readers:

> You promise and solemnly engage before God . . . that whenever you shall enter the public library of the University, you will frame your mind to study in modesty and silence, and will use the books

and other furniture in such manner that they may last as long as possible. Also that you will [not] steal, change, make erasures, deform, tear, cut, write notes in, interline, wilfully spoil, obliterate, defile, or in any other way retrench, ill-use, wear away or deteriorate any book or books, nor authorise any other person to do the like.[23]

In its current version readers find themselves promising not to "kindle a flame" within the library's precincts. I have to admit that until these words were presented to me at the age of eighteen the thought had not occurred to me. But of course, once such an idea enters your head, the power of suggestion is strong.

This apart, perhaps the most interesting aspect of Bodley's morbid imagination of the ill-using of his books by his readers, with their habits of scribbling and willful spoliation, was the new emphasis on silence. The Renaissance library was a noisy place—a place for conversation and display, rather than for study and contemplation. It was only in the seventeenth century, with these new institutional collections, that the library began its long descent into silence, emerging as that new phenomenon of the nineteenth and twentieth centuries, the library as mausoleum, a silent repository of countless unread books, its principal purpose the protection of books from the ravages of human contact. This is the library that has been such a powerful spur to the literary imagination, most recently in Carlos Ruiz Zafón's international bestseller *The Shadow of the Wind*; most famously, of course, in Umberto Eco's evocation of the library as a vast repository of hidden treasures in the medieval blockbuster *The Name of the Rose*.

But such fictional creations do have their basis in fact. The descent into obscurity and irrelevance was a fate that seemed in the mid-twentieth century even to have enveloped the French Bibliothèques Municipales, the great network of the libraries set up with the plunder of the French Revolution, to build a new network of readers and informed, enlightened citizens.[24] By the middle of the twentieth century little of this original purpose remained. A report in the 1930s characterized these libraries as cold, forbidding places, with an out-of-date stock and few readers. With the inherited revolutionary inheritance the principal purpose seemed to be to keep the older stock from ever being seen. Some of this spirit, I regret to say, lives on in some of the world's great libraries today, where the staff will hand over books only with the greatest reluctance. This of course is the greatest nonsense. Most sixteenth-century books are extremely hardy. If anything they benefit from use.

The French municipal libraries were saved by a total reorganization, reenvisaged as the Mediathèque, with furniture and facilities to encourage the widest public use. Some of the happiest reading experiences of my career have been in these libraries, where sixteenth-century books are often delivered to general reading areas, with the infants toddling through to the children's library and alongside war veterans with their daily papers. One of the pensioners kindly stopped by my desk to assure me that I would get far more enlightenment from his illustrated magazine than the text I had in front of me. I did not share my own thought that my robust folio would be far more likely to make it through another four hundred years than his reading material.

This is not of course what Bodley had in mind, for all his suspicions of the dangers of youthful enthusiasm. His drive and energy allowed the University of Oxford to build very quickly a formidable collection, almost wholly through donation and purchase. Other continental libraries took a more direct route. The University of Uppsala in Sweden, founded in the fifteenth century, had no university library until 1620. But from that date it grew very rapidly, stocked by books plundered by the Swedish armies in the Thirty Years' War. Erfurt, Eichsfeld, Mainz, and Würzburg were all looted in 1631. The first great prize had been the Jesuit library of Braniewo (Braunsberg) in northern Poland. The Jesuit college was founded in 1565 by the prince Bishop of Warmia, Stanislaus Hozius. Hozius was one of the great figures of the Polish Counter-reformation, a diplomat and pugnacious polemicist whose published works achieved considerable popularity throughout Europe. The establishment of the Collegium Hosanum in Braunsberg, located perilously close to German East Prussia, was a deliberate effort to counter the creeping spread of the Reformation. An important part of this missionary endeavor was the building of a library: the establishment of such religious foundations was in fact one of the principal spurs to the development of new institutional collections in the sixteenth century.

In 1626 the Swedish army of Gustavus Adolphus conquered Braunsberg as part of its triumphant campaign in the Baltic region. The army laid waste the town, but the library of the Jesuit college was treated with some care. The entire collection was crated up and sent to Uppsala, where it was incorporated into the recently established university library. The collection has remained in Uppsala ever since, clearly distinguished by its original marks of ownership. Recently, perhaps as a belated act of atonement, its Swedish custodians have published a detailed scholarly catalogue.[25] Given this history of predatory collecting there is a certain poetic irony that the Swedish Royal Library lost three quarters of its stock (eighteen thousand books and one thousand manuscripts) in a disastrous fire in 1658.

It must also be said that in this vastly destructive conflict in the early seventeenth century the Catholic armies had shown the way, by ransacking the library of the University of Heidelberg, Germany's premier mediaeval university. Three thousand manuscripts and twelve thousand printed books were carefully crated up, loaded onto mules, and sent over the Alps as a gift to the Vatican library: where they remain today.[26] At least they are well cared for. What remained in Heidelberg was destroyed by the troops of Louis XIV in 1693.

These turbulent events found their echo in the destructive conflicts that engaged Europe's nation-states in more recent centuries. The French revolution brought the confiscation of around ten million books from France's abolished religious orders. Some were torn up to make cartridges for the muskets of the revolutionary armies; others ended up in the new French municipal libraries. Napoleon rebuilt the cultural capital of France by helping himself to the treasures of Italy. In the twentieth century aerial bombing posed a new and deadly hazard to the books that had survived from the first age of print. Several million were lost, and others removed as plunder. The chaos at the end of the Second World War led to the destruction or dispersal of many of Europe's greatest scholarly collections, painstakingly assembled over four hundred years. A few years ago staff at the Universal Short Title Catalogue received a batch of records of the sixteenth-century books presently in the collection of the State Library of St. Petersburg. While integrating this material into the project files, an unusual convergence was noticed between these records and the holdings of the State Library in Berlin. In fact, a high proportion of these books turned out not to be traceable in Berlin but are marked in the Berlin catalogue, with pained resignation, as "possibly lost in the war": "*Kriegsverlust möglich.*" A test identified a group of some three hundred titles that were not in fact lost at the end of the war—they were simply removed to the Soviet Union.

So the book world of Renaissance Europe presents us with a strange paradox. By 1600 an almost unthinkable number of books had been published, and even ordinary citizens could amass a considerable library. But four centuries of conflict since and the normal depredations of time have taken a heavy toll. The data collected by the USTC project indicates that by 1600 around 345,000 separate books had been printed. An average print run is normally calculated at around seven hundred to one thousand copies—this is something over two hundred million copies all told. But for each edition the average number of copies that survive is around 3.5. That is, far less than 1 percent of all the books printed in the first age of print have made it through to the present day.

Furthermore, we need to bear in mind that some types of books were far more likely to survive than others. Some fifteenth- and sixteenth-century books are really quite common. The *Nuremberg Chronicle*, published in 1493, is a magnificent book and was recognized as such at the time of its publication—which is why more than five hundred copies have survived. Thirty percent of the copies of the Gutenberg Bible published are still extant. But the tendency of great libraries to collect the same sorts of books means that whole categories of book have been lost altogether. About 30 percent of the books now known to have been published before 1601 survive in only one copy, and many have disappeared completely.

How are we to recapture this lost world of knowledge? In so far as it can be done, it will be done through the employment of new technology. The books of the sixteenth century, particularly the little books, are dispersed around some six thousand libraries and archives worldwide. No one can visit them all; but thanks to the Internet it is now possible to access remotely a large number of their catalogues. That done one can download, digest, and compare the information, creating ultimately one master list that should comprise the complete corpus of known books. But we can go further than this. Many of these books have notes of ownership, or provenance. By recording these, and comparing them, we can begin to rediscover some of the lost libraries of the Renaissance: wherever in the world these books may now be disposed. A fine example of this sort of work is Malcolm Walsby's reconstruction of the library of René de Bourgneuf from data drawn from the three hundred French libraries visited in the early stages of the USTC project.[27]

Another source of information on lost books is the numerous manuscript book lists, or inventories, that survive from the sixteenth century. These were compiled for many reasons: when the stock of a bookseller was investigated for heretical texts, or when it was assessed for value after the owner's death. This was also the most common reason for the listing of a personal collection.[28] Toward the end of this period we also see the first printed catalogues of personal book collections, sometimes where a very large collection was to be sold at auction. When we begin to incorporate this data, which includes many thousands of references to books whose present location is unknown, we can begin to create the complete profile of a sixteenth-century book. We can tell not only where these books are now to be found, but who their sixteenth-century owners were, and how much they paid for them. This process has also added to the USTC database many thousands of books known to have existed, but where a surviving copy has not yet been located.

This is work that will take our knowledge of the sixteenth-century book world far beyond what has been possible in conventional bibliographical projects. For very good reasons—reasons of national library politics and funding priorities—the study of early books has proceeded essentially within national compartments. That has ensured a degree of progress in the compiling of data from many different libraries—in the case of the splendid Italian national bibliography over one thousand collections, some of them very small.[29] But this separation of the book world into national compartments does little justice to the realities of trade in sixteenth-century Europe. It mattered little to a sixteenth-century collector whether the text he desired was published in Venice, Paris, or Basel—so long as they could get hold of it at a reasonable price. The international book market was organized to make this possible. For this reason the market in Latin books was essentially one pan-European integrated market. A very high proportion of the Latin books published during the century were produced in a small number of well-capitalized printing entrepôts—all of them well situated for distribution along Europe's major arteries of trade, or through the great international book fairs. From these central markets texts in Latin were distributed throughout Europe, and beyond. And despite the advances in vernacular literature, and vernacular reading communities, the Latin market remained very large—at least 50 percent of the total output of books, and a larger proportion when calculated by volume, remained in the scholarly languages.

The Universal Short Title Catalogue will, for the first time, recreate this single integrated market of the sixteenth-century book trade. It will also make it possible for some of the limitations of the present national bibliographies to be corrected. Most established national bibliographical projects incorporate information only from libraries within their own national domain—the German from German libraries, the Belgian from Belgian libraries, and so on. But books were meant to travel. In the sixteenth century Low Countries books formed a major part of their export trade: it would be most surprising if all the books printed were still represented in Belgian libraries. When French-language books were surveyed, it was found that 30 percent are extant only in libraries outside France. We would not expect that to be any less with Latin books, which had an obvious international readership. And so it has proved. A survey of books published in the Low Countries has added a further eight thousand works to those known from published national bibliographies.[30]

So the USTC will advance the knowledge of the world of early printed books in ways scarcely envisaged when the project began. There is an added pleasure to be found in using the twenty-first-century information revolution to unlock the secrets of the last great technological breakthrough, the invention of printing. But this comparison should also give us pause. Technological innovation is frequently accompanied by excitable rhetoric and totally false prophecy. So it was with printing in the fifteenth century. Scholars and investors created elaborate hymns of praise to the marvelous new invention. None were more enthralled than the humanist scholars who, until this point, had worked so hard to gather together their collections of manuscripts. The new art of printing would create a new world of scholarship, where accurate texts were freely available in multiple copies. Print, they wrote, would be itself the Renaissance of letters—it would turn darkness into light.

In fact the major areas of innovation through print turned out to be in areas where scholars had little interest—the development of a market for news for instance, or the popular religious literature that encouraged wide public debate and incited religious discord. Humanist scholars did not want this at all. They wanted a larger, more convenient supply of texts for people like themselves. If they had known how the market for printed texts would evolve, they would probably have heartily disapproved.[31]

Now we are told that we must imminently expect the death of the book. Yet more books are published with every passing year. When I embarked on my PhD in 1979 my tutor cheerfully predicted that I would never write a book. I think, in the context of the conversation, that this was a judgment on the likely speed of technological change rather than on my caliber as a scholar. Whatever, he was wrong. Thirty years later, the book remains an essential aspect of both scholarly life and public recreational culture, and whole forests are sacrificed every year to bring books to an eager public.

The book survives because it is an object of technological genius, refined through two millennia since the Romans decided that there must be a better way of storing information than on scrolls of papyrus. The invention of printing was a critical moment of evolution, but the shape of the physical artifact was already determined, and remarkably similar to the books we own today.

The sixteenth century represented a critical era, not because this was a moment of technological change, but because following this technological change the book became commonplace. This empowered whole new classes of reader. Men and women who could previously not have hoped to own a single book could now own many. But this process—the democratization of a previously luxury item—dealt a heavy blow to the Renaissance library. It would be several generations before the library would find a new role, in a world where the book was suddenly commonplace.

The Universal Short Title Catalogue project provides an unrivalled opportunity to study this whole process: how print conquered Europe, and sent out into the market new texts for new readers. It shows us how this flood of new materials first seemed fatally to undermine the social role and importance of the library—as a place where great men gathered to display their wealth, their books, and only incidentally their erudition. Only in the seventeenth century was the library re-created as a physical space with a new role, as a center of scholarship. If this was a change for the better, it was one not without significant missteps along the way.

NOTES

1. Marcella Grendler, "A Greek Collection in Padua: The Library of Gian Vincenzo Pinelli (1535–1601)," *Renaissance Quarterly* 33 (1980): 386–416. Marcella Grendler, "Book Collecting in Counter-Reformation Italy: The Library of Gian Vincenzo Pinelli (1535–1601)," *Journal of Library History* 16 (1981): 144–51.

2. Anthony Hobson, "A Sale by Candle in 1608," *Library*, ser. 5, 26 (1971): 215–33.

3. For the general context of these events, see Andrew Pettegree, *The Book in the Renaissance* (London: Yale University Press, 2010). This interpretation challenges the generally more optimistic narrative of, for instance, Elizabeth Eisenstein, *The Printing Press as an Agent of Change: Communications and Cultural Transformations in Early Modern Europe* (Cambridge: Cambridge University Press, 1979). Elizabeth Eisenstein, *The Printing Revolution in Early Modern Europe* (Cambridge: Cambridge University Press, 1983).

4. Christopher de Hamel, *A History of Illuminated Manuscripts*, 2nd ed. (London: Phaidon, 1994).

5. For accounts of what kinds of books and manuscripts were on the shelves of Renaissance libraries, see Phyllis Walter Goodhart Gordan, ed., *Two Renaissance Book Hunters: The Letters of Poggius Bracciolini to Nicolaus de Niccolis* (New York: Columbia University Press, 1974), and Pettegree, *The Book in the Renaissance*, especially chapter 1, "The Book before Print."

6. Hanno Wijsman, *Handschriften voor het hertogdom: De mooiste verluchte manuscripten van Brabantse hertogen, edellieden, kloosterlingen en stedelingen* (Alphen: Uitgeverij Veerhuis, 2006).

7. Marcus Tanner, *The Raven King: Matthias Corvinus and the Fate of His Lost Library* (New Haven: Yale University Press, 2008). Csaba Csapodi, *The Corvinian Library: History and Stock* (Budapest: Akadémiai Kiadó, 1973).

Ilona Berkovits, *Illuminated Manuscripts from the Library of Matthias Corvinus* (Budapest: Corvina Press, 1964).

8. As famously reported by the supplier of many of his manuscripts, the Florentine stationer Vespasiano da Bistichi. See William George and Emily Waters, eds., *The Vespasiano Memoirs: Lives of Illustrious Men of the XV Century* (London: Routledge, 1926).

9. David McKitterick, *Print, Manuscript and the Search for Order, 1450–1830* (Cambridge: Cambridge University Press, 2003), 48–52.

10. An estimate derived from an analysis of the British Library's Incunabula Short Title Catalogue: http://www.bl.uk/catalogues/istc/.

11. Universal Short Title Catalogue at http://www.ustc.ac.uk/.

12. M. Connat and J. Mégret, "Inventaire de la bibliothèque des du Prat," *Bibliothèque d'Humanisme et Renaissance* 3 (1943): 72–128.

13. Lotte Labowsky, *Bessarion's Library and the Biblioteca Marciana: Six Early Inventories* (Rome: Edizioni di storia e letteratura, 1979).

14. Anthony Hobson, *Great Libraries* (London: Weidenfeld and Nicolson, 1970), 143.

15. Hobson, *Great Libraries*, 98.

16. Colón's books have been extensively studied by Klaus Wagner. See, for instance, "Le commerce du livre en France au début du XVIe siècle d'après les notes manuscrites de Fernando Colomb," *Bulletin du bibliophile* 2 (1992): 305–29.

17. Hobson, *Great Libraries*, 109.

18. Henry Harrisse, *Excerpta Colombiniana: Bibliographie de 400 pièces du 16e siècle; précédée d'une histoire de la Bibliothèque colombine et de son fondateur* (Paris: Welter, 1887). Klaus Wagner, "Judicia Astrologica Colombiniana: Bibliographisches Verzeichnis einer Sammlung von Praktiken des 15. und 16. Jahrhunderts des Biblioteca Colombina Sevilla," *Archiv für Geschichte des Buchwesens* 15 (1975), cols. 1–98.

19. Pettegree, *The Book in the Renaissance*, 20.

20. Kristian Jensen, "Universities and Colleges," in Elizabeth Leedham-Green and Teresa Webber, eds., *The Cambridge History of Libraries in Britain and Ireland*, vol. 1, to 1640 (Cambridge: Cambridge University Press, 2006), 345–62.

21. E. S. Leedham-Green, *Books in Cambridge Inventories: Book Lists from Vice-Chancellor's Court Probate Inventories in the Tudor and Stuart Periods* (Cambridge: Cambridge University Press, 1986), vol. 1, 234–44.

22. Ian Philip, *The Bodleian Library in the Seventeenth and Eighteenth Centuries* (Oxford: Clarendon Press, 1983).

23. Mary Clapinson, "The Bodleian Library and Its Readers, 1602–1652," *Bodleian Library Record* 19.1 (2006): 36–37.

24. *Histoire des bibliothèques françaises*, vol. 2, *Les bibliothèques sous l'ancien régime, 1530–1789* (Paris: Promodis, 1988). Andrew Pettegree, "Rare Books and Revolutionaries: The French Bibliothèques Municipales," in his *The French Book and the European Book World* (Leiden: Brill, 2007), 1–16.

25. Josef Trypucko, *The Catalogue of the Book Collection of the Jesuit College in Braniewo Held in the University Library in Uppsala* (Warsaw and Uppsala: Uppsala Universitetsbibliotek and Biblioteka Narodowa, 2007).

26. Elmar Mittler, *Bibliotheca Palatina: Katalog zur Ausstellung vom 8. Juli bis 2. November 1986* (Heidelberg: Braus, 1986).

27. Malcolm Walsby, *The Printed Book in Brittany*, 1484–1600 (Leiden: Brill, 2011), 177–79.

28. The sale of the library of a heretic fugitive is recorded in Pierre Jourda, "La bibliothèque d'un régent calviniste (1577)," in *Mélanges d'histoire littéraire de la Renaissance offerts à Henri Chamard* (Paris: Librarie Nizet, 1951), 269–73.

29. Istituto Centrale per il Catalogo Unico delle biblioteche italiane e per le informazioni bibliografiche (ICCU), Edit 16 (Census of Italian 16th Century Editions): http://edit16.iccu.sbn.it/web_iccu/ehome.htm.

30. Andrew Pettegree and Malcolm Walsby, eds., *Netherlandish Books: Books Published in the Low Countries and Dutch Books Printed Abroad before 1601* (Leiden: Brill, 2011), xi.

31. As indeed some did. See, for instance, the remarks of the Venetian Benedictine Filippo de Strata. Filippo de Strata, *Polemic against Printing*. Translated by Shelagh Grier with an introduction by Martin Lowry (Birmingham: Hayloft Press, 1986).

❦

CHAPTER 4

From Printing Shop to Bookshelves

HOW BOOKS BEGAN THE JOURNEY TO ENLIGHTENMENT LIBRARIES

Robert Darnton

As Wayne Bivens-Tatum neatly puts it in his introduction to *Libraries and the Enlightenment* (2012), "without Enlightenment there might still be libraries, but without libraries there can be no Enlightenment."[1] This essay is meant to open a seam of investigation parallel to, but at a short remove from, the primary one of library history, and to show how the book trade supplied the works that now sit on library shelves, bearing testimony to the Enlightenment along with a great deal of other literature that accompanied it.[2]

There was some convergence in the activities of booksellers and librarians during the eighteenth century. True, booksellers were tradesmen, whose main concern was to make money. But like librarians, they also devoted themselves to the task of making knowledge available to the public. In an age of intellectual daring, in which "all things must be examined, debated, investigated," and in which scientific researchers pressed toward new understanding of nature, booksellers and librarians operated at a more modest level, bringing the results of research within the reach of the general reading public.[3]

While the great classifiers were at work pulling together the multifarious strands of eighteenth-century human knowledge—Diderot with his *Encyclopédie*, Linnaeus with the world's flora, Réaumur with insects,

Leclerc with wildlife and minerals, van Haller and Blumenbach with human anatomy, Montesquieu and Bentham with social and legal systems—booksellers and librarians worked to push that knowledge out to an eagerly waiting world. Booksellers purveyed the knowledge in the form of books, and librarians organized it onto bookshelves.

The early modern period was a golden age for libraries, in which many large and prestigious collections flourished in Britain and the rest of Europe. The Bodleian Library in Oxford had its origins in the fourteenth century and began to trace a continuous history from 1602. Chetham's library in Manchester opened in 1653, and other city libraries began serving readers in Norwich (1608), Ipswich (1612), Bristol (1615), and Leicester (1632). The British Library originated in 1753 from within the British Museum. In France the Bibliothèque Mazarine had been open to scholars since 1643, while the Biblioteca Nazionale Centrale di Firenze was opened in 1714, the Prussian State Library in Berlin served scholars under the direction of the Prussian Academy of Sciences from 1735, and the Biblioteka Załuskich was built in Warsaw 1747–95. Increasingly, too, at this time, libraries were becoming institutions that would lend their stock. There was a gradual migration from the "private and parochial" library to the more open "subscription" model, especially in northern Germany, where *Lesegesellschaften* permeated urban society.

Not all philosophers rejoiced in the growing access to books. Far from advocating universal literacy, Voltaire insisted that peasants should till the soil. But the most progressive thinkers, notably Condorcet and his friend Thomas Jefferson, identified Enlightenment with the diffusion of books and understood the printed word as the most powerful force for the liberation of humanity. The busy presses of Enlightenment Europe ensured that library shelves were filled with volumes recording not only the new scientific discoveries and inventions of the age, but also writings on the new subjects now emerging—economics, political science, psychology, and sociology. The mathematics of Euler, the physics of Newton, the chemistry of Black, the medical experiments of Jenner, the biology of Lamarck, all were pressed into book form and shipped to share library shelf space with the philosophy of Hume and Voltaire, and the politics of Paine and Rousseau.

The process of Enlightenment as it was envisioned by philosophers can be understood in a concrete, down-to-earth manner by following the trail of books as they left printing presses and spread through the distribution system of the book trade. The ways they were read and their effects on readers remain difficult to determine, but the diffusion process can be studied in detail, and it shows how literature penetrated into the social order during the eighteenth century before filling the shelves of libraries today. Two exceptionally rich sources, the papers of an important French Swiss publisher, the Société typographique de Neuchâtel (STN), and the archives of the Book Trade Administration in Paris, make it possible to reconstruct this crucial phase in the history of literature and libraries.

In July 1778, Jean-François Favarger, a "commis voyageur" ("sales rep" or travelling salesman) of the STN, mounted a horse in Neuchâtel, Switzerland and set off on a five-month journey, selling books and inspecting the book trade in every town along a route that ran across the Jura Mountains into eastern France, down the Rhône Valley, through all the cities of the south and southwest, then back through the Valley of the Loire, Burgundy, and the Franche-Comté to the STN's headquarters. It was an extraordinary *tour de France*. When Favarger arrived back in Neuchâtel in December, he knew more about French literature, *terre à terre*, as it was dispensed in bookshops and discussed in shop talk, than any historian could ever hope to know.

Fortunately, historians can follow the paper trail that Favarger left behind.[4] He was a responsible, intelligent, and diligent clerk whom the directors of the STN had recruited from the highly literate common people of greater Neuchâtel, which then was a semiautonomous Swiss principality under the ultimate sovereignty of Prussia. Before he set out on his journey, Favarger had come to know the book business from the inside by handling the STN's commercial correspondence; and during his travels, he sent regular reports to the home office, received fresh instructions in reply, and kept a diary with a detailed expense account: 10 sols for refurbishing his pistols in Marseille (the road to Beaucaire was infested with bandits), 26 livres for new breeches in La Rochelle (the old pair did not hold up against the friction in the saddle), and 8 louis d'or for a new horse in Poitiers (the old one kept collapsing on the muddy trails and finally had to be sold.)

On July 7 Favarger crossed a pass through the Jura Mountains into France and spent the night in Pontarlier. On this leg of the journey, he concentrated on inspecting supply lines at the border, because the STN did a large business in illegal and pirated books, which had to be smuggled from Switzerland into France. Favarger negotiated over costs and risks with a half dozen smugglers in villages on both sides of the border.

Two basic kinds of smuggling had evolved in the course of the eighteenth century. The first was called "insurance" (*assurance*). Self-styled *assureurs* guaranteed to get shipments of books from taverns on the Swiss side of the border to secret storehouses on the French side. They hired teams of "porters" (*porte-balles*), who received a stiff shot of schnapps in a Swiss inn—a favorite launching site was chez Jannet in the hamlet of Les Verrières—and then set off along tortuous mountain trails with the books on their backs. A backpack weighed sixty pounds (approximately thirty kilos) under normal conditions, fifty pounds when the snow was deep. The men got 25 sols (the equivalent of a day's labor by a worker in Paris) for a successful crossing. If caught, they could be branded with the letters GAL for "*galérien*" and sent to row for nine years as a galley slave in Marseille. Their boss, the insurer, would then have to reimburse the STN for the full value of the merchandise. On January 23, 1784, Ignace Faivre, an insurer in Pontarlier, signed a contract with the STN that committed him to get its shipments across the border "at my peril and risk for 15 livres per hundredweight.... In case of any unhappy event ["*événement facheux*"], I will reimburse the value of the merchandise within one year according to the prices on the bill of lading."[5]

But Faivre had to compete with rivals from the second type of smuggling, a paralegal system. The publishers hid forbidden and pirated books in normal shipments and sent them through the legal channels of the trade. They used many tricks—for example, "marrying" books or larding the leaves of prohibited works inside the leaves of inoffensive ones. This was easily done, because books were shipped in sheets, not bound in volumes. One particularly happy marriage was a French translation of *Fanny Hill* (*La Fille de joie*) hidden inside the Bible. The crates were sealed by French customs officers at the border (the customs operated *bureaux d'entrée* on all the main routes into France, e.g., Frambourg in Franche-Comté), inspected by officials of the booksellers' guilds in cities located at commercial crossroads (they were known as *villes d'entrée*, e.g., Lyon), and then sent to their final destination, where they might be inspected yet again. Specialized forwarding agents (*commissionnaires*) like Jacques Revol in Lyon often bribed the inspectors to do a superficial job of examining the crates. To be safe, however, they sometimes arranged for the wagon drivers to stop at an inn on the outskirts of the *ville d'entrée*—Aux Trois Flacons in the Croix Rousse suburb of Lyon, for example—where they would unpack the illegal books, replace them with legal works, bind the crate back up under a counterfeit seal, and send it on for inspection in the guild hall. Then they would forward the "philosophical books" (a term in the trade for everything dangerous, from pornography to atheism) along another route, disguised as domestic merchandise.

This system worked well so long as the shipping agents and the wagon drivers coordinated their activities. But things were always going wrong. The STN often dealt with Jean-François Pion, a shipper in Pontarlier, who had a great stable of horses. He could yoke up five at a time to haul loads over the Jura Mountains at the height of winter. His business suffered from one drawback, however: his stupidity. He once sent a crate to Nantes instead of to Rennes. On another occasion he forwarded a barrel of sauerkraut to the wrong address in Lyon, and it was devoured before the mistake could be corrected. So despite the excellence of Pion's horses, the STN constantly tried to find a substitute for him among the brainier peasants of the border towns—François Michaut and the Meuron brothers of Les Verrières and St. Sulpice, for example. But the small farmers could not supply enough horses during spring planting and what they called "the cheese season" in the fall. As a consequence of all these complications, the STN kept readjusting its smuggling operations. It was always playing off one smuggler against another, hoping to find cheaper rates and safer service, while calculating factors such as snow, horses, and the maturing rate of cheese.

The calculations involved every city in France, because the conditions were different everywhere. Favarger reported on them in detail. He described the routes, the techniques, and the persons involved. He even wrote character sketches and minibiographies. In Marseille, for example, he warned the home office in Switzerland that the police inspector was unusually nasty: "one of those men who, in order to have meat on his plate, would eat his brother." There was a commercial war among the booksellers, who were attempting to drive each other out of business. One, a tough entrepreneur named Mossy, seemed to be winning. Another, Caldesaigues, had just gone under. All the booksellers corresponded with the STN, so Favarger's reports can be compared with their dossiers, which reveal many aspects of their business throughout the period 1769–89. In Caldesaigues's case, his correspondence can be supplemented by letters from bill collectors and family members, making it possible to piece together the commerce of a small-time book dealer in the capillary system of the trade.[6]

It begins with a love story: Caldesaigues wins the daughter of a well-off carpenter, collects a good dowry, and sets up shop. But soon he overplays his hand, ordering more books than he can sell. As the bills of exchange become due, he panics, runs away with a load of books on a ship to Spain. His wife returns to her father, engineering a kind of divorce—"separation of bodies and goods"—in order to protect the remnants of her heritage. Then Caldesaigues decides to fight back. He comes back clandestinely to Marseille, woos his wife, fights his father-in-law, and hides from his creditors, while negotiating a settlement of his debts that will permit him to resume his business. It turns into a drawn-out drama, and in the end Caldesaigues loses everything. He disappears like many bankrupt booksellers: "left the keys under the door." Many dossiers end in that manner: "enrolled in the army"; "gone to Russia"; "shipped out to the American war"; "his wife and children are begging on the steps of the church." Capitalism was cruel in the early modern period, when limited liability did not exist.

Much of the fascination in this kind of research comes from the sense of making contact with vanished segments of humanity in a Balzacian world that existed before Balzac. More important, however, is the attempt to reconstruct patterns of behavior and the interrelated parts of an overall system: what could be called the information society of the eighteenth century.

The best way to see the system as a whole is to consider it from the perspective of the final stop in Favarger's tour de France: home base in Neuchâtel, the headquarters of the STN, where the publisher tried to cope with every aspect in the production, marketing, and sales of books.

After reading thousands of letters by the most important director of the STN, Frédéric Samuel Ostervald, I have come to appreciate the enormous complexity of the book industry in the eighteenth century. A publisher had to keep many balls in the air while the ground was shifting beneath his feet. Aside from the difficulties on the production side—a matter of bargaining over paper, recruiting workers for the printing shop, and balancing the accounts—he had to deal with endless complications in other aspects of the business: the possibility of buying manuscripts from best-selling authors, the vagaries of politics in the French Book Trade Administration (Direction de la librairie), the trustworthiness of signatures on bills of exchange, the availability of specie (money in the form of coins rather than notes) in the quadrennial fairs of Lyon, the changing rates of shipping on the Rhine and the Rhône, even the date when the Baltic was likely to freeze over, forcing him to send shipments to St. Petersburg and Moscow overland.

To illustrate these complexities, I would like to discuss the example of a crucial but poorly understood aspect of eighteenth-century publishing: piracy. Copyright was established in England by the statute of Anne in 1710, but it did not exist on the Continent, where the rights to books were usually determined by royal "privileges" valid only within the territory of the sovereign who granted them. To receive a privilege in France, a book had to be approved by a censor and clear many hurdles within the Book Trade Administration. Books with anything that challenged official values or that might offend anyone in authority were generally printed in the publishing houses located everywhere around France's borders. These foreign producers of French books also reprinted everything legal that sold well in the French market. To them, reprinting was a legitimate business. To the French publishers who owned the privileges to those books, it was piracy—piracy, not counterfeiting, a point that is often misunderstood. Pirate publishers rarely attempted to produce a book that would look like the original. They churned out down-market editions, eliminating "typographical luxury," as they called it. They used relatively cheap fonts of type, eliminated ornaments and often illustrations, and frequently abridged the text. Because they paid no author's fees and had access to inexpensive paper, they could undersell the privileged edition, even when they had to smuggle their works into France.

And they developed alliances with provincial dealers, who resented the dominance of the guild of printers and booksellers at the center of the trade in Paris. Probably half the books sold in France during the twenty years before the Revolution—current literature of all kinds but not chapbooks, religious tracts, or professional treatises—were pirated.

The books that sold best differed from modern best sellers in a fundamental way. Instead of being produced in large quantities by one publisher, they were printed simultaneously by many houses in small editions, usually of about a thousand copies, all of them pirated. Piracy was a race to cream off the market by rival entrepreneurs located in a fertile crescent of printer-booksellers (the term "publisher" or "*éditeur*" was not then in use), which extended around France's borders from the Low Countries, through the Rhineland, into Switzerland and down to Avignon, which then was papal territory. (It also was widely practiced in a few provincial centers, especially Rouen and Lyon.) But how did it actually take place?

Not simply by guesswork but by systematically sounding the market and calculating demand—that is, by an early variety of market research. One episode can serve as an example of the calculations. Soon after going into business, Ostervald developed an extensive correspondence with Pierre Gosse Junior of The Hague, one of the biggest booksellers of the Netherlands who knew the trade as well as anyone, having dealt with wholesalers and retailers inside and outside France for thirty years. Gosse advised the STN about what to pirate, and he ordered large quantities of books, receiving in exchange a discount and an exclusive arrangement for their sale in his region. The correspondence between him and Ostervald therefore evolved into a dialogue in which one can follow two professionals assessing literary demand.[7]

As a newcomer to the trade, Ostervald adopted a deferential tone and sent a constant stream of proposals.

What would Gosse say to a *Dictionary of Animals*?

"No" was the answer. "We strongly advise you against this enterprise."

A *Description of Swiss Glaciers*?

No. "It is an interesting work, but it isn't selling well these days."

A refutation of d'Holbach's notorious *System of Nature* by Jean de Castillon?

Gosse had imported the Berlin edition, which had sold badly; and he did not want any more, because "we judge according to our sales." Furthermore, "the people who buy those kinds of books couldn't care less about refutations."

Bougainville's *Voyage Around the World*?

Gosse pronounced it "a very good, an excellent enterprise." But he would commit himself to an advance order of only 50 copies because ". . . the book trade is doing so badly everywhere these days."

A *History of Field Marshall Saxe* and a *Supplement to the Roman comique*, or *Life of Jean Monnet, Director of Acting Troupes*?

No, and no again. "Those are books that nowadays sell only for a short time after their first publication. We don't want to fill our stockrooms with them."

It may seem that Gosse was a crusty, congenital naysayer. But he speculated heavily on books he thought would sell, and he certainly knew the market, which he treated in a strictly commercial manner: "Today, Monsieur, it is absolutely necessary to conform to current taste, to the taste of the public, in one's business. Men of learning often get that wrong. A bookseller with a large trade is far better than a scholar at assessing the public's taste."

As a scholar, I have a great deal of respect for Gosse's judgment. I was therefore keen to know what he would say when he smelled a potential best seller. In March 1770, Ostervald informed him that the STN soon would print a major new work by Voltaire, *Questions sur l'Encyclopédie*. Dazzled by this news, Gosse replied with a letter that, unlike the others already cited, fairly quivered with enthusiasm:

[From your letter], we have seen with surprise that Voltaire at seventy [he was actually seventy-seven] is laboring on a major work with incredible speed and application; that it is to be a new *Encyclopédie* in his manner, which will correct the one that exists and will include everything that the author knows and thinks. . . . You ask, Monsieur, what I think of such an enterprise. I have the honor to answer that it is an enterprise of solid gold and that never in its existence will the [STN] come across another nearly as good or better. . . . Furthermore, I will tell you right away that we commit ourselves to taking a large number. . . . Certainly, Monsieur, as you say, this work will contain all kinds of things that are new, curious, and extraordinarily powerful, and it will be snapped up at any price as soon as it appears. . . . There are prohibitions to be feared, and one will not be able to sell the book openly, but that will only make it sell faster and better. . . . The [STN] is sure to make a great coup.[8]

So, yes, there was a demand for the Enlightenment, a huge demand, among readers in prerevolutionary France and everywhere in Europe. They also wanted a great many books that have dropped out of literary history and that were written by authors who have also disappeared.

It was by helping to satisfy this demand that librarians of the eighteenth century shared the task of eighteenth-century publishers and booksellers. After their treacherous journey over mountains and past customs inspectors some of the books might have ended up on the shelves of, for example, the Advocates' Library in Edinburgh, where philosopher David Hume held the Keepership from 1752 to 1757, rejoicing in his mastership "of 30,000 volumes."[9] If so, their difficult journey would by no means have been over. Minutes of a meeting of the Library Curators on June 27, 1754, record the outcome of Hume's efforts to have three French books ordered from London bookseller Thomas Osborne added to stock—La Fontaine's *Contes*, Bussy-Rabutin's *Histoire amoureuse des Gaules,* and Crébillon's *L'écumoire.* The curators objected, ordaining "that the said Books be struck out of the Catalogue of the Library, and remov'd from the Shelves as indecent Books, & unworthy of a Place in a learned Library."[10] Hume's struggle to make the books available to his readership illustrates the last phase of a process that began when publishers like the STN tried to get them across the border to booksellers in France. Just as the continental publishers had to work around the many inspections their wares encountered in their journeys toward the bookshelves, eighteenth-century librarians had to deal with the restrictions and interferences of their conservative-minded academic masters. (Hume was later in trouble again for having sanctioned the sale of a duplicate book without the signatures of the all-controlling curators).[11]

Then as now, librarians built collections in the same way as publishers constructed their lists, doing "market research" on their readership and buying what they knew would be appreciated by patrons. In the Library Company of Philadelphia for instance, founded in 1731 by Benjamin Franklin, librarian Louis Timothee worked with purchasing agent and fellow of the Royal Society Peter Collinson to acquire an impressive collection, consisting of 375 historical works, geographies and travel books, some literature (poems and plays rather than fiction), some science and some theology and sermons.[12] Again in the Library of the Inner Temple in London, eighteenth-century librarian Joshua Blew was permitted to spend £20 a year on books, and having "all the instincts of a good bibliographer," used this wisely to purchase not only law books but also antiquarian, historical, and literary works that he knew would be of interest to the society's members. Higden's *Polychronicon*, Strutt's *Sports and Pastimes* (1810), Hakluyt's *Voyages* (1598–1600), Clarendon's *History* (1702–4), Saxton's *Atlas of England and Wales* (1579), and Seller's *Atlas maritimus* (1678) are all testament to the diversity of that Enlightenment interest.[13]

"The point of librarians is to help people find information," writes twenty-first-century librarian David Bedford in his blog.[14] The definition applies equally to eighteenth-century librarians who worked hard to put books on their shelves and to booksellers who suffered the vicissitudes of mountain trails, adverse weather, and gimlet-eyed excisemen to get their books to the point of sale. Both knew that knowledge is power; both struggled to make that knowledge accessible to a broad audience; and in doing so, both created the foundations for the world of knowledge that is available to readers today.

NOTES

1. Wayne Bivens-Tatum, *Libraries and the Enlightenment* (Los Angeles: Library-Juice Press, 2012), 45.

2. This essay is based on many years of research in the archives of the Société typographique de Neuchâtel (STN) in the Bibliothèque publique et universitaire de Neuchâtel in Neuchâtel, Switzerland. I published an early version of this research as *The Literary Underground of the Old Regime* (Cambridge, MA: Harvard University Press, 1982), and I am now completing work on an open-access website, which will make available hundreds of the STN documents, including the diary and correspondence of Jean-François Favarger discussed in the lecture. I would like to thank Dr. Alice Crawford, digital humanities research librarian at the University of St. Andrews Library, for furnishing material on eighteenth-century libraries and librarians.

3. Darnton, *Literary Underground*, 7.

4. The following discussion is based on Favarger's "carnet de voyage," and his letters to the STN in the STN archives, ms. 1059 and 1150.

5. Archives of the STN, ms. 1148.

6. The following account is based on the dossier of Caldesaigues, STN archives, ms. 1131 and of Mossy, STN archives, ms 1185.

7. The following account is based on the dossier of Gosse, STN archives, ms. 1159 and the STN's replies to Gosse recorded in its "Copie de lettres," ms. 1095.

8. Gosse to STN, 9 March 1770, STN archives, ms. 1159.

9. Quoted in Brian Hillyard, "The Keepership of David Hume," in Patrick Cadell and Ann Matheson, eds., *For the Encouragement of Learning: Scotland's National Library 1689–1989* (Edinburgh: HMSO, 1989), 103.

10. J. C. Hilson, "More Unpublished Letters of David Hume," *Forum for Modern Language Studies* 6 (1970): 323.

11. The book in question may have been H. Noris, *Cenotophia Pisana Caii et Lucii Caesarum dissertationibus ilustrata* (Venice, 1681); see Hillyard, 107.

12. Information from the website of the Library Company of Philadelphia at http://www.librarycompany.org/.

13. Information from the website of the Inner Temple Library at http://www.innertemplelibrary.org.uk/.

14. From *The Singing Librarian Talks* blog at http://thesinginglibrarian.com/. Blogpost for August 28, 2010, "What does a librarian actually do all day?"

CHAPTER 5

❧

"The Advantages of Literature"

THE SUBSCRIPTION LIBRARY
IN GEORGIAN BRITAIN

David Allan

On December 27, 1784, a meeting took place at Perth, its purpose to discuss a document, previously drafted, bearing the self-explanatory title "Articles for Establishing a Public Library at Perth." Forty people were present, and they duly endorsed the document, each adding a signature to the master copy. By the following spring, a fully fledged membership-based organization, funded by subscription and known simply as the Perth Library, had resulted.[1] The minute books, notably of the first so-called ordinary general meeting held on April 7, 1785, allow us to paint a clear picture of what was actually happening and who was involved.[2] There was a core group of clergymen, including Reverend Adam Peebles, an Episcopalian minister, elected the library's first president that spring, and his two Presbyterian colleagues, Reverend James Scott, incumbent of the town's principal church, St. John's, and Reverend John Duff: all three were also active in the recently formed Perth Literary and Antiquarian Society, of which Scott was president and Peebles vice president.[3] Academic participation came from Alexander Gibson, master of Perth Academy, and his colleagues Duncan Macgregor, the French teacher, and John McOrmie, the drawing master. There were two surgeons, George Johnston and George Craigdallie, and eight lawyers, led by David Black, the library's founding secretary. Several public officials were also involved, including the sheriff of Perthshire and nearby land-owner James Murray; his relation, the local laird and collector of customs, Mungo Murray; Perth's burgh clerk, Patrick Duncan; and James Ross, the town's procurator fiscal. But the largest single occupational group, sixteen strong, were the "merchants," a catch-all contemporary label for businessmen. They included John Maxton, the Perth Bank's cashier (the library's first treasurer), and Andrew Keay, who ran the newly established cotton mill at neighbouring Stanley, as well as members of the powerful Sandeman business dynasty and several other important civic figures like John Caw and Alexander Fechney, who combined mercantile interests with prominence in burgh politics, including serving as provost several times between them in the coming years: Fechney in due course became the library's great early benefactor, leaving it £50 in his will.[4] By the fol-lowing year, working through a subcommittee, the library had purchased its first books, housing them in the long-term accommodation that, after the original gatherings in the town's tollbooth, it had procured in the academy building by St. John's. Borrowing had also commenced and the accumulating books had started to increase the quantity as well as to broaden the range of the subscribers' own reading.

This brief sketch of the Perth Library's founding is useful not only be-cause of the local color it offers nor merely because its extensive surviving records made it the focus of an article I published some years ago.[5] Its greatest value for the present purpose is that it provides a convenient way into thinking about a crucial infrastructural feature of British culture in the long eighteenth century that was genuinely nationwide in its extent. For the subscription library (sometimes then called a "public library" or a "general library," or even, by more recent historians, a "proprietary li-brary") was an institution found the length and breadth of Britain, usu-ally in urban settings but also serving wider hinterlands, from Kirkwall in Orkney to Penzance in Cornwall, from Stranraer on the west coast and Belfast across the water in Ulster to Chichester on the south coast and Hull on the east. In the east Lowlands of Scotland by the end of the Georgian period they had emerged in every sizeable town—not just Perth but also Dundee, Forfar, Falkirk, Stirling, Kirkcaldy, Edinburgh, Haddington, Dunbar, Cupar, and St. Andrews—as well as in dozens of smaller communities across the same region like Elie, Strathmiglo, Milnathort, Auchterarder, Dysart, Burntisland, Largo, and Inverkeithing.[6]

Those who founded such institutions were generally not bashful about their intentions. Some positively flaunted their vision for the transformative role of subscription libraries. The members of the Carlisle Library, for example, boasted that their organization had secured what they called the "advantages of Literature," which they claimed were ethical and social as much as purely intellectual:

> The advantages of Literature to the population of a large and opulent city are obvious to every one capable of appreciating them. An advancement in morals, manners, and taste, is a never-failing attendant upon a habit of reading and reflection: the rapid extension of the CARLISLE LIBRARY, therefore, may be placed foremost in the list of the many judicious and salutary improvements which, within a few years past, have been carried into effect in Carlisle, much to the comfort and convenience of its inhabitants.[7]

The rhetoric was obviously impressive, the ambitions great. And Carlisle's subscribers were, it must be underlined, by no means exceptional in the extravagance of their claims. There is a need, however, to get behind these rhetorical flourishes and to better understand the essential features of the libraries that resulted. This clearly requires a particular focus on what might be called the "nuts and bolts" of the subscription model itself—the structure and its operations, in other words, which reveal a great deal about what these organizations were really like. But the aim in what follows is also to cast a wider look at the cultural context and to see what these institutions, and the aspirations and preoccupations that lay behind them, might tell us about the peculiar nature of British society in the Georgian age.

❦

The subscription library's roots evidently lie in rather earlier and simpler organizations.[8] The key ancestor is what contemporaries knew as the "book club" (or occasionally "book society" or even "reading society"). Quite unlike the term's modern use, describing either a vehicle for those who wish to discuss what they have read (as in the Richard and Judy Book Club, linked to a recently popular television program) or, in a very different context, a commercial publisher's device for persuading people to buy books they may not really want (as in the Reader's Digest Book Club of fond memory), the Georgian book club was, like its eventual progeny the subscription library, fundamentally proprietorial—which is to say that it was a circle of individuals who contributed their own hard-earned cash so as to be able to choose and buy certain books collectively. The first examples seem to have arisen among clergymen in neighboring rural parishes in Huntingdonshire, Cambridgeshire, and Bedfordshire soon after 1700, but the phenomenon soon broadened out considerably so that by later in the century there were at least several hundred book clubs active across the country, and they had clearly become so widespread and so popular that they attracted knowing mockery in Charles Shillito's satirical *The Country Book-Club* (1788).[9] A crucial characteristic, however, was the principle that, once an individual text had been read, it would be sold, usually to a member, and the proceeds used to facilitate new purchases. In short, a book club, at least in theory, had no permanent book collection. Indeed, so important was this defining feature that some subscription libraries alluded to their purposeful avoidance of it in their own formal names: the Lichfield Permanent Library in Staffordshire, the Hereford Permanent Library, the Gloucester Permanent Library, and so forth—the word "permanent" here signalling that these institutions were emphatically not mere book clubs of the older kind. Not surprisingly, however, many subscription libraries nevertheless did coalesce out of preexisting book clubs. The Liverpool Library, for example, was founded in May 1758 when two book clubs, and possibly a third, came together for that very purpose, as their members finally decided to retain the books they had been buying.[10] Some book clubs, confusingly, even retained their old monikers despite mutating into subscription libraries, such as the so-called Huntingdonshire Book Club Society, founded in 1742 but with a sizeable permanent collection in its possession by the 1780s.[11] This had clearly become, in all but name, a large and flourishing subscription library.

The first wave of subscription libraries to emerge, whether ex nihilo or from out of prior book clubs, belongs to the 1740s and 1750s, with the famous Leadhills Library, founded in November 1741 by Lanarkshire miners, having a credible claim to be the earliest.[12] Some of them also provided influential models for emulation, and there is much evidence of blatant copycat activity as aspiring founders often simply followed a precedent from elsewhere. At Leeds in 1768, for instance, it was the Liverpool Library across the Pennines to which the original proposers made explicit reference when promoting their own scheme.[13] Similarly when Manchester's Portico Library was established in 1806 and Nottingham's subscription library was created ten years later both sets of founders based their plans on Liverpool's second major library, the Athenaeum, active since 1800.[14] Imitation also seems the only possible explanation for the rash of subscription libraries across southern Lancashire and in the neighboring West Riding of Yorkshire, where the unusual nomenclature of "circulating library" was adopted despite that term mainly suggesting to Georgian ears a commercial venture owned by a bookseller and hiring out books to fee-paying customers for a profit: the unique concentration of slightly discordant names like Halifax Circulating Library, Manchester Circulating Library, Warrington Circulating Library, and Ashton-under-Lyne Circulating Library in this one region hints strongly at founders simply spotting something interesting in a nearby town and enthusiastically following suit.[15]

From the permanency of their book collections, once established, several implications followed that shaped the subscription libraries and determined how they would operate. One, dictated by their growing assets and by membership numbers that quickly exceeded those of mere book clubs (which only rarely had even twenty participants), was a tendency to greater formalization: after all, the Liverpool Library by 1800, for example, had 893 subscribers and 8,157 books, while at Carlisle in 1819 there were 163 members and 1,463 books.[16] The enhanced rigor that resulted is nicely captured in the rulebook of the library at Dalkeith near Edinburgh, founded in 1798, with its strict laws on such things as penalties for members losing a book or, even worse, passing on borrowed items illicitly to third parties.[17] But rule making can, of course, all too easily become a habit of mind. At its most extreme the increasing officiousness led some libraries to legislate about the most unexpected things: for example, domestic animals. Thus at Wolverhampton in 1795 a polite reminder was issued that "Members are requested not to bring dogs."[18] At Halifax the problem of canine misbehavior was so great that a specific fine was introduced, sixpence for every member entering with a dog, while at Huntingdon the regulatory response was the memorable rule that "No dog shall be suffered to come into the Club Room, under the penalty of the Owner's forfeiting a bottle of Wine."[19] As well as the proliferation of regulations pertaining to a variety of potential scenarios, the increasing scale of operation also entailed the creation of executive subcommittees and the election of individual officers, as at Perth from the outset, to act on behalf of the wider membership—subject, naturally, to constitutional checks and balances prescribed in the regulations. This is what had clearly happened at Stamford in Lincolnshire, for example, where the 1787 library rulebook listed the officers and committee members for the benefit of all forty-six current members.[20] Formalization also meant the periodic creation of printed catalogues as a guide to the ever-expanding book collection. These, such as one that survives from Macclesfield in Cheshire in 1800, are often the only substantial documentary evidence historians now possess of a specific library's activities.[21] Most of the larger institutions also quickly identified a need for at least one employee to act as paid librarian, producing these catalogues, looking after the books and managing access and borrowing by the subscribers.

Much the most important consequence of owning a growing permanent collection was, however, the need for a permanent home. A book club could easily meet monthly on a reasonably casual basis in a tavern or coffeehouse: in Nottinghamshire the Newark Book Society, for example, long met at the town's Kingston Arms.[22] It might even persuade a friendly proprietor to let them keep a locked trunk on the premises containing their not very many current books. The subscription library's requirement for accommodation for at first hundreds and then eventually thousands or in some cases even tens of thousands of books on a permanent footing obviously created logistical problems of a wholly different order of magnitude. Formal renting, perhaps in a bookseller's back room as for the Amicable Society at Lancaster in the 1780s, or, as in Perth in the same decade, wangling a favorable tenancy from the corporation or a school, was one obvious recourse. This would have been true also of the many smaller libraries like those mentioned earlier in the eastern Lowlands: leasing a room would generally have been all that was possible. But in certain cases, especially later in the period, constructing dedicated premises was the solution of choice wherever feasible, since only this could provide full and exclusive control over access to the building in which a library's increasingly valuable property was housed. It is to the architectural decisions made at a time when the Grecian style was all the rage that the names of some of the most prepossessing of these institutions, like the Portico in Manchester and the Lyceum in Liverpool (the latter a name change for the old Liverpool Library to reflect its brand-new, purpose-built accommodation), are owed. Other groups, especially by the 1820s, embraced the Gothic with equal enthusiasm: the Carlisle Library's building is a good example. Many of the resulting edifices, often prominently positioned in the townscape, reflected the towering ambitions as well as the considerable self-regard of those involved: these were articulate statements about the importance of the institution, and, perhaps, of its proprietors, rendered unmistakably in fine masonry.

The financial affairs of the larger libraries also tended to be correspondingly complicated. A building, especially if bespoke, did not come cheap: £914 at Tavistock in Devon in 1822, for example, for a Grecian confection known as the Propylaeum, and a reported £1,850 at Hull a decade earlier.[23] Fitting them out could also be expensive. Taking into account the perceived need for a suitably high-quality finish—Corinthian capitals, false ceilings, balconies, even grand pediments, and glazed domes were often regarded as essential—it is not hard to appreciate how the costs could often mount: overruns, as original estimates proved wildly over-optimistic and continually needed raising, were a normal part of the experience for libraries undertaking these sorts of building projects. And the routine running costs of operating a library, whether in its own building or not, were also substantial, not infrequently stretching well into the hundreds of pounds each year: annual expenditure of £357 at the Bristol Library Society, for example, in 1810.[24] This in turn is why membership costs were sometimes so high: at the Lyceum in Liverpool it was already half a guinea per annum by the 1790s with an initial joining fee of a further five guineas—the same prices as at York.[25] Accordingly it is easy to understand why concerns about fair and open decision making, about keeping officers and subcommittees on a tight rein, about maintaining proper accounts and producing accurate documentation, and about managing and monitoring access to the institution's property all bore heavily on the thinking of participants. It was because the scale of operation in many cases and the consequent costs for those involved had comprehensively outgrown the simple book club format where a handful of people met periodically in the back room of a hostelry to put a little money into a pot to fund some additional reading matter.

ॐ

Brief allusion has already been made to the sorts of people involved in these institutions, at least to the limited extent that the Perth Library might be regarded as a classic example. But there is actually no such thing as a standard model for the membership of a Georgian subscription library. There is, moreover, a methodological problem when reconstructing the social composition of these institutions, and that is the difficulty, familiar to historians as to statisticians, created by survivor bias in the run of evidence. For it is precisely the grandest, most well-heeled, most prosperous, largest, and longest-lasting libraries in the more significant urban centers that tended to compile and conserve the most prodigious quantities of self-referential documentation. And it is therefore these that also tend to be heavily overrepresented in the historical evidence that has come down to us. Hence, for example, we can enumerate the founders of the Perth Library—and even add some interesting biographical color in many cases—but we cannot name the people who patronized many of the smaller libraries that sprang up across rural Fife. As a result it is necessary for us to talk instead in rather more general terms about the broad types of membership base found in different kinds of institutions, usually but not always reflecting local demographic patterns.

English cathedral cities, for instance, constitute a particularly well-defined subgroup, with the clergy from the chapter, the town churches, and the surrounding district often amounting to between 10 percent and 20 percent of all library members: at Norwich in 1792 the proportion of clergymen stood at 12 percent, at Worcester in 1818 it was 13 percent, while at York five years later sixty-five of the 477 members (or 14 percent) were reverend gentlemen, including the archbishop himself and the dean.[26] Another recognizable pattern that is readily illustrated from the surviving records is that of what might be described as the county or country town library—the institution located in the sort of urban center that chiefly functioned as an administrative, economic, social, and cultural focus for the population of a substantial rural area. Such memberships tended to be dense with local landowners, mainly prosperous farmers and country gentlemen: Stamford is once again a very good example, with its sprinkling of squires, as are Shrewsbury, Penzance, and Bury St. Edmunds.[27] There are also, meanwhile, clear signs of a type of library that was particularly heavily patronized by the new middle classes—people, in other words, involved in the expanding commercial and industrial activity of the Georgian era, including gratifying confirmation of what even then were emerging as familiar occupational stereotypes for certain towns and localities. At Wolverhampton, for example, at the time increasingly known for its role in the Black Country's metalworking industries, the subscribers included toolmakers and toy makers; at Lancaster, a port town especially noteworthy for its American hardwood imports, the founders of the Amicable Society included numerous Quaker ship owners and also Robert Gillow of the great local furniture-making dynasty; and in the early Liverpool Library there were, as one might predict, a smattering of chandlers, rope makers, sailmakers and sugar importers.[28]

The involvement of female readers was also commonplace. In fact, like the clergy, women frequently made up a sizeable minority of subscribers: for example, 18 percent at Norwich in 1792, 21 percent at Lancaster in 1812, and 20 percent at Worcester in 1818.[29] The formal admission of female proprietors was, it seems, invariably welcome, even though this only occasionally was made explicit (as at Lewes in Sussex, where the library's regulations expressly permitted their inclusion, and also at Lancaster in 1775, where the minutes preserve the moment when the initial proposal that women should be enrolled as members was accepted).[30] Yet there is a complicating factor when attempting to gauge levels of active female participation from the surviving membership lists: the phenomenon of group subscription. For it was very common indeed for one member of a household to subscribe and for this to confer borrowing privileges on the entire family. Documentary proof of this survives in one case because the library characteristically bureaucratized it. At Wolverhampton a pro forma certificate carried the following formulation: "I certify that the bearer [blank space for a handwritten name] is an inmate of my family, and as such is authorized by me to frequent the library, and to have books from it as for myself."[31] The same happened at the Portico, with the rule-book confirming that "The Library and Reading-Room shall be open to the Ladies of the respective families of the subscribers."[32] Another suggestive piece of evidence comes from what is missing from the registers: at many institutions (at Lancaster in 1812, for example) there are no instances of female subscribers sharing a surname with the men—so no wives, no unmarried daughters or spinster sisters. This either demonstrates that none of the men had any close female relations who wanted to join or, as seems infinitely more likely, that only women who did not already have a husband or father or brother who was a member bothered to subscribe, and pay the necessary dues, independently.[33] There is therefore every reason to think that actual female users of the subscription libraries were almost certainly far more numerous than the recorded female subscribers.

We need also to consider, of course, despite the huge problems with the lack of evidence for the humblest institutions, the scope that existed for the involvement of working-class readers. Two developments in particular are worthy of mention in this regard because they did bring readers from poor backgrounds into the subscription library's ambit. The first was the authentic working-class membership-based library, usually small in scale, such as the one at Luddenden in the West Riding around 1830, about which we know because one member, William Heaton, a Methodist weaver and an autodidact entomologist, subsequently published some poetry along with a memoir; or the self-improvement society and library founded at Failsworth near Manchester by the weaver and future journalist Ben Brierley; or in the same decade the library at Edwinstowe in Nottinghamshire of which the artisan painter—and, again, working-class autobiographer—Christopher Thomson was a cofounder.[34] How many of these institutions existed we do not know and never will, because virtually none left durable evidence. The second avenue into this world for the reader of limited means about which it is still possible to say something was, of course, for the costs of participation to be transferred to someone else. In practice this meant the formation of subscription libraries where patrons or employers paid on behalf of working-class users or at least subsidized them. Often designated artisans' or apprentices' libraries and probably quite widespread by the end of the Georgian period, when they were linked to the emergence of full-blown mechanics' institutes, there are a small handful from which documentation is still extant, in places like Nottingham, Liverpool, and Birmingham.[35] The difficulty with this sort of institution, however, was that, unlike the orthodox proprietorial libraries in which Heaton, Thomson, and Brierley participated as owners, by introducing the philanthropic involvement of nonusers they also potentially compromised the conventional rights of the readers to exercise exclusive control both over the library in general and over book selection in particular. This awkward state of affairs brings us neatly to the question of the kinds of reading experience that subscription libraries in practice actually made possible.

❦

Broadly speaking the books acquired by subscription libraries tended to be the outcome of two conflicting impulses. On the one hand there was the freedom of readers who were also owners and members to decide, by some combination of individual proposal and collective approval, the books that the library would buy: this expectation, of course, implied a potential for glorious chaos as the collection would inevitably reflect individual subscribers' myriad wishes and whims. On the other hand there was the strong desire for order imposed by prevailing notions of taste, decency, and propriety. These constraints were especially potent in practice because Georgian culture was not notably open-minded about appropriate reading material. Indeed they gave rise to a series of specific anxieties that the construction of an institutional collection was always liable to exacerbate. One was closely related to the commitment of many participants, as we have seen, to the strict emulation of precedents from elsewhere, which were accepted as in some sense establishing standards to which other libraries needed to aspire: as the minutes at Nottingham record, for example, it was agreed shortly after that institution was founded in 1816 "That the Librarian [should] make out a list of books marked in the Liverpool catalogue & that Mr Almond Mr Hutton and Mr Pearson be requested to look over such catalogue and mark against them the prices at which such books can be obtained"—in other words, the early members assumed that the Athenaeum's catalogue defined the sort of collection to which they too should aspire.[36] A further concern when shaping a burgeoning institutional collection was the whole thorny question of dubious literature. In some cases this meant merely texts of an inherently argumentative nature that might inflame tempers or trigger unseemly disputes between members. This was why at Newark, for example, a rule declared books of "party politics and polemical divinity" strictly inadmissible.[37] But the commonest problem, at least as it was understood by contemporaries, was the novel, a literary form that from midcentury, the era of Fielding's *Tom Jones*, Richardson's *Pamela*, and Mackenzie's *The Man of Feeling*, was sweeping all before it in public taste, much to the horror of many critics.

The issue with novels was, or was usually held to be, twofold. One concern was that narrative fiction seemed to be so constructed by manipulative and morally bankrupt authors as to sensationalize or whitewash bad behavior and encourage emotional incontinence among readers through blatant titillation. The other worry, closely related to the first, was that such literature was also simultaneously much more likely to appeal to and therefore to lead astray those vulnerable readers with the weakest constitutions, specifically women, the young, and—a fascinating Georgian perception—servants, as a consequence threatening not just public morality but also the social and political order. This set of deeply rooted prejudices about the dangers of fiction meant that the place of the novel in subscription library collections was inherently and inevitably contentious, with many institutions laying down obiter dicta on the subject: "No Novel or Play shall be admitted into the Library, but such as have stood the test of time, and are of established reputation," as the nervous founders of the Leicester Literary Society put it in 1790.[38] Between the right of members to choose, however, and the fear of what might happen when they did, libraries continually struggled to negotiate. Usually this entailed committees receiving general policing powers in relation to questionable titles. But inevitably disputes could arise, since the difference between acceptable and unacceptable work is almost always in the eye of the beholder and in any case the very idea of censorship being imposed by a subgroup ran counter to the democratic ethos and proprietorial expectations of the paying membership as a whole. At

Uxbridge in Middlesex in 1819, for example, it is almost possible to hear the conflicting impulses at work as the members objected to the high-handed way in which one new text, bought at one member's suggestion, had then been removed by another, but also found themselves agreeing with the underlying moral judgment about Byron's writing that had caused the incident in the first place. As the minutes record, the members "decidedly object to and blame the manner in which Don Juan has been withdrawn—as being a direct infringement of the Rules of the Society, but fully convinced of the impropriety and licentious nature of the book itself do not think proper to repurchase it."[39]

Such qualms, however, did not stop the novel, reputable or otherwise, finding a significant place in most subscription library collections. A good example is again from the Macclesfield catalogue from 1800: among the so-called twelves—the duodecimo format, typically used for small-size multivolume editions of popular novels—there are numerous instances of narrative fiction, including imaginative works that remain much loved, like Richardson's *Clarissa* and Ann Radcliffe's newer novel *The Italian*, as well as some less well remembered books such as *Henry Somerville* and the gothic romance *The Children of the Abbey*.[40] But turning back to the first page of the same catalogue we would also find more of the other types of material that subscription libraries tended to supply, because of their intense commitment, as we have seen, to "the advantages of Literature"—an ideal always implying edifying, improving books that would inform and educate. History, biography, and travel literature were extremely common everywhere. So too were essays, poems, philosophical works, and scientific texts. There was, in other words, an invariable emphasis on more serious forms of literature, the kinds of things with which a knowledgeable person needed to be familiar, whether Ben Brierley in Failsworth, who with his working-class friends was apparently ploughing through Shakespeare, Burns, and Locke, or genteel Cheshire squires and silk manufacturers, as in the case of the Macclesfield subscribers, immersing themselves in Michel de Montaigne's sixteenth-century meditative essays or devouring the autobiography of the recently deceased historian Edward Gibbon.

Before moving toward a conclusion it is necessary to say something in addition about why these people did what they did. This is the more

important because explaining the popularity and vibrancy of the subscription library model across Britain from the 1750s onward lays bare
some hugely significant Georgian idiosyncrasies. Superficially, of course,
they did it simply because they wanted to get their hands on more books:
membership of a voluntary association of fellow readers generated far
greater purchasing power and, over time, at least in the case of a proper
subscription library, offered the use of a sizeable lending collection of
texts. But there was clearly more to it than that. After all, there were
many instances of individuals who almost certainly did not engage in
this kind of associational activity mainly, or even at all, because they required more or easier access to books. Wordsworth was one, a keen user
of the so-called Kendal Book Club, another library in disguise, who had
his own large personal collection at Rydal Mount that even served as a
private lending resource for friends like De Quincey and Arnold (indeed so capacious was it that Wordsworth actually needed to create his
own borrowing records to keep track of the comings and goings).[41] Less
celebrated but no less revealing is the case of Reverend Thomas Clarke,
mainstay and sometime president of the Hull library, who, when his own
books were auctioned on his death in 1798, owned a good five thousand
titles.[42] Evidently neither Wordsworth nor Clarke, both of them regular
attenders of their respective libraries over many years, was exactly short
of reading material.

The Kendal institution in particular gives us an important clue as to
why this type of organization attracted such people, for in addition to
the opportunity to borrow books it also offered a venue for meeting
friends and acquaintances as well as an annual Book Club Ball and a Venison Feast. The Huntingdonshire Book Club Society fulfilled much the
same function, serving as a focus for social gatherings, including formal
events like its well-attended monthly dinners, held, apparently, for three
hours in the evening of the Tuesday before full moon.[43] In other words,
these libraries were also convivial organizations that provided plentiful
opportunities for sociability—for meeting and interacting with others.
But sociability was not just a casual pleasure. For some participants in
the subscription libraries, like the Earl of Exeter, a committee member at
Stamford, involvement was a way in which local dignitaries could confer
patronage and acknowledge their social obligations, especially necessary

given the claims that were frequently heard, as at Carlisle, for the moral benefits of such institutions to the wider public. Social interaction in the libraries could also involve attending instructive lectures or taking part in enlightening debates. Occasionally these formats caused their own problems, such as when the subjects covered strayed into divisive territory: they clearly did this at Lancaster in 1775, as, with the prime minister's disastrous American policy triggering outright revolution, the members felt obliged to pass a subsequent resolution regarding the relevant entry in their minute book that "that part of the society's discussion of the Subject No 26 respecting Bribing Lord North be erased."[44] More often, however, members' discussions, formal or informal, clung to the principle made explicit at Wakefield, that they should "cherish and maintain, on all occasions, a profound reverence for the principles of revealed religion, and . . . refrain from the expression of any sentiments or views hostile to the British constitution."[45]

Sociability, then, mattered intensely to the participants in subscription libraries. But it was generally properly structured and intentional in character, not random and accidental. In particular it was organized and given coherence by conversations on reading-related questions, by discussion of the library's own internal affairs, by debates on appropriate topics, and by regular dinners and periodic dances. It was also sociability that was consciously directed, in keeping with the influential doctrines of commentators like Joseph Addison and Lord Shaftesbury, toward the cultivation of what contemporaries knew and prized as "politeness"—that is to say, it was considered as constructing an amiable and emollient disposition, resolutely rational in outlook and accepting of others, always interested and inquisitive about the world and about other people but determined to avoid disagreeable conflict and seeking to form secure interpersonal relationships that would in turn become the very building blocks of peaceful and prosperous wider communities.[46] Politeness, in this sense, was profoundly ideological, concerned with stabilising eighteenth-century society after the disastrous upheavals of the seventeenth century that had been marked throughout the British Isles by civil war and revolution resulting from irrational fanaticism and endemic mutual intolerance. And politeness, the necessary antidote to these devastating pestilences, could best be nurtured by a concerted commitment to sociability, in effect by joining and participating in associational organizations—not just subscription libraries and book clubs but also masonic lodges (which were proliferating rapidly at this time), literary societies, antiquarian societies, music societies, even cricket clubs (the latter again spreading like wildfire, at least in England).[47] This was in fact, as Peter Clark has argued, a golden age of British associationalism, and we miss something vital about the subscription library phenomenon if we view it in isolation, merely as a question of people wanting to read more books, and if we divorce it from this broader cultural and ideological context peculiar to Georgian Britain, which was positively obsessed with organized sociability, structured interaction, and the pursuit of politeness.

So why, finally, did the subscription library craze eventually fizzle out? Why are there so few of these institutions—the Portico in Manchester is one—still around today? In particular, why did so many close their doors for good between around 1870 and the Second World War—like the Lyceum in Liverpool, for example, which ceased to operate in 1942 and whose splendid city-center building is now regrettably unoccupied? Partly the simple answer must be that, over time, the Georgian preoccupation with politeness dissipated. Victorian people found new things to fret about and devised new solutions in which polite sociability—so crucial to Addison and Shaftesbury, looking nervously over their shoulders at the violent and chaotic world of Cromwell and the Covenanters—no longer played a meaningful part. But partly also the problem for the subscription library by the second half of the nineteenth century was one of rival attractions, above all the result of parliamentary legislation that, in concert with Mr. Carnegie's good works, provided late Victorian and Edwardian Britons with a compelling alternative to the relatively expensive private subscription library model: which is to say, true public libraries, run by local government, ratepayer-funded, and free at the point of use, which may usually have lacked dances and drinking sessions and, one presumes, venison feasts—indeed much of the characteristic paraphernalia of Georgian sociability—but that did provide automatic access at no cost to large and growing book collections for enthusiastic readers of all social classes. And to appreciate how these new institutions generally replaced the preexisting subscription libraries even in the affections of most of the more prosperous book-lovers, to the extent that they had largely killed them off by the 1940s, we need to recall that the Victorian or early twentieth-century public library was a quite different creature from its early twenty-first-century descendant with its DVD collections and vast reams of council literature.

Most crucially we should understand that those who first conceived and built Britain's public libraries entirely shared the burning vision of edifying literature and learning—of reading as an ennobling and morally uplifting experience—which had previously animated the idealistic subscribers at Carlisle and at Perth. Public libraries of the new kind were often architecturally at least as striking as the grandest of the old-style subscription libraries, and certainly as powerful a statement of cultural self-confidence on the part of those who erected them. But they were free, and they also rapidly accumulated book collections on a very large scale indeed, facts that quickly made them overwhelmingly preferable even to many well-to-do readers. Something of the glorious ambition of this movement is captured in the former Crumpsall Library on Cheetham Hill Road in Manchester.[48] The building is an exquisite example of corporation Edwardian Baroque and Grade II–listed, although it is now sadly derelict, its future in jeopardy. In its heyday, however, it possessed wonderful stained-glass windows, which when the sun shone through them created a cathedral-like atmosphere within, quite deliberately reminding the seated rows of hushed readers of the stars in the literary firmament whom they were there to venerate: Keats, Gray, and Burke from these islands; Homer, Euripides, and Cervantes from the Continent. And on the exterior cartouches, clearly cut into the stone so as to draw in the passing public from the busy high street, were the names of the four patron saints of British literature as viewed from the vantage point of late-Victorian high culture, the dedicatees of this temple of classless, publicly funded scholarship: Scott, Milton, Shakespeare, Dickens. Crumpsall Library, it should be noted, was planted in an unremarkable inner suburb of Manchester, just a couple of miles from where Ben Brierley and his friends two generations before had organized their own subscription library at Failsworth and only a short Edwardian tram ride from the Portico in the city center. And once this type of facility was available to everyone in the local population—in Cheetham Hill, to an eclectic mix of working-class Jews newly arrived from Eastern Europe and also a middle-class enclave of factory managers and office workers— the attractions of reading became even more obvious, in fact irresistibly alluring, to even greater numbers than before. But as the most effective and convenient way for eager readers to seek the "advantages of Literature," the emergence of proper public libraries meant that the proprietary subscription institution, a peculiar monument to Georgian Britain's distinctive cultural moment, had very largely had its day.

NOTES

1. Perth: A. K. Bell Library, Perth and Kinross Council Archive, MS 4: Perth Library 1784–1874, "Minutes I, 1784–1819": 1–3.

2. Ibid., 4–5.

3. David Allan, "The Scottish Enlightenment and the Politics of Provincial Culture: The Perth Literary and Antiquarian Society, ca. 1784–1790," *Eighteenth-Century Life* 27 (2003): 1–31.

4. *Guide to the City and County of Perth* (Perth, 1805), 16.

5. David Allan, "Provincial Readers and Book Culture in the Scottish Enlightenment: The Perth Library, c. 1784–1800," *Library* 3 (2002): 367–89.

6. My source for the existence of individual subscription libraries is the Library History Database, formerly provided online by the late Robin Alston. This is currently off-line as it is transferred to the website of the Institute of English Studies in the School of Advanced Study at the University of London.

7. *Rules for the Regulation of the Carlisle Library* . . . (Carlisle, 1819), iii.

8. David Allan, *A Nation of Readers: The Lending Library in Georgian England* (London: British Library, 2008), chs. 2 and 3. The urtext for modern students of the subscription library's emergence remains Paul Kaufman, "The Community Library: A Chapter in English Social History," *Transactions of the American Philosophical Society* 57 (1967), pt. 7: 3–67.

9. Keith Manley, "Rural Reading in North West England: The Sedbergh Book Club, 1728–1928," *Book History* 2 (1999): 78–95 (at 79); Keith Manley, "The S.P.C.K. and English Book Clubs before 1720," *Bodleian Library Record* 13 (1989): 231–43.

10. M. Kay Flavell, "The Enlightened Reader and the New Industrial Towns: A Study of the Liverpool Library, 1758–1790," *British Journal for Eighteenth-Century Studies* 8 (1985): 17–35.

11. Allan, *Nation of Readers*, 56.

12. John C. Crawford, "Leadhills Library and a Wider World," *Library Review* 46 (1997): 539–53.

13. Frank Beckwith, *The Leeds Library 1768–1968*, 2nd ed. (Leeds, 1994), 4–6.

14. Allan, *Nation of Readers*, 64; Nottingham: Bromley House: "Proceedings of the Library Committee, 1816–1830," fol. 5v.

15. Allan, *Nation of Readers*, 110n.

16. Ibid., 65, 97.

17. *Rules for the Regulation of the Dalkeith Subscription Library* . . . (Dalkeith, 1798).

18. Stafford: William Salt Library, MS. 101/31, Minute Book of Wolverhampton Subscription Library, 1795–1828, fol. 2v.

19. E. P. Rouse, "Old Halifax Circulating Library, 1768–1866," *Papers, Reports, etc. Read before the Halifax Antiquarian Society* (1911), 45–60 (at 46); *Laws and Regulations of the Huntingdonshire Book Club Society* . . . (Huntingdon, 1814), 8.

20. *Rules for Regulating the Subscription Library at Stamford* . . . (Stamford, 1787).

21. *Supplement to the Catalogue of the Macclesfield Library* (Macclesfield, 1800).

22. Nottingham: Nottinghamshire Archives, D463/22, Newark Book Society: "Accounts, 1784–1836," fol. 1v.

23. *A Catalogue of the Books in the Tavistock Public Subscription Library* . . . , 8; Keith Manley, "Lounging Places and Frivolous Literature: Subscription and Circulating Libraries in the West Country to 1825," in John Hinks and Catherine Armstrong, eds., *Printing Places: Locations of Book Production and Distribution Since 1500* (New Castle, DE, and London: British Library, 2005), 107–20 (at 118); *An Account of the Rise and Progress of the Subscription Library at Kingston-upon-Hull* . . . (Hull, 1810), 11, 26, 28.

24. Kathleen Hapgood, "Library Practice in the Bristol Library Society, 1772–1830," *Library History* 5 (1981): 145–53 (at 148).

25. Allan, *Nation of Readers*, 92.

26. Ibid., 67–68.

27. *Catalogue of Books Belonging to the Subscription Library in Shrewsbury* . . . (Shrewsbury, 1812); *Rules and Catalogue of the Penzance Library* . . . (n.p., 1824); *Laws for the Regulation of the Suffolk Public Library, Bury St. Edmunds* (Bury, 1791).

28. Minute Book of Wolverhampton Subscription Library, 1795–1828, fol. 1v; Lancaster Public Library: MS.5147, "Laws for the future regulation of the

Amicable Society . . ."; *A Catalogue of the Present Collection of Books in the Liverpool Library* (n.p., n.d.), 12–15.

29. Allan, *Nation of Readers*, 78.

30. *Catalogue of the Books Belonging to the Lewes Library Society* . . . (Lewes, 1827), iv; "Minutes of the Amicable Society," January 10, 1775.

31. *Catalogue of Books Belonging to the Wolverhampton Library* . . . (Wolverhampton, 1835), xiii.

32. *Catalogue of the Books Belonging to the Portico-Library* . . . (Manchester, 1810), 3.

33. *A Catalogue of the Amicable Society's Library* . . . (Lancaster, 1812).

34. William Heaton, *The Old Soldier, The Wandering Lover; and Other Poems* . . . (London, 1857), xviii–xix; John Host, *Victorian Labour History: Experience, Identity and the Politics of Representation* (London, 1998), 83; Christopher Thomson, *The Autobiography of an Artisan* (London, 1847), 335.

35. *Catalogue of the Books Belonging to the Nottingham Artisans' Library* . . . (Nottingham, 1824); Thomas Kelly, *A History of Adult Education in Great Britain*, 2nd ed. (Liverpool: Liverpool University Press, 1970), 127–28.

36. Nottingham: Bromley House: "Proceedings of the Library Committee, 1816–1830," fol. 5v.

37. *A Catalogue of the Newark Library* . . . (Newark, 1825), 17.

38. *Laws for the Regulation of the Literary Society. Leicester* . . . ([Leicester], [1790]), 11.

39. Uxbridge: Uxbridge Central Library, Mus. 5, Book Society Minutes, 1811–36, fols. 30v–31r.

40. *Supplement*, pp. 1–4.

41. Manley, "Rural Reading," 90; *Wordsworth's Library: A Catalogue*, ed. Chester L. Shaver and Alice C. Shaver (New York and London: Garland, 1979).

42. *Catalogue of a Valuable and Curious Collection of . . . the late Rev. Thomas Clarke, D.D.* . . . (York, 1798).

43. *Laws and Regulations*, 3.

44. "Minutes of the Amicable Society, 1769–85," January 6, 1775.

45. *Rules and Regulations of the Wakefield Literary and Philosophical Society* . . . (Wakefield, 1830), 32.

46. Lawrence E. Klein, *Shaftesbury and the Culture of Politeness: Moral Discourse and Cultural Politics in Early Eighteenth-Century England* (Cambridge: Cambridge University Press, 1994); Lawrence E. Klein, "The Third Earl of Shaftesbury and the Progress of Politeness," *Eighteenth-Century Studies* 8 (1974): 186–214; Lawrence E. Klein, "Liberty, Manners and Polite-

ness in Early Eighteenth-Century England," *Historical Journal* 32 (1989): 586–603.

47. Peter Clark, *British Clubs and Societies 1580–1800: The Origins of an Associational World* (Oxford: Oxford University Press, 2000).

48. Arthur Jones and M. Barry King, "The Effect of Re-siting a Library," *Journal of Librarianship and Information Science* 11 (1979): 215–31.

CHAPTER 6

Literature and the Library
in the Nineteenth Century

John Sutherland

THE LANDSCAPE

Viewed in its half-millennial totality the history of the printed book in Britain—its manufacture, distribution and reception—presents a pattern of precariously achieved stabilities lasting decades, sometimes centuries, punctuated by seismic shifts and, after turmoil, new long stabilities emerging to replace the old.

The reasons for the constitutional inertia are self-evident. The producing and merchandising of books is costly and returns are notoriously slow. Commercial success for any one book is, often, as unpredictable as a stake at the gambling table. The traditional book lore is that of five books three lose money, one breaks even and one makes profit. The everswollen ranks of "remainders" testify to the truth of the mournful trade wisdom. Many titles do not enjoy even the half-life of "broken price." One reads in trade papers the daunting statistic that as many as 40 percent of printed books are destined to be pulped, unbought, unread, unwanted.[1] Few industries could survive such a casualty rate.

Uncertainty stimulates a reluctance to innovate until innovation becomes absolutely essential for survival. Conservative strategies, old ways of doing things, keep the applecart steady. Many steadying strategies emerged in the nineteenth century. The Net Book Agreement (a Victorian innovation, introduced in the 1890s, abolished in the 1990s, long after rpm, retail price management, in every other retail commodity) was one of the longer standing.[2] The retention of the NBA for books was successfully defended in court in the mid-1960s. Gradual refinements in copyright legislation, and contractual practice, were introduced throughout the century, cooling author-publisher friction. Book trade institutions—the Society of Authors, the Publishers' Association, the Booksellers' Association, came into being, adding their steadying influences. The growth to dominance of "dynastic" publishers was another stabilizing force. These dynasties eventually merged into other elites, following the classic Vico pattern. Macmillan, a firm that grew out of provincial bookselling and "tobacco parliaments" on the fringe of Cambridge University, would eventually produce a prime minister of England—the most literature loving of his kind since Gladstone.[3] It was a significant moment when Thackeray nominated his publisher George Smith (nicknamed "The Prince of Publishers") for election (successful) to the Reform Club[4] and another significant moment when Smith, in his later years, put a massive part of his wealth into the *Dictionary of National Biography* (arguably the greatest institutional venture of the period—taken over after Smith's death by Oxford University Press). By the early twentieth century it was Oxbridge lore that "wine and publishing" were the two leading "trades" a gentleman graduate could decently enter.

It is painfully clear that we are currently in one of the intervals of all-change turmoil—arguably the most tumultuous since the fifteenth century. The large conduits that have supplied reading matter in traditional printed codex form for over half a century, many institutionalized in the nineteenth century, are shutting down en masse, with a speed that evokes extinction rather than evolution. I pass two decaying public libraries on my everyday way to work. The last independent booksellers in the part of London that I live in have gone under. I note the same disappearance in the North American system—including those libraries called, within living memory, "Carnegies," after Andrew Carnegie, a living witness to the historical supremacy of the Scottish reverence for self-improving reading, who devoted a large portion of his wealth to the establishment of some twenty-five hundred public libraries.

Paradoxically, these extinctions have been replaced, instantaneously, by a vastly greater availability of reading matter. The electronic sale of new books and new e-libraries have created an Aladdin's Cave, no "open sesame" required. An extraordinarily reenergized secondhand book market booms, via web operators such as ABE and Amazon "pre-owned" (delightful euphemism).

One recalls Catherine Morland's wonder, on being introduced to one of Bath's select circulating libraries, that she could read whatever she chose to read. (And much good it did her, Jane Austen implies.) There were, as the nineteenth century opened, some thousand small "circulating libraries," concentrated where literary and leisured people concentrated—spa towns prominently.[5] The Reverend Morland's library in Wiltshire was, one suspects, short on Mrs. Radcliffe's tales of terror.

One of the more interesting nineteenth-century clergyman's libraries that we have any record of, that of the Reverend Patrick Brontë, is stultifyingly Christian and instructional—but one title jumps out—Byron's *Don Juan*, acquired in 1835, as Gondal and Angria were hatching.[6] One can make much of that volume, and the sisters' cultivation of the Heathcliff-Rochester Byronic antihero. Irritatingly one does not know the content of the Reverend George Austen's private library.[7] It was sold off, for needed expenses, when the family moved to Bath. What one can assume is that, like Mr. Bennet's, it was more ecumenical than the Reverend Brontë's, with more than Scott and Byron available for the young ladies of the household. It was there, one assumes, that Jane came across Tom Jones and other reading matter that might have been thought downright poisonous by Sir Anthony Absolute.[8]

If one wanted a telegrammatic account of the six-hundred-year history of the codex printed book it would be "ever more access, ever more readers." The inexorable line extends from the anonymous genteel bookseller in Bath to the Google Library Project, catering to modern Ms. Morlands by the billion.

Upheaval and change, such as we are now going through, can be similarly observed in the new structures and systems of book delivery and access that came into being in the mid-nineteenth century. There were many forces driving change, but one of the most reformative was industrial. In the show window of the British industrial revolution, the Great Exhibition of 1851, book manufacture featured prominently. Processes had advanced rapidly from the 1820s onward, refining and cheapening the machine production of embossed, ribbed, and relief cover designs, on dyed cloth (using heated rollers), along with gilding and block work. New rag-quality paper and improved typography enhanced the page quality of the better class of product. John Leighton, a craft leader, was a starred exhibitor under the panes of the Crystal Palace.[9] The new book could be that beloved Victorian thing—a cheap luxury. Decorative, eye-catching covers verged on the exotic in the second half of the century. They were forerunners of the modern illustrated dust jacket, the least of whose purposes is to protect against dust. Michael Sadleir was a pioneer in appreciating the art and craft of these florid excrescent features (Sadleir's magnificent library rests in its bibliophile shrine in UCLA).[10]

The illustrated "cover" was integrated into the printing and library and retail distribution process. The hardback made feasible the "circulating library," with sturdy wares good for an estimated 150 loans (with three-decker novels, which could satisfy three end users simultaneously, the economics of the initial outlay of thirty-one shillings and sixpence—a guinea and a half—typically discounted by 50 percent for bulk orders, are self-evident).

It was not all flux. The nineteenth century, as the decades unrolled, developed skeletal stabilizing factors. The three-volume novel (which lasted an incredible seventy years, from 1821 to 1894) was clearly one such binding element. The recurrent bans on retail underselling by united publisher boycott (eventually wholly successful with the NBA in the 1890s) preserved the country's network of bookshop outlets from destructive competition with each other. There evolved, in the midcentury the forerunner of a two-tier pattern of publication with an inhibitingly expensive first issue (e.g., the guinea-and-a-half three-decker, the half-guinea poetry volume) followed, after a year or two (shortened to months in the 1890s) by a "cheap edition" costing a disinhibiting few shillings.[11] This pattern survived through the twentieth century as the ubiquitous hardback/paperback sequence.

The expensive first form of book, beyond most pockets, fostered the growth of circulating and municipal public libraries. Borrowed books. The cheap follow-up fostered the widespread growth of personal "libraries"—the poor man's treasury. They often carried the suffix "library"—as in the longest lived of the series, J. M. Dent's Everyman Library (still, in mutated form, with us). Everyman texts carried the flyleaf motto:

> Everyman, I will go with thee
> and be thy guide,
> In thy most need to go
> by thy side.

Ownership is assumed.

There were thriving firms with specialist lines in such things as law, medicine, music, and school texts. But the nineteenth century saw the growth to central prominence of houses specializing in "general trade publishing," with patterns of cross subsidization between intrinsically different kinds of book. The nineteenth-century dynastic general trade publisher has, in the last one hundred years, become the multinational "agglomerated" combine—the mountainous feature of today's publishing landscape.

Libraries: Metropolitan, National, Institutional, and Affiliational

Industrialization, urbanization, and countrywide railway connection created a national framework in the nineteenth century for the British book trade. Wherever congregations of human beings form (in churches, schools, universities, cities, clubs), libraries—centralized pools of books —form alongside them as surely as barnacles on the hulls of ships. Britain's new metropolitan cities, growing at explosive speed, were the largest such congregations, with one metropolis, London, becoming as unofficially the capital of the book trade as the city itself was capital of the country. Readers supplied by London were a countrywide constituency (worldwide if one extends perspective to the colonies—steam, by ship and train, made both national and international distribution possible).

There is a moment in Disraeli's *Coningsby* when the sage, Sidonia, thrown together with the ingenuous hero in a storm (the author loved operatic grandeur), learns that the young man longs to undertake the grand tour:

> "I never was in the Mediterranean," said Coningsby. "There is nothing I should like so much as to travel."
>
> "You are travelling," rejoined his companion. "Every moment is travel, if understood."
>
> "Ah! but the Mediterranean!" exclaimed Coningsby. "What would I not give to see Athens!"
>
> "I have seen it," said the stranger, slightly shrugging his shoulders, "and more wonderful things. Phantoms and spectres! The Age of Ruins is past. Have you seen Manchester?"[12]

If London was the country's capital, Manchester could trump its preeminence as the workshop not merely of a country, but of the midcentury world. Confirming Sidonia's acclamation, Manchester became the first civic authority to establish a rate-supported (misnamed "free") public lending and reference library under the 1850 Libraries Act. The institution opened, with appropriate pomp, at the Hall of Science, Campfield, on September 2, 1852. The opening address was given by Lord Lytton, or, to give him his full title: Edward George Earle Lytton Bulwer-Lytton, first Baron Lytton. It's worth quoting (not for nothing has Bulwer-Lytton given his name to the prize for worst opening sentence of the year). No vindication of the library could have been loftier:

> I call it an arsenal, for books are weapons, whether for war or for self-defence; and perhaps the principles of chivalry are as applicable to the student now as they were to the knight of old.

A more temperate Dickens, the other godfather attending the project, declared:

> In this institution, special provision has been made for the working classes, by means of a free lending library this meeting cherishes the earnest hope that the books thus made available will prove a source

of pleasure and improvement in the cottages, the garrets, and the cellars of the poorest of our people.[13]

Five years earlier Marx and Engels addressed their *Communist Manifesto* to the world's working classes (not least those in Manchester, where Engels did his fieldwork). It's nice to record that the two fathers of communism put their heads together to compose the manifesto in Manchester's Chetham's Library—the oldest free public reference library, by centuries, in Britain. When Marx and Engels collaborated it had sixty-thousand books. The economics books Marx consulted are honorifically shelved, and the window nook in which they worked together is memorialized.

Dickens, interestingly, came to have second thoughts about the Manchester Free Library. The city, among its other preeminences, was the world center of statistical analysis, and a record of borrowings and measurable usage was duly published after the first year of the free library's operation in the *Statistical Journal*.[14]

The figures made for interesting reading. There were twice as many volumes in the reference (all nonfiction) as in the lending department. In the lending section:

> The demand for prose fiction was more than half of the aggregate circulation in the latter department, while in the former it constituted only one-seventh of the whole.

The report noted that "of the works of individual novelists, those of Scott and Defoe were most in demand" and "of individual works the *Thousand and One Nights*." The library's collection of fiction was, despite the clear appetite for it, meager in the extreme and universally that of dead authors. A literary graveyard. The living poet laureate, Tennyson, was deemed admissible.

Dickens, very much alive and kicking, made his irritation clear in a digression in *Hard Times* (his Lancashire novel, serialized in 1854), a work dedicated to the need for "amuthement" (as the circus master Sleary lisps it). Mill workers, he scathingly noted, with a glance north to Manchester:

wondered about human nature, human passions, human hopes and fears, the struggles, triumphs and defeats, the cares and joys and sorrows, the lives and deaths of common men and women! They sometimes, after fifteen hours' work, sat down to read more fables about men and women, more or less like themselves, and about children, more or less like their own. They took DeFoe to their bosoms, instead of Euclid, and seemed to be on the whole more comforted by Goldsmith than by Cocker.[15]

The seventeenth-century mathematician, Edward Cocker, author of the ubiquitous text-book *Cocker's Arithmetic*, was the congenial source of Mr Gradgrind's war cry, "Facts, facts, facts." Dickens's retort was fiction, fiction, fiction.[16]

Fiction, particularly new fiction (like *Hard Times*) was regarded by the Free Library's custodians as something dangerous to the working-class mind—too exciting. They were not alone in their prejudice. Samuel Smiles, in his gospel of self-help, aligns novel reading, delicately, with self-abuse. Both, he instructs, should be avoided by the young self-improver. He concurred, in his manual for the aspiring young, with John Sterling (and Sterling's biographer, Carlyle):

> Periodicals and novels are to all in this generation, but more especially to those whose minds are still unformed and in the process of formation, a new and more effectual substitute for the plagues of Egypt, vermin that corrupt the wholesome waters and infest our chambers.[17]

The public must, in Smiles's verdict, avoid "the garbage with which the shelves of circulating libraries are filled." And, he might have added, public libraries benignly quarantined from.

The prejudice expressed so loftily by Smiles was, as we now say, in the DNA of the free library institution and its successors. When I used it as a boy, my library, in Colchester, Essex, applied 75 percent of its acquisition budget to nonfiction while 75 percent of borrowings were novels. Free public libraries always practiced (one can almost talk about them now in the past tense) a mild Britannic equivalent of the Papal Index. And alongside this well-meaning nervousness lurked a more primitive fear—a terror of the unwashed mob. It was not violence but plague, that other rider of the apocalypse that was most feared. The lower classes, as did my Victorian-born grandmother, licked their unwashed index finger to turn the page—the TB bacillus was passed on with an efficiency the master of Poe's Red Death would have envied. The rational French prefer sanitary uncut pages (each one guillotined with a special knife)—something that has never been thought acceptable in Britain. A quaint "fumigator" in which Victorian public libraries could decontaminate their stock is illustrated in Leah Price's discussion of the potentially disease-carrying book.[18] It was introduced into late Victorian public libraries and was still puffing away until the 1950s at least.[19]

Towns were constitutionally reluctant to follow the opportunities offered by the 1850 Public Libraries and Museums Acts, and by the "penny on the rates" provision, which allowed the establishments, if the ratepayers consented. Manchester led the way. Others were slow to follow, even after the Universal Education Act of 1870 and the increase in rate revenue made the library an asset to even small towns.

As early as 1860, Colchester (then around ten thousand strong) was encouraged to invest by similarly sized Kidderminster, whose town clerk wrote:

> A large majority of our readers are young men from fourteen to thirty years of age, chiefly belonging to the working classes, and who are exceedingly well-conducted and particular in observing the rule with regard to cleanliness.[20]

Colchester did not, however, get its public library until 1894. Ratepayers balked.

Despite the common saw, "the public library was my education" (most recently proclaimed by Adrian Mole creator, Sue Townsend) very few nineteenth-century authors of note (William Hale White and Richard Jefferies are possible exceptions) were directly nourished by local public library lending departments—although many probably made use of reference rooms. But, whatever their shortcomings, the public libraries served to raise into literacy the other side of the equation, a mass reading public. As John Cheever neatly put it: "I can't write without a reader. It's precisely like a kiss—you can't do it alone."[21]

At exactly the same moment as Manchester's free public library opened, the dominant commercial lending library in England was raising itself to "leviathan" status. Charles Edward Mudie had begun as a newsagent in Bloomsbury's Southampton Row, with a small section of books on display. Students, then as now, would browse and not buy. It is a peculiarity of the retail book trade. Supermarkets such as Tesco's and Vons do not install armchairs (as do Barnes and Noble in the United States, and Waterstone's in the UK) where uncertain customers can open a can of beans, to see if it is to their taste, decide "no," and leave having bought nothing.

Mudie drew the obvious conclusion and prudently put his book stock behind the counter and charged borrowing fees. With the *embourgeoisement* of west central London, his clientele expanded well beyond the student population. Mudie's sales hook was the one guinea per annum, one volume per loan, charge. Unlike the free libraries, he had not the slightest prejudice against new fiction. It was in fact his main line of goods.

In 1852 he moved his library to grand new premises, in New Oxford Street, alongside the British Museum. Having dragged the circulating library business into the mid-nineteenth century he formed himself into a limited liability company in 1864. His was the first library in Britain to do so.

By now he was claiming to purchase eighteen thousand volumes a year, supplying one hundred thousand subscribers. His orders had a palpable effect on the British publishing industry and the authors serving it. What in the twentieth century would be called the "safe library sale" became something publishers counted on, and it translated as pressure on authors, particularly novelists, to supply the ("safe") kind of thing Mr. Mudie wanted—a pressure depicted, savagely, in George Gissing's *New Grub Street*'s attack on "Mudieitis." Branch outlets were opened in Birmingham's New Street and (inevitably) Manchester's Cross Street. London home deliveries were by van, country deliveries by train. Books were also shipped abroad in tin boxes. Mudie was, if sea monsters were the appropriate analogy, as much a giant octopus as a leviathan. He himself preferred the "Pegasus" device, which was attached to all his publicity materials.[22]

Mudie's only significant rival over the following years would be W. H. Smith, which had expanded gigantically from their humble paper stall at Euston, to enjoy a virtual monopoly on purchased reading matter at major train stations in England.[23]

Railway termini created the most fluid congeries of reader in the Victorian period and fostered two distinct kinds of library. One was the uniform cheap book, pocket-sized, ideal for a long journey or two. To answer the demand Routledge's one-shilling "Railway Library" was launched in 1848. The series took off, aided by shrewd advertisement. Four years later, George Routledge complacently noted seeing all six other passengers in his first-class compartment reading "his" edition of *Uncle Tom's Cabin* (pirated, of course, there being then no international copyright agreement with the United States). Routledge's advertisements saucily guaranteed his purchasers, travelling in whichever coaches, "First Class" books. Antimacassars for the common man were evoked. Enriched by his theft of Harriet Beecher Stowe's property Routledge purchased a ten-year lease on twenty of Bulwer Lytton's still-fresh fiction titles for the unprecedented sum of £20,000. It paid off for both parties.

Smith's, with their foothold in stations, were the principal retail supplier of Routledge's library. Wide-awake authors, wanting to "work their copyrights," were keenly conscious of the importance of railway sales. Not least Lytton—thanks to Routledge the most popular "literary" novelist in the country. A constitutionally querulous (noble)man, he wrote to his publisher to complain that he did not find his novels being sold "in any station along the Birmingham line . . . not even [in] the London one Euston Square were there any of my works in the cheap editions—and I heard one passenger ask if they had any—and the reply was no we don't have them."[24]

Smith's moved on to specialize in the sale of so-called yellowbacks,— books twice as expensive as Routledge's one-shilling items, but racier and with garish illustrated board covers.[25]

It was necessary for books to leap out and catch the passing eye. Rail travellers do not browse—they snatch, pay, and run. Since there was a cloak of invisibility for the typical single male passenger, more libertine wares could be offered: even French novels. There were regular rumblings about yellow-back immorality, mild as W. H. Smith's offerings were.[26]

In other ways Smith's served as a dynamic literary generator. One of the sights of the central London terminals was "magazine day" at the end of the week and month when novels in monthly parts (Dickens's, prominently) and literature-carrying magazines were disseminated country-wide from the London stations. Railroads, and the up-to-the-minute communication they afforded, made possible the spectacular success of George Smith's *Cornhill Magazine*, launched in January 1860 with a sale of 120,000 copies at a cover price of a shilling. Edited by Thackeray, the magazine launched Trollope into fame with *Framley Parsonage*, illustrated by Millais. The magazine became, over the successive years, the monthly anthology of what was best in current literature.[27]

Challenging Mudie head-on, Smith's myriad railway outlets offered books ("of the day," prominently) that could be borrowed at a departure station and returned at the destination station.[28]

Conversely, one of the features in which Mudie had had a distinct advantage over Smith's was that his outlets were (like the antique genteel circulating libraries catering for the Misses Morland and Thorpe) woman-friendly. Counter service was as discreetly civil as at a haberdashers, and books could be ordered and delivered by van to female customers.

Public libraries were much less accommodating to female users, and they did not deliver to homes. Unaccompanied women never felt entirely comfortable at railway stations—hence the "ladies only" carriage and similarly protective waiting rooms. Smith's proclaimed motto was "that he who rides may read"—not "she," or even "they."

Massive and constantly renovated as their stocks were (old books being sold off before the bloom was quite off them), Charles Mudie and W. H. Smith, brought up in evangelical backgrounds, were "select" in their favored stock. Selectivity was increasingly felt as something censorious as the century wore on. The need to protect children, susceptible servants, and, above all, womenfolk was the leviathans' paramount justification—and a sales point. It was increasingly felt as a clog on their creativity by authors. George Moore—whose novels were routinely "selected" out (*A Mummer's Wife*, 1885, which led to an outright Mudie ban)—made the point polemically in his pamphlet *Literature at Nurse: Circulating Morals* (1885).

Moore, a Francophile, was, along with the publisher Henry Vizetelly, an admirer of Zola—an author no more likely to be stocked by Mudie than Karl Marx. Vizetelly, an aged, frail bookman, went to prison in 1889 for publishing the French novelist in translation. The punishment shortened Vizetelly's life. Moore, and advanced literary spirits like him, felt the public needed something stronger than mother's milk. Pressure built, leading to the demise of the three-volume novel in 1894, to the end of "Mudie's half century" and a literary culture dominated by borrowing.

A few yards away from Mudie's emporium was the British Museum and, at its heart (like the library in Eco's *abbaye de la source*), the "Reading Room"—the nuclear core of the country's literary culture.[29] The BMRR began as what A.N.L. Munby would call "the library of an eminent person."[30] The most eminent person of all, in fact, the King.

By the midcentury the Reading Room had become a central driver of the "March of Mind" that Rosemary Ashton chronicles in her recent monograph *Victorian Bloomsbury*.[31] Dominance of the square mile's constellation of "progressive institutions" was shared with the BMRR's neighbor, the University of London (after 1836 "UCL"), "the Godless Place in Gower Street." Both were explicitly "open" institutions, founded on the enfranchising impulses of 1832. The ungowned openness of the University of London was not merely to the admission of Jews, nonconformists, atheists, and—after a decade or two—women. The institution was open to new, and newly devised, disciplines. So too was the BMRR open to all (even German fathers of communism) who could show plausible reason to use it.

Open access created bursting strains as did the ever growing book stock, swollen annually by legal deposit that by the 1850s had become a torrent. The BMRR sorely needed more space and better internal order. Antonio Panizzi, the newly appointed keeper of printed books, was the driving force behind the construction of Robert Smirke's Round Reading Room in what had previously been the empty central courtyard of the museum building. It was completed by May 1857. The entrails, on which hundreds of books were shelved, was iron—good Sheffield ware.

The dome itself was in Smirke's favored ancient Greek style. Thackeray gloried in the architectural allusion:

> I have seen all sorts of domes of Peters and Pauls, Sophia, Pantheon—what not?—and have been struck by none of them so much as by that Catholic dome in Bloomsbury, under which our million volumes are housed.
>
> What peace, what love, what truth, what beauty, what happiness for all, what generous kindness for you and me, are here spread out! It seems to me one cannot sit down in that place without a heart full of grateful reverence. I own to have said my grace at the table, and to have thanked Heaven for this, my English birth-right, freely to partake of these bountiful books, and to speak the truth I find there.[32]

Thackeray was a particularly favored reader. Panizzi gave him stack privileges—specifically access to the Burney newspaper collection, essential for the composition of *Henry Esmond* (Thackeray left pen marks on some of the collection's pages—a privilege too far less indulgent librarians than Panizzi might think). An early adopter, the author of *Esmond* was one among many. A whole literary pantheon drew sustenance from Panizzi's remodelled reading room: and still does—in its new St. Pancras location.[33]

Internal order was achieved by the readers' ticket system and, more effectively, by the reformed catalogue—the task for which Panizzi (a professor of Italian at the University of London) had first been recruited in the 1830s. The resolution had been made to produce a new catalogue. Battles were fought over what its form should be. Panizzi was adamant for an author-title system, not one that was subject-based (the so-called inventory concept). He was also fiercely opposed to printed catalogues, wanting something more fluid. Card catalogues were not in universal use until the 1870s, although they would thereafter rationalize library book organization and access until the end of the twentieth century. The BMRR, under Panizzi, went for ledgers (elephant-sized) with pasted entries and room for page inserts. The system lasted, efficiently, until the great move from the British Museum to St. Pancras in the 1990s and the current electronic catalogue—whose digital fluidities Panizzi, one suspects, would have applauded.

The catalogue and request form system made finding the required book, and facilitating its delivery to a user's numbered desk, a smooth operation, accompanied by the soothing thuds of the arriving volumes (a sound I have heard nowhere else).

Post-Panizzi efficiency had, inevitably, its price. It could mean the kind of conveyor belt slavery—one thinks of Henry Ford and the copyists in the medieval scriptorium. The Reading Room, when working at full capacity, could be seen not as a privileged haven—a foretaste of heaven, as Thackeray implies—but a place of soul destroying drudgery, a literary factory. Gissing's *New Grub Street* describes luckless hackette Marian Yule, slaving in the grim trade of higher journalism and low circulation, tied to her futile work like a galley slave to the oar:

> The days darkened. Through November rains and fogs Marian went her usual way to the Museum, and toiled there among the other toilers.
>
> One day at the end of the month she sat with books open before her, but by no effort could fix her attention upon them. It was gloomy, and one could scarcely see to read; a taste of fog grew perceptible in the warm, headachy air. She kept asking herself what was the use and purpose of such a life as she was condemned to lead. When already there was more good literature in the world than any mortal could cope with in his lifetime, here was she exhausting herself in the manufacture of printed stuff which no one even pretended to be more than a commodity for the day's market.[34]

David Lodge, seventy years later, offered a similarly jaundiced view of ticketed servitude in the BMRR in his comic novel, *The British Museum Is Falling Down*. He originally wanted to call it "The British Museum Has Lost Its Charm."[35] For Gissing it most certainly had.

The British Museum inspired a nostalgic offshoot, infused with an obstinate determination by the privileged to retain privilege. The London Library, as it grandly called itself, defiantly maintained the ethos of the book club, a character it is only just now, in the twenty-first century, beginning to shed (to older members' chagrin). The foundation of the library was urged in 1841 by Thomas Carlyle. He was infuriated by the man with the bassoon nose, in the pre-Panizzi British Museum (he is still there, trumpeting away in St. Pancras. I sat next to him just the other day). The brochure put it more politely. The London Library, it said, would be a "great benefit to all followers of literature and science who cannot study with comfort and advantages in a public room."

Carlyle's founding vision was of an institution that would allow paying, and elected, subscribers to enjoy the riches of a national library in their own homes. Thackeray was the London Library's first auditor. Early members included Charles Dickens and George Eliot. An eccentric subject-based cataloguing system was adopted—no Panizzi nonsense. Clubbish disregard for the etiquette of the public library—about such things as defacing books—was tolerated.[36]

The recent remodelling of the London Library has provoked debate about preservation of Edwardian sanitary ware and the provision of red-leather armchairs. The library is located in the heart of St. James clubland and has much of the exclusive club about it. Panizzi was not welcome—the "Italian outsider" was similarly blackballed from the Athenaeum.

Many authors—major, minor, and hopeful—drew literary sustenance from the London Library.[37] The club ethos, traditionally slightly unwelcoming to women (there are still holdout institutions in St. James—as was the Athenaeum until recently), and the fee (a hefty £8 in the late century) meant that women writers of independent spirit were marginally more likely to use the BMRR.

PERSONAL LIBRARIES

Every cluster of books has its fascinations, none more so than the privately assembled collection by a person in whom one has some interest. The most necessarily private collections are of pornography—a criminal practice until the late twentieth century. Two nineteenth-century names are famous for their encyclopedic erotica. One is Richard Monckton

Milnes (1809–85), the first Baron Houghton, a politician most remembered as a persistent suitor of Florence Nightingale. The other is Henry Spencer Ashbee (1834–1900).

Both the connoisseurs' collections eventually found their way, by bequest, to the BMRR, initially in the mysterious "Private Case," now, following 1960s liberation, openly shelved, although still with the usefully historic PC pressmark. Monckton is plausibly supposed to have shared his forbidden treasures, lodged at his Fryston Hall country house (where he too, presumably, had a securely private case), with friends such as Thackeray, Dickens, and Wilkie Collins. Not, presumably, Miss Nightingale. Collins offers an oblique cameo portrait of his friend as the dilettante collector, Mr. Fairlie, in *The Woman in White*. Milnes's sexual preference was the English vice, and he is suspected of being behind the journal *Rodophilia*.[38]

Ashbee was morbidly, and successfully, secretive and, from the bibliographic point of view, the more interesting collector. Born in south London, he was, by profession, a trader in cloths and textiles. His line of work involved travel and encouraged a worldly, not to say underworldly, view of the human condition. Ashbee, as cultivated as he was prurient, collected Cervantes and erotica. He wrote on the latter under the pen-names "Fraxinus" (Latin for "Ash"), "Apis" ("Bee"), and the bawdily punning "Pisanus Fraxi," under which pseudonym he wrote his classic three-volume bibliography of "Prohibited Books." Ashbee left both his Cervantes and pornographic collections to the British Museum with the provision that neither should be destroyed or sold on.

It is plausibly suggested, although no definitive evidence survives, that Ashbee was the author of the monumental work of pornography *My Secret Life*, published between 1888 and 1894 in eleven volumes in Amsterdam. Only twenty-five sets were printed, at a deterrent cost of £60 apiece. The work, clearly as fictional as it is factual (it purports to be an authentic memoir and work of sexology) is, of its peculiar kind, a masterpiece of Victorian literature.

More innocent, but undeniably, by Victorian cultural measurement "low," is the collection of "bloods" and "penny dreadfuls" bequeathed to the British Library by the music-hall performer Barry Ono, who trod the boards in the late century. Few authors trouble to preserve the ephemeral reading matter that they read as children, even when it demonstrably had a formative influence on their later development. In the sales catalogue of Dickens's Gad's Hill library, drawn up by Sotheran's, there is no relic of the primal reading matter that reverberated, traumatically, throughout his writing life.[39] He himself tracked his lifelong fascination with cannibalism ("the unpardonable sin"—monographs have been written on the subject) to gruesome fairy stories, notably *Jack and the Beanstalk* (curdling reference to which surfaces in his last, incomplete novel, *Edwin Drood*). He found added fuel for this, and other sinful things, in *The Terrific Register*, a weekly "penny dreadful" he came across aged twelve. It made him, he said "unspeakably miserable," and frightened "my very wits out of my head." But he eagerly spent his penny a week for the latest issue, "in which there was always a pool of blood, and at least one body." Sometimes more than one, as in the *Register*'s description of the cannibalistic Sawney Bean family (accompanied by a graphic woodcut):

> The Men had their privy members thrown into the fire, their hands and legs were severed from their bodies, and they were permitted to bleed to death. The wretched mother of the whole crew, the daughters and grandchildren, after being spectators of the death of the men, were cast into three separate fires, and consumed to ashes.[40]

Strong stuff for a twelve-year-old.

Dickens, in his triumphal years at Gad's Hill, it is worth noting, regarded his library as something to display—aggressively. Humphry House records that prominent over his shelves was a set of faux volumes: *The Wisdom of Our Ancestors: I. Ignorance; II. Superstition; III. The Block; IV. The Stake; V. The Rack; VI. Dirt; VII. Disease.*[41]

Private collections have flavors as individual as their collectors. For some, they are intimate parts of themselves. Keats, in his poignant last testament, on leaving for Italy where he would die, willed: "My chest of books divide among my friends." It was a quasi-sacramental bequest. The most charming introspection on the erotics and intimacies of bibliophilia I know is that by Jacques Bonnet, *Phantoms on the Bookshelves*. Bonnet is a distinguished French journalist. In his spare time he is a self-confessed bibliomane (well past bibliophilia); he has amassed "several tens of thousands of books." *Phantoms on the Bookshelves* is a loose barrage of musings as he conducts the reader on a voyage round his library. There are chapters on adventures in book hunting, dilemmas of classification, the secret codes of marginalia, innumerable curiosities, and good anecdotes.

Bibliophilia, like other kinds of love, will appear preposterous to those not in thrall to it. "There is," Bonnet recalls, "a lithograph by Daumier" called " 'the Book Lover in heaven,' "

> which perfectly illustrates the fascination rarity holds for the bibliophile. It shows a man thumbing through a little book and explaining to another book-lover, "I can't tell you how happy I am.... I've just found the 1780 Amsterdam edition of Horace for fifty *écus*—it's worth a lot of money because every page is covered with misprints!"[42]

How important are books to those truly in love with them? Rick Gekoski opens his bibliomemoir, *Outside of a Dog* (2011), with the teasing suggestion that if his wife fell out one side of the lifeboat and his books out of the other side, the true bibliophile would be strongly inclined (so long as no one was looking) to rescue the books first.

Harry Elkins Widener, legend has it, was drowned on the *Titanic* because he insisted on rushing back to his state room for his treasured volume of Bacon's *Essays*. "Women, rare books, first-class passengers, and children first!" the young bibliophile might have bawled, had he made it back to the first-class deck. One of the world's great libraries—the Widener at Harvard—commemorates Harry's fatal love.

Trollope tells us in his *Autobiography* that, having recently been obliged on doctor's orders to give up hunting, his one consolation in life was his library:

> I own about five thousand volumes and they are dearer to me even than the horses, which are going, or than the wine in my cellar, which is very apt to go, and upon which I also pride myself.[43]

The Chronicler of Barsetshire gallantly refrains from putting a valuation on Mrs. Trollope. One hopes she would, at least, outrank the horses.

Trollope went to the trouble of printing three catalogues of his volumes, in 1867, 1876, and 1880. Pride of place, in the Waltham Cross library was a collection of his own works, privately printed and bound in leather, which he bequeathed to his son, Henry.[44]

For the Trollopian these catalogues are treasure trove; not merely for what they contain, but for showing odd vacancies on the shelf. As the critics who have examined them most carefully note,

> Trollope apparently did not own the book of Bagehot's *English Constitution* (serialized, however, in the *Fortnightly*), nor E. A. Freeman's *Growth of the English Constitution*. There is hardly a trace in 1874 of the Reform controversy or the public debate of the period on the Trades Unions—no copy, for instance, of *Essays on Reform* (1867), to which Hutton contributed. Even *Culture and Anarchy* is present only in its *Cornhill* serialization.[45]

Of course Trollope knew these works. The Palliser parliamentary sequence is suffused with them. He most probably read them at his club, the Garrick or the Reform.

There is a monograph waiting to be written on the gentleman's club library and British literature. Thackeray's personal library copy of Macaulay's third volume, the historical bedrock of *Henry Esmond*, is, apparently, similarly unmarked.[46] But since sizeable portions of the novel's manuscript pages carry club crests (Garrick and Reform) it is safe to assume that Thackeray used their library copies of the books he needed.[47]

There are, however, very interesting annotations and illustrations to Thackeray's personal volumes. The antiquarian Joseph Grego managed to locate several, after they had been dispersed by auction, and reproduced them in his volume *Thackerayana*.[48] Among the more interesting things turned up by Grego is a cartoon adorning Thackeray's copy of *Rollin's Ancient History* that shows Clio, the muse of history, leaning on a pillar of works of fiction.[49] This supremely ironic sketch, with its implication of generic indivisibility, was done before Thackeray wrote any historical novel (a contradiction in terms, if one thinks about it, as the author of *Henry Esmond* obviously did).

That we can date the Clio sketch as a late-juvenile ebullition confirms that knowing when a writer acquired a book is as important as the fact that it was owned. Sometimes dates of acquisition and usage are clearly deducible. The fact that there are scholarly volumes of Celtic history in Tennyson's library (now in the Tennyson Research Centre in Lincoln) can confidently be seen as reading preparation for his last epic great work, *The Idylls of the King*. Based as he often was on the Isle of Wight, and as reclusive as its other royal resident, it was not convenient for him to go to the BMRR or the London Library.[50]

These Tennyson items were not décor but "tools of the trade," as Jack London brashly called his collection of books.[51] So too was George Eliot's massive ten-thousand-strong book-hoard a toolkit. It is largely dispersed, but an illuminating portion ended up in Dr. Williams's library, in Bloomsbury (a proper home for it). It bears out Eliot's notion of the library as a "quarry," something to be laboriously dug in.[52] Ingenious scholars have traced her source books' transmission, via commonplace books and preparatory notes, into the fabric of her published fiction. Other ingenious scholars have reconstructed authors' libraries from textual and ancillary materials.[53] Grateful as one is for their labors it is a wonderful moment when one sees the spark actually jump from an author's library book, to the literary text. Sharp-eyed editors noted, for example, that entered in the sales catalogue of Dickens's library was a second, January 1860, edition of Darwin's *Origin of Species*. One of the book's chapter titles (the phrase "universal struggle") is echoed in the second paragraph of the novel Dickens was serializing, *Great Expectations*. The link adds a whole new (Darwinian) narrative dimension to the novel.[54]

It is no surprise that Hardy should have had thumbed volumes of Schopenhauer on his shelves. He was of a mind with the German philosopher. What is significant is that he read Schopenhauer on the "Vanity of Existence" just before embarking on the writing of *Tess of the d'Urbervilles*. The most tantalizing item in Hardy's books, now enshrined in Dorchester, is a copy of Einstein's pamphlet on the theory of relativity. How this affected the author's many ruminations on time has inspired much exegesis.[55]

Faustus's forlorn shriek as he's carried off to Hell—"I'll burn my books"—makes clear that they are second only in value to his immortal soul. For most authors, no igniting match is necessary. The auctioneer's hammer will do it. The effect of the public library auction is uniquely pulverizing. Very seldom are libraries, in their entirety, bought by institutions. They are, in bulk, too expensive. Souvenir hunters, ravenous for "association copies," tear the years-long collection to fragments like vultures.

The scholar who has chronicled the postmortem (or post–other disasters) dismantling of eminent persons' libraries most scrupulously is A.N.L. Munby.[56] His multivolume record of sales is like a maritime record of wrecks. Among the most poignant catalogues is the hugger mugger disposal of Oscar Wilde's exquisitely well-chosen library, after his court conviction, in April 1895. It was, Munby says, "one of the worst-conducted dispersals on record."

Eyewitnesses report theft, wanton damage, and the inability of bidders to communicate their offers to the rostrum. R. H. Sherard in his *Life of Wilde* quotes a description of the scene given him by "an Irish publisher:"

> I went upstairs and found several people in an empty room, the floor of which was strewn, thickly strewn, with letters addressed to Oscar mostly in their envelopes and with much of Oscar's easily recognisable manuscript. This looked as though the various pieces of furniture which had been carried downstairs had been emptied of their contents on the floor. . . . After I had been in the room some time a broker's man came up and said: "How did you get into this room?" I said: "The door was open and I walked in." Then the man said: "Then somebody has broken open the lock, because I locked the door myself." It was no doubt from this room that various of Oscar's manuscripts which have never been recovered were stolen.[57]

It's heartbreaking. But stoics will recall that the Alexandrian fate is the ultimate destiny of all libraries, of whatever kind.

NOTES

1. Regular confirmations of the grisly statistic can be found in the trade journal the *Bookseller*.

2. Ronald E. Barker and G. R. Davies, *Books Are Different* (London: Macmillan, 1966).

3. For the early history and growth of the house of Macmillan, see Charles Morgan, *The House of Macmillan* (London: Macmillan, 1943).

4. This was during the writing of *Henry Esmond*, which Smith contracted for with Thackeray. See J. Sutherland, *Victorian Novelists and Publishers* (London: Athlone Press, 1976),101–16, "The Shaping Power of Contract."

5. William St. Clair, *The Reading Nation in the Romantic Period* (Cambridge: Cambridge University Press, 2004), 237.

6. See John Alexander Symington, *Catalogue of the Museum and Library, the Brontë Society* (Shipley: Caxton Press, 1927).

7. For a lament on the missing catalogue, see post by Roberta Wedge on her blog *A Vindication of the Rights of Mary*, January 24, 2012, "Lost daughter: Jane Austen, part five (Gilbert)" at: http://avindicationoftherightsofmary.blogspot .co.uk/2012/01/lost-daughter-jane-austen-part-five.html.

8. For a thoughtful essay on what one can suppose Mr. Bennet's library to contain, and the correspondingly grander library at Pemberley, see H. J. Jackson, "What Was Mr. Bennet Doing in His Library, and What Does It Matter?" in *Romantic Circles: A Refereed Scholarly Website Devoted to the Study of Romantic-Period Literature and Culture*, at http://www.rc.umd.edu/praxis/ libraries/jackson/jackson.html. Sir Anthony's famous outburst against the circulating libraries' ever green trees of diabolical knowledge is in Sheridan's *The Rivals*.

9. Leighton has a worthy place in the *Oxford Dictionary of National Biography*. The resource is not searchable by trade, but I suspect he may be the earliest book designer to have earned an entry.

10. The Sadleir collection was acquired in 1951, through the agency of Bradford Booth, for what seems now the incredibly low price of $65,000. Any one of the prize volumes would collect ten times that today. For an account of Sadleir, and his fascination with nineteenth-century bookbinding (among much else), see J. Sutherland, "Michael Sadleir and His Collection of Nineteenth-Century Fiction," *Nineteenth-Century Literature* 56.2 (September 2001): 145–59.

11. See Simon Eliot, "Unequal Partnerships: Besant, Rice and Chatto, 1876–82," *Publishing History* 26 (1989): 73–109.

12. Benjamin Disraeli, *Coningsby: Or the New Generation*, book 3, chapter 1.

13. I take this account from "The Manchester Free Library," *Spectator*, November 12, 1853, 30–31. Online at http://archive.spectator.co.uk/article/ 12th-november-1853/30/the-manchester-free-library.

14. The relevant material cited here is most conveniently reproduced in "The Manchester Free Library," *Spectator*, November 12, 1853, 30–31. Online at

http://archive.spectator.co.uk/article/12th-november-1853/30/the-manchester-free-library.

15. *Hard Times* (1854), chapter 38.

16. At a preliminary stage Dickens thought of calling his novel "According to Cocker," which had become, over the centuries, a catchphrase.

17. Samuel Smiles, *Self Help* (1859), chapter 11.

18. Leah Price, *How to Do Things with Books in Victorian Britain* (Princeton, NJ: Princeton University Press, 2012).

19. Susan Hill in her delightful bibliomemoir *Howards End Is on the Landing: A Year of Reading from Home* (London: Profile Books, 2010) recalls in her girlhood seeing fumigation stamps in her public library loans. She testifies to the value of the library to her education.

20. The letter, dated April 1860, is stored in the Colchester Public Library archive.

21. Quoted in Colin Robinson, "The Loneliness of the Long-Distance Reader," *New York Times Sunday Review*, January 5, 2014, 6. Online at http://www.nytimes.com/2014/01/05/opinion/sunday/the-loneliness-of-the-long-distance-reader.html?ref=books.

22. The authoritative account of Mudie in the nineteenth century is G. L. Griest, *Mudie's Circulating Library* (Bloomington: Indiana University Press, 1970).

23. The authoritative account of W. H. Smith in the nineteenth century is Charles Wilson, *First with The News: The History of W. H. Smith, 1792–1972* (London: W. H. Smith, 1985).

24. Lytton, May 1849. Sutherland, *Victorian Novelists and Publishers*, 66.

25. A comprehensive display and description of yellowbacks can be found in the digital exhibition *Yellowbacks: An Exhibition of Material From the Monash University Library Rare Books Collection*, November 26, 1991–March 2, 1992. Online at http://monash.edu/library/collections/exhibitions/yellowbacks/xyellowbackscat.html.

26. Smith's were given their initial concession on the understanding that their wares for the traveller would be "pure and instructional." They kept to that mission well into the late twentieth century, earning for themselves from the satirical magazine *Private Eye* (which they declined to stock) the vindictive nickname, "W. H. Smut."

27. For the sensational launch of *Cornhill*, see J. Sutherland, "*Cornhill*'s Sales and Payments: The First Decade," *Victorian Periodicals Review* 19. 3 (Fall 1986): 106–8.

28. For a Smith's catalogue, pasted into one of the firm's popular novels, see, for example, *The Madman of St. James*, translated from the German of Philip Galen by T.H. (London: C. H. Clarke, 1861). Online at http://books.google .co.uk/books?id=G8wNAAAAQAAJ&pg=PA1&redir_esc=y#v=onepage& q&f=false.

29. Umberto Eco's international best seller *The Name of the Rose* was first published as *Il Nome della Rosa* in 1980.

30. See A.N.L. Munby, ed., *Sale Catalogues of Libraries of Eminent Persons*, 12 vols. (London: Mansell, 1971–75).

31. R. D. Ashton, *Victorian Bloomsbury* (London: Yale University Press, 2013).

32. Nil Nisi Bonum, *Cornhill Magazine* February 1860: 129–34.

33. The old BMRR finally burst its seams in the 1990s and, in its enlarged and modernized form, reopened alongside St. Pancras station—an appropriately historical Gilbert Scott structure—in 1998.

34. George Gissing, *New Grub Street* (1891), chapter 7.

35. Lodge's favored title was a quotation from the popular song "A Foggy Day in London Town." The Gershwin estate refused permission to use it.

36. To insert a personal note, I picked up a copy of one of my books the other day, and my eye was caught by the marginal comment: "Sutherland can surely write better than this. Is he a member?"

37. Susan David Bernstein, *Roomscape: Women Writers in the British Museum from George Eliot to Virginia Woolf* (Edinburgh: Edinburgh University Press, 2013), 5.

38. See Holly Furneaux, *Queer Dickens: Erotics, Families, Masculinities* (London: Oxford University Press, 2009), 7.

39. The contents list of Dickens's Gad's Hill Library at the time of his death is given in J. H. Stonehouse, *Catalogue of the Library of Charles Dickens and W. M. Thackeray* (London: Piccadilly Fountain Press, 1935). Dickens's recollection of the effect of the *Terrific Register* on him as a child was confided verbally to his biographer John Forster.

40. This account appeared in the *Terrific Register* in 1823, when Dickens was twelve. The lifelong effect of the publication on him is investigated by Harry Stone in *The Night Side of Dickens: Cannibalism, Passion, Necessity* (Columbus: Ohio State University Press, 1994).

41. Humphry House, *The Dickens World* (London: Oxford University Press, 1941), 35.

42. Jacques Bonnet, *Phantoms on the Bookshelves* (London: Quercus Books, 2013), 5.

43. Trollope, *An Autobiography* (1883), chapter 20.

44. The set eventually found its way to the magnificent Robert H. Taylor collection of Trollopiana at Princeton.

45. Richard H. Grossman and Andrew Wright, "Anthony Trollope's Libraries," *Nineteenth-Century Fiction* 31.1 (June 1976): 48–64.

46. Sotheran's auction catalogue. The catalogue contains a large number of history volumes chosen, one supposes, to display in the author's new house at Palace Green, designed in Queen Anne style, to his specifications, which he moved into shortly before his death. It is now the Israeli embassy in London.

47. See Edgar Harden, "The Writing and Publication of *Esmond*," *Studies in the Novel* 13 (1981): 79–92.

48. Joseph Grego, *Thackerayana* (London: Chatto and Windus, 1875). The book was withdrawn (even from access at the British Museum) a few months after publication on account of its copyright infringements.

49. The illustration may be conveniently found in Grego, *Thackerayana*, 29. Online via Project Gutenberg at http://www.gutenberg.org/files/44563/44563-h/44563-h.htm.

50. See P. G. Scott, "Tennyson's Celtic Reading," *Tennyson Research Bulletin* 1.2 (1968): 4–8.

51. The Jack London library is housed in its entirety at the Huntington Library and is the subject of a catalogue raisonné by David M. Hamilton, *The Tools of My Trade: The Annotated Books in Jack London's Library* (Seattle: University of Washington Press, 1986).

52. See William Baker, *The George Eliot–George Henry Lewes Library: An Annotated Catalogue of Their Books at Dr. Williams's Library, London* (New York: Garland, 1977).

53. See William Baker, *Wilkie Collins's Library: Reconstruction* (Westport, CT: Greenwood Press, 2002); Patrick Scott, "Book Ownership and Authorial Identity: Reconstructing the (Im)Personal Library of Arthur Hugh Clough," available on the *Selected Works of Patrick Scott* website, online at http://works.bepress.com/patrick_scott/230/. Scott's article has the fullest bibliography of work in this Victorian area of research.

54. See Goldie Morgentaler, "Meditating on the Low: A Darwinian Reading of *Great Expectations*," *Studies in English Literature, 1500–1900* 38.4 (Autumn 1998): 707–21.

55. See *Thomas Hardy in Context*, ed. Phillip Mallett (Cambridge: Cambridge University Press, 2013), 247–50.

56. See A.N.L. Munby, "The Libraries of English Men of Letters," *Essays and Papers*, ed. Nicolas Barker (Ukley: Scolar Press, 1977). A.N.L. Munby, ed., *Sale*

Catalogues of Libraries of Eminent Persons, 12 vols. (London: Mansell, 1971–75).

57. A.N.L. Munby, ed., *Sales Catalogues of Libraries of Eminent Persons*, vol. 1, *Poets and Men of Letters*, 371–72. The largest surviving collection of Wilde's literary and library remains is held by UCLA's William Andrews Clark Memorial Library.

PART 2

THE LIBRARY IN IMAGINATION

CHAPTER 7

✾

The Library in Fiction

Marina Warner

THE STORY IN THE STONE

The opening paragraph of the earliest work of literature yet known to us evokes the act of its own making: how "the whole story" it tells was engraved on a stone.[1] The narrator declares:

> I will proclaim to the world the deeds of Gilgamesh. This was the man to whom all things were known; this was the king who knew the countries of the world. He was wise; he saw mysteries and knew secret things, he brought us a tale of the days before the flood. He went on a long journey, was weary, worn-out with labour, returning he rested, he engraved on a stone the whole story.[2]

This is from the translation of N. K. Sandars, published by Penguin in 1960, which I read when an undergraduate at Oxford and which became a cult book of my student days. The poem that follows has since been reedited for rendering in English and many other languages, and Sandars's work has been superseded as more fragments have been found and reinterpreted. The epic that is still emerging from these accretions tells the story of the semidivine Gilgamesh, King of Uruk, through his heroic and hubristic adventures until his tragic initiation into the knowledge of mortality. Engraving the story on a stone, this earliest of heroes attempts to stay the moment when he will be forgotten; the stone will become part of the fabric of the city he is building as part of his claim on eternity, a stone that is a book, for his great city will include a library.

The tablets on which the *Epic of Gilgamesh* is written lay in the Assyrian library of Ashurbanipal for millennia. They were unearthed, millions of scattered, battered, and chipped clay pages, between 1850 and 1853, during the excavations of Nineveh (today, near Mosul). Austen Henry Layard was the remarkable archaeologist who supervised the revelations; over subsequent decades, thousands more tablets were found in the ruins of Babylon and Uruk and other lost cities of Anatolia, Armenia, and Khuzestan, formerly Elam. The majority of these findings were deposited in tray loads in the British Museum as part of its collections of objects; the tablets have remained there, after the numerous scholarly works they gave birth to, including the many translations and versions of the poem, were placed in the British Library, which was only formally divided from the museum in 1973, thus instituting a new distinction between stones and books. Pieces of Babylonian, Sumerian, and Akkadian poetry, alongside hoards of legal documents, accountants' audits, tallies of sheep and goats, and other databases of antiquity, continued to be dug up from the desert cities of the ancient civilizations in the region of present day Iraq. Over the last two decades and the two Gulf wars, tons of bombs have fallen on the region. It is one of the several irreversible and melancholy consequences of the conflicts there and the air power brought to bear, that what might have remained buried under the sand will now have been smashed to smithereens.

Although the term "fiction" has come to denote novels and short stories only, I am stretching it here to include works of imagination that tell tales, including narrative poems such as the *Epic of Gilgamesh*, because fiction, with its root in *fingo*, meaning "I fashion," implies invented, made-up things, and the transition between the voice and the page, the storyteller and the writer, involves many degrees of translation between languages and genres. Classical epics, such as the *Odyssey* and the *Iliad*, now exist in multiple transmutations, which often carry the stories they tell as the Diabelli variations remember their source. My last example of the interconnectedness of the library with fiction in the present day will be *Memorial*, a poem of haunting by Alice Oswald, in which the writer retells the *Iliad*.[3] As you read, her work of deconstruction and reconstruction turns the book in your hands into a monument to the fallen, a cenotaph echoing to the sounds of the ghosts it commemorates.

The *Epic of Gilgamesh* holds a pivotal position in the history of libraries and works of the fictive imagination. Most distant from us in time, the poem draws very close to us again through its concerns—with love, sex, friendship, the responsibility of rulers, the relation to nature and growing things, and above all, the knowledge it unfolds about the grief of loss, the costs of violence, and the inevitability of death. But the work also calls attention to itself as a written artifact, set down in stone, as described in that first paragraph. This self-reflexiveness reveals a crucial quality in the character of the fictive: it has always aspired, since these beginnings of literature, to monumentality. It has designs on eternity and, in order to achieve them, must turn itself from the verbal into the graphic, from the narrated story told once upon a time by someone who has since died into an object deposited for those who come after to find and read. The gesture-defying time described in the poem's opening lines was successful: the poem has survived, and Gilgamesh's name and his deeds have not been forgotten. But the story of the epic's preservation could be told another way round, for the poet is actively providing, with hindsight, a plausible origin for the poem's survival: the permanence of the medium, its preservation as an element in a building. The text survives in tablets, which were inscribed much later than the events they recount, even though the poet pretends that he was there; the later scribes/ compilers seem aware of this, when they dramatize how the epic came to be set down in writing. The story in the stone gives precious eyewitness authority to the poem and merges its historical truth with its state as an object: something that will last, an item that can be kept safe in a library. The library becomes an archive, enshrining those fugitive, mobile, airy webs of words that make up stories, and its existence—its survival— provides the necessary warranty for the work's value and its imperishability. Without the library to preserve its creations, the imagination is mortal, like its protagonists.

The implied library also extends a claim on truth. When the narrator of the *Epic of Gilgamesh* states that the poem will give an account of the king's deeds, and that Gilgamesh himself set them down for posterity in retrospect, he (the narrator is characterized as a he, the mouthpiece of the king himself) is bringing about what is now called a reality effect— the writing of the story by its principal actor persuades us of the truth

of what we are about to read. We know the name of one of the many re-
dactors who must have worked to create the poem, for he names himself
on a surviving tablet, Sin-leqi-unninni, a scholar-priest, an exorcist and
diviner, and he announces his presence working in the role of recorder,
placing himself in the position of someone working from the primary
source, the stone that Gilgamesh inscribed. He was writing sometime in
the thirteenth to eleventh centuries B.C., and he was less an originator of
what follows than a collator or editor, braiding and splicing myths and
legends for the poem. This way of making is important with regard to
the library in fiction, viewed not only as a particular place where single
titles or book-objects have been collected, but as a metaphor for literature itself, a polyphony of voices, laid down on multiple tracks, looping
and converging over time, sometimes over great vistas of time. What we
know as the *Epic of Gilgamesh* does not have a fixed form; the numerous, very different translators work from different textual arrangements.
Andrew George, in the 1999 Penguin Classics edition, has far more archaeological primary material than N. K. Sandars had for her version
of 1960, and in his introduction to his Penguin edition of Gilgamesh,
he writes, "Seventy years ago we possessed fewer than forty manuscripts
from which to reconstruct the text and there were large gaps in the story.
Now we have more than twice that number of manuscripts and fewer
gaps. Slowly our knowledge of the text will become better and better, so
that one day the epic will again be complete, as it last was more than two
thousand years ago."[4] This last may be a hope against hope that we can
only pray will be granted.

In Andrew George's opening section, the stone on which Gilgamesh
writes his story acquires a specific, sensuous character, and significant
continuity is established between the city Gilgamesh has built and what
it contains in the form of stores containing treasures, such as the book we
are reading, the one in which the story of his epic life has been set down:

> He saw what was secret, discovered what was hidden,
>   He brought back a tale of before the Deluge.
>
> He came a far road, was weary, found peace,
>   And set all his labours on a tablet of stone.

He built the rampart of Uruk-the-Sheepfold,
   Of holy Eanna, the sacred storehouse.

. . . .

Climb Uruk's wall and walk back and forth!
   Survey its foundations, examine the brickwork!
Were its bricks not fired in an oven?
   Did the seven Sages not lay its foundations?

. . . .

[See] the tablet-box of cedar,
   [release] its clasp of bronze!
[Lift] the lid of its secret,
   [pick up] the tablet of lapis lazuli and read out

The travails of Gilgamesh, all that he went through.[5]

The book as artifact, playing a part in its own plot as a thing charged with power, leaps out of these lines: the secret that Gilgamesh learned through his ordeals becomes the secret that we are promised to unlock by reading the book in our hands.

The efflorescence of the epic includes many languages and many versions by many poets. Recently, English poets who have revisited it include Stephen Mitchell[6] and Philip Terry, both of whom treat the tablets like elements of code to be cracked open for contemporary eyes and ears. Terry's version does not try to mend the fragments into a legible whole but remembers the poem's shattered state; this poet responds to the roots of written language in accounts and law and has also adopted, as its corresponding present-day vernacular, the austere minimalism of Globish, or business speak. This draws harsh music from the clay as it invokes the place of safekeeping—the casket:

Find the | metal | box full | of cut | stone + + +
slide op | en the | steel lock

open | the mouth | that hold | the + + + | secret
Take out | the blue | stone and | read it | out loud

How DIC | TATOR | suffer | every | hard ship [7]

As the nursery rhyme goes, "How many miles to Babylon? Here is a candle to light you there." How many miles from the tablet of lapis lazuli to the tablet of the I-pad or the Kindle? And are they both the candle that lights up the dark?

The epic has not come down to us on lapis lazuli but on clay, impressed with a reed pen—hence cuneiform, a form of writing invented c. 3000 B.C. in the cities of Mesopotamia, in the valleys of the Tigris and Euphrates; the poem has been pieced together from surviving passages in Akkadian, the language of the "Standard Version," and Sumerian, which has no connections to any other known language and was gradually superseded by Akkadian. One of the "tablet houses" built to enshrine works of literature was part of the legacy of King Shulgi (2094–2047 B.C.), who seems to have patterned himself on the hero of the epic in some ways, but surpassed him in his sophisticated cultural ambitions.

Soon after leaving university and reading the *Epic*, I wrote a libretto for a rock opera, called *Babylon*, with music by a composer who was a friend. It was a hugely enjoyable endeavor, and we made a tape with professional singers and bands. The first big number was a hymn to the goddess Ishtar, Aida-like in its vastness, with a chorus that sang out her praises: "'What is her power?'" some asked. "'It is desire, it is desire!'" others replied.[8] "Desire" was then, unexpectedly, a rather daring word. The script never reached production, but the composer and my sister fell in love during the process of our collaboration, and so the goddess showed her power, in at least one important and long lasting way, since my sister has been married to the musician in question for over thirty years.

At that time, we were early readers of the *Epic*, as it had lain unread for eons. In several significant ways, Gilgamesh belongs to modernity because it resurfaced so belatedly, rescued in the nineteenth century by archaeologists, and then, in the course of the twentieth, reassembled like the dismembered corpse of Osiris from the breaking and dispersal of its parts. One of the most remarkable figures in the story of its res-

Plate 1. An *armarium* (book cupboard): detail from the mosaic in the so-called Mausoleum of Galla Placidia, Ravenna. Photograph by R. Gameson.

Plate 2. Scribe (Ezra) and *armarium* from Codex Amiatinus. Firenze, Biblioteca Medicea Laurenziana, MS Amiatino 1, fol. Vr. Su concessione del MiBACT. E'vietata ogni ulteriore riproduzione con qualsiasi mezzo.

Plate 3. *Bibliotheca* in Hrabanus Maurus's *De rerum naturis*. Montecassino, Archivio dell'Abbazia, MS132, p. 96, and reproduced with kind permission.

Plate 4. *Bibliotheca* in Hrabanus Maurus's *De rerum naturis*. Vatican City, Biblioteca Apostolica Vaticana, Pal. Lat. 291, fol. 43r. (c) 2014 Biblioteca Apostolica Vaticana. Reproduced by kind permission of Biblioteca Apostolica Vaticana, with all rights reserved.

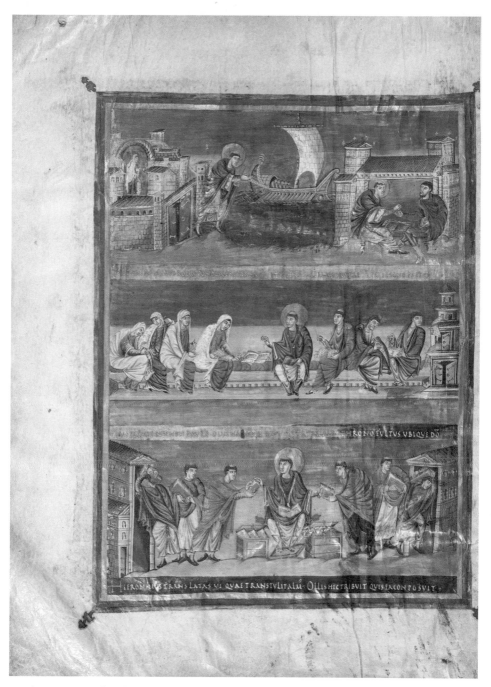

Plate 5. Jerome distributing his Vulgate from the Vivian or First Bible of Charles the Bald. Paris, Bibliothèque nationale de France, lat. 1, fol. 3v. Reproduced with kind permission of the Bibliothèque nationale de France.

Plate 6. Frontispiece of the *Vita Ansberti* in the *Chronique majeure* of Saint-Wandrille. Le Havre, Bibliothèque municipale, ms 332 (A34), fol. 41 v. Reproduced with kind permission of the Bibliothèque municipale, Le Havre.

Plate 7. Frontispiece to a lectionary. Cologne, Diözesan-und Dombibliothek, 59, fol. 1r. Reproduced with kind permission of the Diözesan-und Dombibliothek, Cologne.

· Corncinus ·

E le batailles maintenir.   P oz ses paz son denunamet.
c om les nes furet establies.   E r an panser r an torment.
Z a grans istorie eles nauies.   E ce uoz reduirai apres.

Plate 8. Benoît of Sainte-Maure, *Roman de Troie*. Paris, Bibliothèque nationale de France, Fr. 782, fol. 2v. Reproduced with kind permission of the Bibliothèque nationale de France.

Plate 9. King Charles V of France. Prefatory miniature to French translation of John of Salisbury's *Policraticus*. Paris, Bibliothèque nationale de France, Fr. 24287, fol. 2r. Reproduced with kind permission of the Bibliothèque nationale de France.

Plate 10. Petrarch: prefatory miniature to a copy of his *De viris illustribus*. Darmstadt, Universitäts-und Landesbibliothek, MS101, fol. 1v. Reproduced with kind permission of the Universitäts-und Landesbibliothek, Darmstadt.

Plate 11. Statutes of Ave Maria College, Paris. Paris, Archives nationales, MM406, fol. 10v. Photograph: Atelier photographique des Archives nationales; reproduced with kind permission.

Plate 12. Statutes of Collegium Sapientiae. Freiburg-im-Breisgau, University Archives, MS a, fol. 44r. Reproduced with kind permission of Freiburg-im-Breisgau University Archives.

Plate 13. Statutes of Collegium Sapientiae. Freiburg-im-Breisgau, University Archives, MS a, fol. 44v. Reproduced with kind permission of Freiburg-im-Breisgau University Archives.

Plate 14. *Thomas Aquinas in Prayer*. Predella panel from Sassetta's altarpiece for the Arte della Lana, Siena. Photograph by R. Gameson.

Plate 15. Jacques le Grand, *Le Livre de bonnes meurs*. Chantilly, Musée Condé, MS297, fol. 71v. Reproduced with kind permission of the Agence Photographique de la Réunion des musées nationaux.

Plate 16. Boethius (trans. Jean de Meung), *De consolatione philosophiae*, prefatory miniature. London, British Library, Harley 4335, fol. 1r. ©The British Library Board, and reproduced with kind permission.

Plate 17. English translation of Guillaume de Digulleville's *Pilgrimage of the Life of Man*. London, British Library, Cotton Tiberius A. vii, fol. 91v. ©The British Library Board, and reproduced with kind permission.

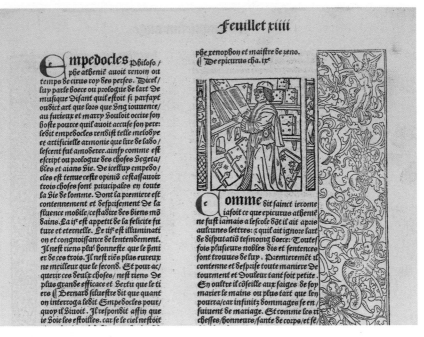

Plate 18. *La Mer des Histoires*. Manchester, John Rylands Library Incunable Collection (19932, vol. 2). © The University of Manchester (image number 1216121) and reproduced with kind permission.

Plate 19. *Roman de Jean d'Avesnes*. Paris, Bibliothèque de l'Arsénal, MS5208, fol. 1r. Reproduced with kind permission of the Bibliothèque nationale de France.

Plate 20. *St. Jerome in His Study*, by Jan van Eyck (circle of). Detroit Institute of Arts, Inv. 25.4. Reproduced with kind permission of Detroit Institute of Arts/Bridgeman Images.

Plate 21. Vincent of Beauvais, *Miroir historiale*. London, British Library, Royal 14E. I, vol. 1, fol. 3r. ©The British Library Board, and reproduced with kind permission.

Plate 22. Fresco in Ospedale di Santo Spirito, Rome. Photograph by R. Gameson. (below)

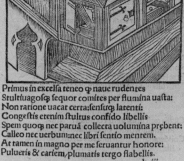

Plate 23. *The Book Fool* from the 1498 Paris edition of the Latin translation by Jacobus Locher Philomusus of Sebastian Brant, *Das Narrenschiff* (Paris: Georg Wolf for Geoffrey Marnet). Manchester, John Rylands Library Incunable Collection (17644). ©The University of Manchester (image number JRL1216124) and reproduced with kind permission.

Plate 24. *The Book Fool* from the 1497 Basel edition of Sebastian Brant, *Das Narrenschiff* in Latin translation by Jacobus Locher Philomusus (Basel: Johan Bergman de Olpe). Manchester, John Rylands Library Incunable Collection (17676). © The University of Manchester (image number JRL1216122) and reproduced with kind permission.

Plate 25. The Flood Tablet, part of *The Epic of Gilgamesh*. From the Library of Ashurbanipal, Nineveh, northern Iraq, Neo-Assyrian, seventh century B.C. © The Trustees of the British Museum, and reproduced with kind permission.

Plate 26. William Henry Fox Talbot, *A Scene in a Library*. In *The Pencil of Nature* (London: Longman, Brown, Green and Longman's, 1844), Plate VIII. University of St. Andrews Library, Photo TR144.T2. Image courtesy of the University of St. Andrews Library.

urrection was George Smith, who was working as an engraver for Waddington's, the producers of playing cards; in Victorian times, they also printed banknotes. George Smith was one of their engravers, skilled at the technical intricacy required to create irreproducible, forgery-proof money; he was also a devout Christian. The British Museum was round the corner from the workshop, and Smith used to pass his lunch break in the Assyrian rooms. The keeper noticed this regular visitor and observed how intently the young artisan scrutinized the shards and clay tablets from Layard's dig at Nineveh. One day he asked him what his interest was. George Smith replied that he was reading them. He was soon seconded to the museum, and put to work in the basement, where trays upon trays of broken clay tablets were laid out like a vast jigsaw that some clumsy giants had casually thrown up in the air and let fall down again through the firmament. But George Smith set to work, impelled by his pious desire to find evidence of the historical truth of the Bible from records made before the Bible was written. He began identifying and ordering the tablets on which the *Epic of Gilgamesh* was inscribed, and then, one day, he came upon a precious piece of evidence for what he was looking for: the tablet that tells the story of the meeting between Gilgamesh and Uta-napishtim, the sole survivor of the Flood. Here was an account of the deluge, as described in the Bible, set down from a separate, prior authority on what has come to be known as the Flood Tablet (see plate 25). The recognition of this piece of the puzzle, which provided Smith with incontrovertible corroboration of scripture as history, filled him with such rapture that he began to tear off his clothes, crying out for joy. He was restrained, and a few months later, on December 3, 1872, he appeared before the Society for Biblical Archaeology, and in all sobriety, presented his discovery to the learned members.

George Smith in 1872 was truly the first person to read Gilgamesh after an unimaginably, mythically, long span of time: the archive of stone, evoked in the poem's opening lines, had kept its story safe—partly safe—until someone with his exceptional gifts at decryption came along. But the poem still did not reach beyond its stone muteness for other readers, not until a team of scholars, under the leadership of Samuel Noah Kramer, working at the University Museum, Philadelphia, after World War II, began to decipher, reassemble, and translate it.

In other ways, in other forms, and in other libraries, both in the physical buildings that exist and in the imaginary granaries of fiction, *Gilgamesh* underwent marvellous metamorphoses and survived. Its own story of transformations and transmission demonstrates the principle that the doyen of translators, Michael Henry Heim, defined: "Literary translation is a primary, necessary form of literary scholarship."[9] The wrath of Achilles, with which Homer begins the *Iliad*, shadows the furious rampage of Gilgamesh the king at the start of his story, where the citizens of Uruk complain to the gods about the excesses of their ruler. The friendship of Achilles with Patroclus resonates powerfully with the passion of Gilgamesh for Enkidu, the wild man whom the gods create in answer to the people's laments in order to contain and tame Gilgamesh. Gilgamesh's devastated grief at Enkidu's death again seems half-remembered by Homer in his epic of loss. When Odysseus meets Calypso, the episode echoes Gilgamesh's meeting with al-Siduri, the wine maiden who helps him across the threshold into the world beyond. And one could continue, although some of the rest of the Babylonian poem also contains the core material of a mythical hero's quest: including the struggle against a monster and a *katabasis* or descent into the Underworld.

However, the work where Gilgamesh continued to be told, mutated, and differently stressed, was in the *Tales of the 1001 Nights*.

THE STORIES OF THE NIGHT

The tale of the hero Buluqiya is told over several nights in a cycle of stories carried on the voice of the queen of the serpents, who gives her name to the tales she tells, themselves nested inside Shahrazad's enchained sequence.[10] Analysing correspondences in the plotting of initiatory romance quests alongside onomastic and phonetic resonances, the scholar Stephanie Dalley argues that "certain close similarity in points of detail can . . . be used to show that the story of Buluqiya is a descendant of the *Epic of Gilgamesh*."[11] She also points out that the close resemblances have not been noticed before because Orientalists and Arabists were not looking at *Gilgamesh*, and neither were Babylonian scholars looking at the *Nights*; fairy tales did not count in academic study, and the *Nights* were not appreciated until recently by literary scholars in their countries of origin. Besides, Buluqiya's cluster of stories anyway falls outside the accepted core of the *Nights* and has been reprinted only in the complete editions of the longest version of the *Nights*, which are not read by many.

The story belongs in the dizzying *mise-en-abyme*, stories within stories that Yamlika, queen of the serpents, tells the protagonist Hasib; it is one of the elaborate sets of Chinese boxes of stories in the book and contains recognizable Biblical, Sanskrit, Persian, and Babylonian elements. Significantly, it opens with an allusion to another compendium, a book of wisdom that prompts Buluqiya's own quest for more knowledge, and sets him off on his travels through different realms; on this journey, he encounters a series of mythological figures—guardians of the threshold, temptresses, helpers, teachers of wisdom, and dangerous monsters. The different worlds described in the story—natural, supernatural, human, and social—retain metaphysical resonances of the lost paradise, lost natural harmony, lost organic enchantments, and lost immortality, as the *Epic of Gilgamesh* dramatizes so powerfully. Buluqiya thirsts for greater understanding, and his story reveals his bitter recognition of human limits.

Further difficulties over recognizing the affinities between Gilgamesh and Buluqiya arise for historical reasons, writes Dalley. "There has long been a certain traditional resistance among many western Europeans to any close links between Semitic and Indo-European material, a prejudice that dates at least from the Renaissance. In addition, cuneiform Akkadian literature has generally been studied by people trained in the Classics and the Old Testament, with the result that Islamic links in particular are scarcely recognized."[12]

The book of the *Nights*, like the *Epic of Gilgamesh*, also acknowledges its dependence on the deposit of stories that precede it. Shahrazad's library, we are told at the very start of the cycle of her stories in the book, is the source of her repertoire. She does not make up the stories. Instead, we discover that she is clever and learned and has "read the books of literature, philosophy, and medicine. She knew poetry by heart, had studied historical reports, and was acquainted with the sayings of men and the maxims of sages and kings. She was intelligent, knowledgeable, wise, and refined."[13] She has a library of a thousand books, and knows all the stories she tells from having read them. As in a mirror in infinite recession, the book imagines its own antecedents, its prior existence in other libraries.

As the thousand and one nights of storytelling elapse, every now and then the Sultan Shahriah (Shahrazad's principal audience), or the legendary ruler of Baghdad, Caliph Haroun el-Rashid, or another fortunate recipient of the tales, remarks that the story he has just heard must be recorded and kept forever. Indeed at different points in the book, we are shown the circumstances in which the tales are recorded: for example, Haroun el-Rashid, after hearing the brilliant cluster of tales told by the five ladies in the house of Zobeide, orders them to be written down and placed in his archives.[14] Haroun's orders are then echoed at the close of the book by Sultan Shahriyar, when he joyfully reprieves Shahrazad and tells the scribes to write down all her stories. According to some versions, Shahrazad's library is then brought from her father the vizier's house to the palace. So the stories have already been collected—the tales of the Arabian Nights that we have been hearing are already in existence. As the Moroccan scholar and fabulist Abdelfattah Kilito points out, this command adds to the dizzy circularity of the *Nights*: this copy will be a copy of something that already exists in the library that Shahrazad collected as a young, unmarried woman. Except for the story of herself and Shahriyar himself—that is the only one she has not told.[15]

The prior existence of this vast body of stories adds to the oneiric quality of the whole: not exactly a collective unconscious, her library seems to stretch in infinite recession, an archive of all the stories. The thousand and one in the book's title hints at infinity, and indeed the stories keep multiplying, podding off into different new stories, as well as into multiple versions and translations. The utopian fantasy of the book includes the possibility that someone could act as the keeper of memories on this vast and labyrinthine scale, that someone like Shahrazad could fulfill the role described by the poet Derek Walcott: "Every collection of human beings gathered for a long time in one place codifies itself, arranges rules of conduct, and makes a calendar for its celebrations of harvest, of the shapes of the moon, with tribal melodies, and preserves its fables and its history in the archives of the shaman and the *griot* and the bard's memory."[16]

This is a hope of survival, too, a wager against history, a stand against entropy and a sighting of a small light in the general darkness. In Italo Calvino's *Invisible Cities*, in which the Italian writer revisits the form and themes of the *Nights*, Marco Polo says to the Great Khan, "This is the aim of my explorations: examining the traces of happiness still to be glimpsed, I gauge its short supply. If you want to know how much darkness there is around you, you must sharpen your eyes, peering at the faint lights in the distance."[17] His Marco Polo is an alter ego, a male writer and teller of tales standing in for Shahrazad, who also tells her stories to the Sultan to pick out faint lights and dispel the thickest part of the darkness around him.

The process whereby a story, such as the adventures of Gilgamesh, moves from the song, the recitation, the performance, and the scene of storytelling into the precious manuscript and the sanctum of the library has been fascinatingly explored by the classical scholar Florence Dupont in her study *The Invention of Literature* (1999). She proposes a different model from the straightforward contrast between the written and the oral, demonstrating that some of the greatest works of human imagination were created as texts, as written literature, but texts to be performed, to be heard. Voicing was an art of living creators, who took a piece of writing and worked with it as singers or players work with a score, or, perhaps, even more closely, as jazz soloists take up a tune and improvise on it. The voice of the storyteller was many and the stories created were all different and the same at one and the same time. Immutable inscription—writing—was used for tallies, the law, and other reckonings intended to be solid and permanent. But narration belonged to the different order of time—flowing time, mutability, chromatic harmony. Every listener became—and becomes—a potential new storyteller. Early literature, she declares, was composed of play scripts and prompt books, storytellers' scrolls, pattern books. She writes, in her commentary on *The Golden Ass*, "The book that moderns have mistakenly called a novel seems in truth to have constituted an intermediary between two kinds of orality."[18]

Literature was a speech act performed by living voices present to their audiences, as in many art events today (this might go some way to explaining the ever-growing popularity of literary festivals). Writing, according to Dupont's reading, represented an attempt to capture those voices—the book was a kind of early phonograph, which would preserve the dead and bring them back, living and audible, into time present. When books established canonical, fixed texts, they turned into death masks, entombing the once living beings that made the sounds of the words. In the absence of those bodies, Dupont writes, literature, when enclosed in a book, was fated to draw attention endlessly to that absence.

In this sense Shahrazad is speaking against death in another way besides her stratagem of endless delay: the appeal of the stories she tells arises from their availability for retelling—the vitality of their lack of definitive form.

The stories are currency, flowing in circulation across cultures and time zones. Only twenty-two manuscripts containing stories from the *Nights* have survived. But the numbers of translations and editions and recensions would not be possible to count. One manuscript collection, now in the Arcadian Library, London, gives a powerful sense of the way the stories lived in the world where they were made: thirty octavo notebooks, written in a variety of hands in the seventeenth century, with a sprinkling of red-letter headings, their boards softened by handling, their pages tattered and torn, in some places patched and edged to stop them falling to pieces—these copies have been read to bits.[19] As with paper money after long use, a fusty, creaturely smell of human hands and breath rises from these working copies. They have every look of a professional storyteller's precious resource. On the inside cover at the back of several of the volumes, sums and a kind of tally appear to have been kept: the numbers of listeners? Receipts?

The manuscripts belong to written literature, but their making precedes print and multiple copies and silent reading, and their form as well as their transmission took shape in relation to audiences, not silent readers. As the wider history of fairy tales reveals, the passage from oral to written and back again is much more complex than a simple division of literature from orature allows.

The Wisdom of the Books

At certain points in the cycle of the *1001 Nights*, someone who, inside the stories, promises to tell a marvelous tale, will open by declaring, "Mine is a tale that, if it were written in lessons at the corner of the eye, would be a needle for those who would be pricked." Sometimes, the listener will echo this strange, disturbing image and exclaim, after hearing a story told, "If you inscribed [this tale] with a needle in the corner of the eye, it would give matter for reflection to those who can understand its lesson."[20] The extended metaphor raises shivers as it searches out an area of ultimate sensitivity, but it also works with the symbolism of the eye, as the organ of discernment, and a vehicle of power. The story earns its place among sacred, apotropaic texts and the ranks of amulets and talismans: like an Egyptian *wadjet* eye or the eye of Fatima inscribed with sacred formulae, it can protect against the evil eye.

Within the stories-inside-stories, several tales dramatize other protagonists saved by storytelling. These "ransom tales" include the tales told within the two opening cycles of "The Merchant and the Genie" and "The Fisherman and the Genie," and many others later in which the narrators subdue their enemies by fascination, like legendary snake charmers. One of the most splendid parables about justice in Shahrazad's repertoire is a story of a book that becomes a weapon, "The Tale of the Greek King and the Doctor Douban."[21] It has a long and reverberating history in literature, with Umberto Eco's best seller *The Name of the Rose* one of its direct progeny.

The story is told by the fisherman who has found in his net a barnacled copper flask, which, when he opens it, exudes fearsome black smoke that gradually gathers into the form of a furious jinni, Sakhr, who threatens to kill him in revenge for the thousands of years he has spent at the bottom of the sea imprisoned in the copper bottle. But the fisherman manages to trick the furious—and highly gullible—jinni back into the copper bottle and is walking back to the water's edge to throw him back into the sea when from within, the prisoner pleads for his life. The fisherman sternly refuses, while the jinni keeps crying out to promise him every blessing. "You are lying," says the fisherman, "Your promises are empty. You and I are like the vizier of King Yunan and Douban, the doctor." "Tell me how we're like them," says the jinni, and so sparks the next story within a story in the cycle.[22]

In Byzantium, a king who has everything in the world—great riches, loyal followers, and vast armies at his command—falls ill with a disease —a kind of leprosy—for which none of his physicians or doctors can find a cure. A travelling sage called Douban happens to be passing through the king's territory; he's very old and very learned in Greek, Arabic, Persian, and Syriac philosophy, medicine, and astronomy and knows the properties of herbs and other things—he has a travelling library with him. When he hears of the king's sickness, he consults his books, arrays himself in his finest clothes, and calls in all submissiveness on the court. When the king receives him, Douban offers to heal him, and in return Yunan, overjoyed, presents him with a ceremonial robe and promises to shower blessings on him and on his entire descendance. The doctor begins his work, renting a house, studying his books; after consulting further, he prepares a mixture, fashions a ball, and, into the shaft of a mallet that he has hollowed out, introduces the mixture; the next day he presents the ball and mallet to the king and tells him to go out to the polo field and ride as hard as he can, holding the mallet tight and swinging it vigorously until he's worked up a lather all over; the salve in the stick will transpire through his whole body. Then he's to return to the palace, and after bathing, he will be cured.

King Yunan does as the doctor tells him. The following morning, when Douban presents himself at the palace, the king receives him royally because, as soon as he left the baths, he found all traces of his leprosy had vanished from his body. His skin has become "as smooth as pure silver." The passing old man is a foreigner, a stranger, and his magic is a form of practical intelligence, rooted in scientific learning. In his joy and gratitude, King Yunan makes a fuss of Douban, sitting him by his side on his ceremonial divan, arraying him in splendid silks, feasting with him, showering him with money and other presents, and giving him his own thoroughbred to ride home.

The same happens the next day: more is lavished on the doctor who has cured the king.

One of the king's viziers looks darkly on these developments. He is particularly ugly, the fisherman says, with a character to match, evil-tongued, jealous, and mendacious. He approaches the king and warns him that he is in danger from someone close to him. "Speak!" says the king. When the vizier names Douban, the king rejects the insinuation angrily and reminds his advisor of the example of King Sindibad, who destroyed his favorite hawk when the bird kept overturning his cup, preventing him from drinking from a stream. But it turned out that a snake was in the tree above, pouring its venom into the water, and the bird had saved Sindibad's life. "You are asking me to do the same," says the king, "and kill the man who has saved me."

The envious vizier rejects the parable and counters with another story of his own: a fairy tale about a prince who meets a young girl weeping in the forest. She says she's the daughter of an Indian king; he takes her up on his horse and prepares to rescue her; seeing a ruined house she asks to be let down, to meet a need of nature; he follows her and finds she is in fact an ogress who has tricked him and is now rejoicing with her children that she's caught a nice fat young man for them to eat.

The doctor Douban, says King Yunan's treacherous vizier, fits the part of the ogress in this story. "If he cured you," insinuates the vizier, "he can kill you as easily." The king is afraid, and the vizier advises him to execute Douban forthwith, before he can spring anything on him.

After these coils within coils, Shahrazad (and the fisherman) return to the main story of the physician Douban.

Summoned to the king's presence, in complete ignorance of the fate that lies in store, Douban salutes him with many fervent praise-poems about just providence, the wise ways of destiny, and the necessity of placing trust in learning and study.

The king tells him he is going to kill him—as abruptly as that. "You are a spy, I've been advised, come to assassinate me." And he orders the executioner to cut off the physician's head.

It is the doctor's turn to plead for his life, as the fisherman originally pleaded for his to the jinni he had delivered (and who had refused him), as the jinni is now doing from inside the bottle, and as Shahrazad is doing throughout the thousand and one nights to the Sultan who wants to execute her like all his other wives.

Douban pleads for justice; he compares himself to the crocodile in the fable—but he does not proceed to tell that story. There is not enough time left. The councillors and courtiers surrounding King Yunan uphold his innocence. But the king is now blinded by suspicion and fear. "You could kill me merely by giving me some perfume to smell," he says. Douban protests the charges are false and again begs for his life.

At this point, the fisherman interrupts the flow of the story and reminds Sakhr that these are the exact terms that he, the fisherman, had used to plead for his life, which the jinni had ignored. "I shall only rest easy when you are dead," continues King Yunan. The doctor warns him, "If you make me die, God will make you die." The doctor weeps; the hangman binds his eyes and lays his head on the block. But one of the courtiers rises and asks that he be spared. The doctor then asks for one last grace: to go back to his house, order his affairs, arrange his burial, and give away his library, especially his medical books. He has one special volume, he adds, that he wants to present to the king. It contains myriad secrets, one of which is truly singular and precious. He gives the king chapter and verse how to discover it, and tells him that after he has been executed, the king should place the head in a basin, with a layer of kohl at the bottom to staunch the blood, and it will answer any question the king puts to it. "Your severed head will speak to me?" the king marvels.

The following day, the court reassembles for the execution in their splendor, so that, the fisherman says, "The room seemed a bed of flowers." The doctor Douban returns from his house with a book and a box of powder, which he sprinkles on a dish, telling the king once more to place his head on the dish once it has been cut off.

The doctor is beheaded. Yunan is eager to open the book and discover the secret, but he finds that its pages are stuck together. He licks his finger and turns a page, then a second, then a third. They can only be separated with great difficulty, and Yunan can see nothing written on them. The head on the dish keeps urging him to turn more, and he does. At the end of a very short time, the king falls into convulsions: the pages are poisoned. Then, as his murderer writhes in his death agony, the head of the physician Douban recites a poem about the workings of destiny on the just and the unjust.

"You see," says the fisherman to the jinni, "that if the king Yunan had allowed the doctor to live, God would have preserved him. But he refused, wanted to kill him and God made him die. It is the same for you, Jinni. If you had intended to keep me alive, God would have preserved your life."

The jinni twists and turns, refusing this interpretation of his behavior and promising, swearing to reform, if only the fisherman will release him. After more to-ing and fro-ing, the fisherman makes the jinni swear he will be good and true to his word and will do him no harm.

Sakhr swears, and the fisherman unstoppers the bottle; smoke pours out and the jinni materializes, horrible of aspect; he tramples the copper bottle in fury, and throws it into the sea. The fisherman is terrified and reminds the jinni of his promise, and of the lesson of the story of Yunan and Douban. The jinni roars with laughter, and he begins striding way, telling the fisherman to follow him—he is taking him into another country, another story, and eventually, fabulous fortune.

In this cautionary tale the book that the doctor gives to the king who wronged him—the poisoned chalice he so greedily drinks—is active and transformed by the poison the doctor has introduced. But in many ways this magic book that promises to yield unprecedented knowledge is a type of all books, which have the power to ransom and save, to inflict harm and bring danger, like an amulet, or more strictly speaking, with reference to the *Nights*, like a talisman, an Arabic word imported into Europe by means of the stories and other translated texts.

Shahrazad's ransom tale-telling could be described as a single, prolonged act of performative utterance, by which she demonstrates the power of words to affect reality—her own fate and by extension others'. She exchanges stories against goods—against her survival and the survival of others. As when dreams materialize in reality on waking, words are made flesh throughout the stories of the *Nights*.[23] Such speech acts take place as part of the plots themselves, and they also constitute a strong claim for the effects of the storyteller or writer's methods. The enchantments of the *Arabian Nights* depend on this self-mirroring, magical technique, whereby the audience experience illusions summoned by the words on the page or in the ear, in the same way as the characters in the stories move in a landscape where magic keeps turning illusions into reality and inward apprehensions turn out to be truthful signs, propitious and cautionary.

"Open sesame," the robber chief calls out, and he is overheard by Ali Baba, who uses the magic formula to open the entrance to the treasure cave. The verbal form of this charm does not conform to other spells or charms in the *Nights*, which mostly depend on well-known sacred names, especially the ninety-nine names of God, Solomonic allusions in words and ciphers, and other riddling and talismanic verbal combinations. Sometimes the words form mysterious images, as on the carnelian that

Princess Maryam rubs to summon the flying bed. By comparison, "Open sesame!" is simple and heightens the fun when the wicked brother cannot remember it to escape from the cave and keeps listing different cereals in vain. But the underlying principle, that words can operate effectively to do things in the world, remains. "To hear is to obey, o Master," says the genie of the lamp. Vows, blessings, curses, apotropaic and expiatory formulae, repeated and performed in the correct way, place language at the center of ritual; these verbal, literally spellbinding, rituals occupy the heart of fairy tale.

The Library in the Story

No exploration of libraries and fiction could overlook the literary imagination of Jorge Luis Borges, who was a fervent advocate of the *1001 Nights* and himself chief librarian at the National Library in Buenos Aires; Borges found in the world of the library a microcosm of the world, the universe as encyclopedia, a book of all books, and a labyrinth in which readers find themselves while they are getting lost. Borges created works about libraries. He assembled virtual libraries of books he loved and wrote several obsessive tales about libraries, in which they achieve a monstrous, overwhelming reality like some vast organism, the root system of the world tree, on which we depend but which also drains all the vitality out of us. In one of his stories, called "The Library of Babel," he imagines an infinite library, composed of books made of every combination of twenty-three letters of the alphabet, in which every book is unique if only by virtue of a differently placed space or comma, a vertiginous, queasy vision of plenitude and multiplicity.[24] In an even more celebrated tale, "Tlön, Uqbar, Orbis Tertius," Borges follows a conjecture from his friend, the writer Adolfo Bioy Casares, that there exists a parallel world of Tlön, as attested in an encyclopedia found by Bioy in a certain library. By the end of the account, given in Borges's favored dry factual manner, like a bookkeeper's ledger, the imaginary and virtual realm of Tlön has insinuated itself into reality so thoroughly that it has become reality. "Reality 'caved in' at more than one point," the story tells us. "The truth is, it wanted to give way."[25] The word and the world are intersheaved and cannot be unravelled.

In this light, I think one can interpret an entry in Borges's splendid anthology *The Book of Imaginary Beings*, in which he evokes, with copious references, every mythological and legendary creature ever brought into existence in imagination, from well-known examples—sirens, unicorns—to singular specimens, "an animal imagined by Edgar Allan Poe," for instance.

His "The Fauna of Mirrors" tells a legend about a distant time when the inhabitants of the looking-glass world on the other side of the mirror are free, autonomous beings.[26] But they transgressed and were punished by imprisonment behind the glass, condemned forever to repeat the actions of those who had imprisoned them. The emperor stripped them of their power and of their forms and reduced them to mere slavish reflections.

Nonetheless, says the narrator, at the end of this concise riddle of a tale, "a day will come when the magic spell will be shaken off. The first to awaken will be the Fish. Deep in the mirror we will perceive a very faint line and the color of this line will be like no other color. Later on, other shapes will begin to stir. Little by little they will differ from us; little by little they will not imitate us. They will break through the barriers of glass or metal and this time will not be defeated. Side by side with these mirror creatures, the creatures of water will join the battle. In Yunnan they do not speak of the Fish but of the Tiger of the Mirror. Others believe that in advance of the invasion we will hear from the depths of mirrors the clatter of weapons."[27]

The tiger of the mirror—these fauna are empowered to move by Borges's words, and they embody, to me at least, an approach to words and stories that this indefatigable reader, this librarian of infinite libraries, absorbed from the *Nights*: that mimesis—reflection—has ceased to be their destiny, and *poesis*—making—has taken its place. In literary terms, naturalism has been superseded by fabulism, and representation by agency. The word is a coil in the battery of a book, and the library a huge generator. No surprise that Borges is the inspiration of the *Matrix* films.

THE STORY AS MONUMENT

In conclusion I will turn to Alice Oswald's *Memorial*, as mentioned before. Her subtitle terms her poem "An excavation of the *Iliad*," drawing attention to her work of exhuming pieces of the poem and reassembling them in a different shape and sequence as if they were shards in a puzzle. By shuffling the constituent elements of Homer, she claims she has distinguished three different layers in its archaeological depths: a seam of pastoral poetry that gives the epic its famous, lyrical extended similes from scenes of domestic and daily existence both of people and of animals; another seam, which gives a roll call of the dead; and a third, closely associated, that is a threnody, singing of the dead in the manner of professional mourners of antiquity who remember the ways the heroes died. She parts the strands and sets them out distinctively on the pages of her book. The first strand gives a simple litany of the fallen, by name. This list unfolds over many more pages than one could imagine possible, and through the paper the reader can see the phantom traces of those who have gone before and those who are to come. The mourning songs account for the particulars that Homer gives for each death (the javelin through the cheek, the spear in the groin); these leap up in the mind's eye like filmic flashes of violence, each one distinct and terrible. The third stratum Oswald excavated, as she pursued her form of poetic archaeology, yielded a corpus of buried pastoral lyric; she separates the celebrated Homeric similes from their referents in the narrative and turns the images into depth charges of elegy, evoking the passing of seasons and other cyclical events in nature that memorialize an eternal law of transience:

> Like a wind-murmur
> Begins a rumour of waves
> One long note getting louder
> The water breathes a deep sigh
> Like a land-ripple
> When the west wind runs through a field
> Wishing and searching
> Nothing to be found
> The corn-stalks shake their green heads [28]

The imagery here strikes the ear, and Alice Oswald has drawn attention to the incantatory and oral character of Greek poetry (she often performs her poem by heart). Other Homeric similes in her renderings shift between the acoustic and the written: the autumn leaves that offer an image of dead souls in classical literature are turning into the pages of books:

> Like leaves who could write a history of leaves
> The wind blows their ghosts to the ground [29]

The similes' role as an oblique chorale gains strength from repetition: each of the stanzas beginning "Like a . . ." is repeated exactly. The pared-down simplicity gives the epic in this variation an illuminist character, like the poetry of Eugenio Montale or Giuseppe Ungaretti. But the emotive repeat, avoided by these Italian precursors, produces an effect of uncertainty, as if summoning the healing vision once cannot do enough, but saying it twice only draws attention to the insufficiency, ultimately, of lament.

The result is a book that is a tombstone and a hymnal, a collection of epitaphs and a lyric anthology of songs. It is a stone inscribed with praise and lament, a memorial with the secret of death at its heart. It can be downloaded onto a Kindle or into a laptop, or read on paper inside the hard covers of a book. But figuratively it's a clay tablet or a lapis lazuli stone enclosed in a casket of cedar and kept safe in a library, mine or yours, in a public or a personal collection. The poem is doing the work of keeping the story of the past, moving it into a permanent present, as the sultan requested should be done for Shahrazad's acts of propitiation, her ransom tales.

NOTES

1. The earliest fragments extant, known as the Old Babylonian version, are thought to be from the eighteenth century B.C.; the largest number of tablets, from the later tenth to eighth centuries version, were found in the Library of Ashurbanipal, seventh century B.C.

2. *The Epic of Gilgamesh*, trans. and ed. N. K. Sandars (London: Penguin, 1960), 61. For an alternative translation, see "The Epic of Gilgamesh" in *Myths from Mesopotamia: Creation, The Flood, Gilgamesh, and Others*, trans. and ed. Stephanie Dalley (Oxford: Oxford University Press, 1989), 39–135.

3. Alice Oswald, *Memorial* (London: Faber and Faber, 2011). The relentless death toll in the *Iliad* has been drawn up by Ian Johnston of Vancouver Island University and is available at http://records.viu.ca/~johnstoi/homer/

Iliaddeaths.htm. I am grateful to Professor Nicholas Lowe for directing me to this site.

4. Andrew George, Introduction, in *The Epic of Gilgamesh*, ed. and trans. Andrew George (London: Penguin, 1999), xiv.

5. Ibid., lines 7–12, 18–21, 24–28.

6. Stephen Mitchell, *Gilgamesh: A New English Version* (London: Profile Books, 2004).

7. Philip Terry, "DICTATOR," forthcoming. Terry acknowledges the inspiration of various translations and editions, including, above all, John Gardner and John Maier, *Gilgamesh Translated from the Sin-Leqi-Unninni Version* (New York: Alfred A. Knopf, 1984).

8. "Babylon," music by Brian Gascoigne, libretto by Marina Warner (1976).

9. Esther Allen, "Michael Henry Heim: A Theory," from *The Man Between: Michael Henry Heim and a Life in Translation*, eds. Esther Allen, Sean Cotter and Russell Scott Valentino (Rochester, NY: Open Letter, 2014), 289.

10. "The Tale of Bulukiya," in *The Arabian Nights: The Book of the Thousand Nights and One Night*, vol. 3, trans. Powys Mathers, from the French trans. by J. C. Mardrus (London: Folio Society, 2003), 256–68. See also "The Queen of the Serpents," in Ulrich Marzolph and Richard van Leeuwen, *The Arabian Nights Encyclopedia*, vol. 1 (Santa Barbara, CA: ABC-Clio, 2004), 348–50.

11. "The name can be explained as a hypocoristic of Gilgamesh's name in a pronunciation attested both in Sumerian and in Hurrian: Bilga mesh. In the element *bilga* the third consonant exhibits a standard change, from voiced G to unvoiced K, the Akkadian hypocoristic ending -*ya* is added, and the second element *mesh* is omitted. The name Gilgamesh is presumed to be Sumerian, although it does not conform to any clear type of name in that language. The affix -*ya* is typical of Akkadian names, and it corresponds very closely to the Sumerian hypocoristic affix -*mu*." Stephanie Dalley, "Gilgamesh in the *Arabian Nights*," *Journal of the Royal Asiatic Society*, ser. 3, 1.1 (1991): 8.

12. Ibid., 10.

13. "Prologue: The Story of King Shahrayar and Shahrazad, His Vizier's Daughter," in *The Arabian Nights*, trans. Husain Haddawy (New York: W. W. Norton, 1990), 11.

14. *The Arabian Nights: Tales of 1001 Nights*, trans. Malcolm C. Lyons, with Ursula Lyons (London: Penguin, 2009), 121.

15. Abdelfattah Kilito, *Dites-moi le songe* (Arles: Actes Sud, 2010), 67–70.

16. Derek Walcott, "A Frowsty Fragrance," *New York Review of Books* June 15, 2000, 57–61.

17. Italo Calvino, *Invisible Cities*, trans. William Weaver (London: Picador, 1974), 48.

18. Florence Dupont, *The Invention of Literature: From Greek Intoxication to the Latin Book*, trans. Janet Lloyd (Baltimore: Johns Hopkins University Press, 1999), 11.

19. Marina Warner, *Stranger Magic: Charmed States and the Arabian Nights* (London: Vintage, 2012), 11; Alastair Hamilton, *The Arcadian Library: Western Appreciation of Arab and Islamic Civilization* (London: Arcadian Library in association with Oxford University Press, 2011), plate 172, 357.

20. From the preamble to "The Tale of the Young Man" ("The Prince of the Black Islands"), *Mille et une Nuits*, trans. Jamel Eddine Bencheikh and André Miquel (Paris: Gallimard, 2005), 1: 54; also in preamble to "The First Calender's Tale," in "The Porter and the Three Ladies of Bagdad," *Mille et une Nuits* 1: 82. Sometimes translated as "fine pen" not "needle." See also André Miquel, "Préface," in Abelfattah Kilito, *L'oeil et l'aiguille: Essai sur 'Les mille et une nuits'* (Paris: Le Fennec, Editions de la Découverte, 1992), 7–8, 104–11. Elliott Colla translates the sentence as "Mine is a tale that, if it were written in lessons at the corner of the eye, would be a needle for those who would consider," or "for those who would be pricked." See Elliott Colla, "The Porter and Portability: Figure and Narrative in the Porter's Tale," in *Scheherazade's Children: Global Encounters and the Arabian Nights*, ed. Philip Kennedy and Marina Warner (New York: New York University Press, 2013).

21. Warner, *Stranger Magic*, 191–94.

22. Ibid., 191.

23. Sandra Naddaff, *Arabesque: Narrative Structure and the Aesthetics of Repetition in the 1001 Nights* (Evanston: Northwestern University Press, 1991), 13–57.

24. Jorge Luis Borges, "The Library of Babel," in *Collected Fictions*, trans. Andrew Hurley (New York: Penguin, 1998), 112–18. For an alternative translation, see "The Library of Babel," trans. James E. Irby, in *Labyrinths*, ed. Donald A. Yates and James E. Irby (New York: Penguin, 1962), 78–86.

25. Borges, trans. Hurley, 81.

26. Jorge Luis Borges, with Margarita Guerrero, *The Book of Imaginary Beings*, trans. Norman Thomas di Giovanni (New York: Penguin, 1967), 67.

27. Ibid.

28. Oswald, *Memorial*, 14.

29. Ibid., 73.

CHAPTER 8

❦

The Library in Poetry

Robert Crawford

"Ze zbrojnic udělejte biblioték" (Turn the arsenals into libraries) reads an inscription on a flagstone at the entrance to Palacký University Library.[1] This Czech library, itself a converted Habsburg arsenal in the historic city of Olomouc, has a pale, spacious courtyard punctuated with large black cannonballs. The inscription quotes the seventeenth-century Moravian poet and educator J. A. Comensky, known as Comenius. When he first penned those vatic words, this arsenal had not even been built. Though it may lack the Baroque splendor of the library of the Strahov Monastery in Prague, the Olomouc library, eloquent in its quieter aesthetic and far fuller of readers, is a fine, meditative space. Yet, as poets as different as the Bosnian Goran Simić ("The National Library burned for three days last August") and the Englishman D. J. Enright ("To shoot a man against the National Library wall!") remind us, libraries can be sites of conflict and devastation.[2] They have, as Matthew Battles puts it, "an unquiet history."[3] Their meaning in poetry can be threatening as well as nurturing.

Frequently, libraries are places poets adore. Whether it is Kathleen Jamie in the 1990s showing how the queen of Sheba with her "bonny wicked smile" in Edinburgh "desires the keys / to the National Library" or Les Murray in the previous decade admiring "The softly vaulted ceiling of St. Gallen's monastic library" glimpsed as "beautifully iced in Rococo butter cream," poets love libraries as temples of books.[4] Often, from medieval cathedral libraries to Yale's Sterling Library, these buildings have been designed to invoke the sacred. Book temples are among the stunning examples of "architectural history" photographed by Will Pryce for James W. P. Campbell's *The Library: A World History*.[5] In his poem "El guardian de los libros" (The Guardian of the Books) Jorge Luis Borges, greatest of modern poet-librarians, portrays Hsiang, a heroic but aging and perhaps blind librarian guarding his rescued book stock in a noble high tower, contemplating a city that is turning into a desert. Elsewhere Borges is fascinated by "something / essential and immortal" that his poem's speaker has "buried / somewhere in that library of the past."[6] Yet in his 1939 essay "The Total Library" Borges, who died just as the Internet was born, had imagined an impossibly enormous library in terms of "horror" and "a delirious god."[7]

From Innerpeffray in Perthshire to Jiaojiehe north of Beijing, libraries may look like towers, or Shinto shrines, or Dhaoist or Athenian or Roman temples, or Christian cathedrals or kirks or multistory, monolithic postmodern standing stones; but ultimately they are adored (or feared) by poets less for their architecture than for something more nimbly spiritual and imaginative. To be a poet or a librarian should be a calling: libraries often signal as much in their physical as well as their intellectual design, and some (including Glasgow's Mitchell Library with its Burns Room or the London Library with its T. S. Eliot wing) have a poet as genius loci. Libraries are places, though not the only places, that poets want their collections of verse to find a home in; but they are also sites that shape poets, educating us and giving us sustenance. If specialist libraries devoted only to verse—such as the beautifully luminous Scottish Poetry Library off Edinburgh's Royal Mile or the wood-panelled Woodberry Poetry Room at Harvard—are few in number, then almost all general libraries have a place for poets, and many are places to which, over the centuries, poets have wished to pay tribute.

Charles Bukowski in his poem "they arrived in time" sums up an excited love that modern poets often feel for libraries. Libraries are to be revered; but they are also places of transformational opportunity. Bukowski details the librarians with their serious stares and the hardcover library books he devoured as a young man; he ends by saluting all those people—poets and librarians—who contributed to his imaginative and intellectual education and who in doing so at a time when "there was no chance / gave me one."[8] Another American poet, Rita Dove, paying tribute to the British-accented "improbable librarian" of "Maple Valley Branch Library" with her "*impeccable blouse*," sees the library as a gateway, a portal to knowledge, book by book by book, so that the poem's speaker, encouraged to borrow volumes, comes to realize that she can consume even "an elephant / if I take small bites."[9]

Such a sense of the library as offering incremental excitements—book after book after book—is also why poets want to join the library. They seek both to enroll, and, perhaps even more ardently, they are eager for their works to become further accessions to the library's collection. So the seventeenth-century Metaphysical poet Abraham Cowley, penning an "Ode" that features "Mr Cowley's Book presenting it self to the University Library of Oxford," has his collection of poems exclaim at the start,

> Hail Learnings *Pantheon*! Hail the sacred Ark
> Where all the World of Science do's imbarque!
> Which ever shall withstand, and hast so long withstood,
> Insatiate Times devouring Flood.

Here is a book that wants to be accessioned. It longs to be received as one of the "Sacred throng" of chosen volumes of "the mysterious Library, / The Beatifick *Bodley* of the Deity." For Cowley the library is not just a temple of books; it is heaven with shelving. For his volume to live there is for it to pass beyond the world in which its poet "woo'd."[10] Cowley's book woos the library, seeking the best chance of immortality. As Margaret Cavendish, Duchess of Newcastle, put it a little later in the same century, "In Fame's great Library are Records plac'd."[11]

The idea of the library as a celestial, or at least a prelapsarian paradise is found not infrequently in seventeenth-century verse. From the Latin of poet, dramatist, and theologian Theodore Beza, Thomas Heywood translated a hymn of delight "To his Library,"

> Hayle to my books safe and in sight.
> You, all my mirth; my choice delight.

If such books are an earthly joy, they incite a rapture that verges on worship. From a Classical genealogy that includes not only the great poet-librarian of Alexandria, Callimachus, but also many less well known lovers of libraries, traditions of library praising enter the literatures of the British Isles. Anglo-Saxon poets had written of books and bookworms, but more fulsome praise of book-hoards comes later. The quick-wittedly imaginative Latinist Arthur Johnston, who played a significant part in the making of the first published anthology of Scottish poetry, the 1637 *Delitiae Poetarum Scotorum*, sings of that "Temple of the Muses," the Fife tower house belonging to Sir John Scot of Scotstarvit, patron of the *Delitiae*. Disconcertingly, perhaps, for readers in Scot's library, the leader of a local colony of honeybees

> Delegit certam sibi Scoti in culmine sedem,
>   Servat ubi vates bibliotheca sacros.

> Chose a place on Scot's tower's topmost storey
>   Where his library holds sacred singers' songs.

Yet the sweet, mellifluous honey making is presented as a library adornment, one nurtured by the Classical milieu of Virgil's *Georgics* and adding to this near-celestial library's sacredness. Arthur Johnston regards his own library as a garden of books, yielding the sweetest fruits even in the depths of winter and, if not quite celestial, then certainly Edenic:

> Nil opus his rastris durisve ligonibus, hortus
>   Hic domino nulla poma labore parit.
> Aureus est hortus nobis, hunc protulit aetas
>   Aurea, qua fructus sponte ferebat humus.

> No need for rakes or hoes. My garden grows
> Apples for its owner without work.
> An eighteen-carat golden garden, given
> By a golden age when, once, the soil itself
> Spontaneously blossomed.[12]

This library is a heaven on earth, even if it yields a fruit that is hardly edible. Like Cowley's Oxford, that "Muses' Paradise," Johnston's smaller Scottish library could be seen to be a "living University of the Dead!"[13]

Or, as Henry Vaughan put it more tactfully around 1678 in his poem "On Sir Thomas Bodley's Library," the library was a place where ancient rabbis might be found to be far more than mere "empty Skulls"; thanks to the priestly efforts of librarians, such worthies were "not dead, but full of *Blood* again."[14] The library is a sacred space, a place of resurrection; yet as a location of learning it is also a site of transformational opportunity.

However, while the sacred and the educational continue to resonate, sex and death come to dominate the presentation of libraries in English-language poetry, though books and the naming of them are certainly to the fore. Whether those books are the poet's own, as in Cowley's "Ode," or other people's, as in Don Paterson's late twentieth-century "The Alexandrian Library" (whose "book-clogged" shelves seem to be groaning with titles such as *16 RPM—A Selective Discography* and *Urine—The Water of Life*), repeatedly what those volumes offer is something tinged with mortality, with what Emily Dickinson in her poem "In a Library" terms a "mouldering pleasure":

> A precious—mouldering pleasure—'tis—
> To meet an Antique Book—
> In just the Dress his Century wore—
> A privilege—I think—
>
> His venerable Hand to take—
> And warming in our own—
> A passage back—or two—to make—
> To Times when he—was young—[15]

The implication in this poem is that the author of this "Antique Book" is dead; yet when we and the poet take his hand and feel it "warming in our own" there is that sense of immediate contact that poetry is so good at communicating and that carries here, surely, just a hint of erotic thrill.

Though there are homoerotic moments to be found in English-language poems about libraries and librarians, on the whole the library emerges as a place of mainly heterosexual encounters. Libraries as institutions do figure in English-language poems during the seventeenth century, but those poems tend to involve isolated mentions of the library, as in John Donne's "To Sir Henry Goodyere," which glances toward "All libraries, which are Schools, Camps, & Courts," rather than taking libraries as their principal focus.[16] When Alexander Pope in book 3 of *The Dunciad* writes of "Wits, who like Owls see only in the dark" that "their heads were *Libraries out of order*" he makes this last remark in a footnote, rather than in the body of the poem.[17] Such references are glancing. What seems hard to deny is that it is later in the eighteenth century, around the time when women first become librarians and when libraries become social spaces that admit both sexes, that the library becomes more prominent in Anglophone poetry. Whether there is a causal relationship at work or whether there are other reasons—to do with changes in educational practice and the growth of democratic ideals, for instance—it is hard to say. Yet, strikingly, the first extended "library poem" in English is a flirtatious, mischievous one in which a woman (as well as a host of male readers) plays a prominent part.

Though many women worked as librarians in mid-nineteenth-century America, it was not until the later nineteenth century that female librarians became common in Britain, making libraries among the relatively few social intellectual institutions other than schools in which women might hold positions of authority and so challenge unthinking assumptions about gender roles, education, and professionalism. Nonetheless, David Allan points out in *A Nation of Readers: The Lending Library in Georgian England* that there were certainly a few eighteenth-century women librarians. In poetry, though Allan does not mention her, the most characterful of these was Esther Caterer. Born Esther Saunders, she had become a librarian by inheritance. Her father, Joseph Saunders, was the "first librarian" of the subscription library founded in Sheffield in 1771 and based in his house; a published list of its fifty-nine subscribers in 1778 shows that seven were women.[18] From 1777, after Joseph's death, Esther took over as librarian, receiving a salary, and, after her marriage to William Caterer, went on holding this post until her death in 1818. By then her salary had been raised to £30. Earlier poor pay had meant that she worked only part-time: "The books were in a very dirty and tattered condition in consequence of the librarian's attendance not being constant."

This was a library housed in an industrial city: "the approach was bad; the staircase was winding, the room was dark and inconvenient, but still there was no small number of good books." Some subscribers took advantage of the librarian, taking out more than their quota of volumes. Esther Caterer was a character, and had her favorite readers, for whom "favourite books" were reserved by hiding them from other people; volumes were secreted "in cupboards, drawers, and even in the warming-pan, for the more zealous, eager, and vigilant readers." If that annoyed some folk, in general this pioneering eighteenth-century female librarian was regarded locally with considerable affection.

> She was a great favourite on account of her easy good temper; and she was a great newsmonger too. Marriages were whispered in her little room long before they took place; deaths were known as soon as the bell tolled; and all the affairs of the town and country were amply discussed.

Still, Esther's "death was the signal for reformation. A committee was appointed to consider what measures would most conduce to the improvement of the library." So it was that a man, Isaac Hatfield, was appointed as the next librarian. The library relocated "to a more commodious room in George-street." Its subscription was raised, the number of members increased, and "not a book was lost."[19]

A pioneering woman librarian in a mercantile and working-class man's world, Esther Caterer may not have enjoyed the resources granted to her male successor, but her example was celebrated in poetry. To John Holland, cottage-born author of "Sheffield Park" and admirer of Robert Burns and Robert Bloomfield, is attributed the first published extended English-language elegy to a librarian. Imitating in form and Scots accent Burns's partly mocking laments such as "Poor Mailie's Elegy," this English poet's "Elegy on the Death of Esther Caterer, Librarian of Surry Street Book Rooms" takes from the tearfully grinning Scots tradition of "Standard Habbie" its sometimes unstable mixture of affection and mockery. Dated "*Sheffield, January* 19, 1818," it begins by urging "Ye book worms," the readers of Esther's library, to "a' wi' sorrow meet," bewailing this librarian's passing:

> She was a canty clattering dame,   *lively*
> A servant gude; abroad, at hame,

She had an honest matron's fame;
    Nor could I spread
A mickle stain owre a' her name—   *big; over*
    Auld Esther's dead!

When gentles came, in studious mood,
To fash their brains 'mang learning's brood,   *bother; among*
Or tak' their meal o' mental food,
    Wi' ready head
She ken'd where every volume stood.—   *knew*
    Auld Esther's dead!

An' when the storm blaw'd hard an' reekit,   *fumed*
An' the warm room ye ran an' seekit,
'Tis fearless truth, an sic I speak it,
    Free frae a' dread,
Wi' her the hours like minutes sneakit.—
    Auld Esther's dead!

The books are grievin, 'mang themselves,
From folios fat down to lean twelves,
As if sad ghaists and wailing elves
    A clamour spread;
And sighing a' alang the shelves:
    Auld Esther's dead!

Sigh for her, every ancient book,
Auld Chaucer i' the poet's nuik;
A' ye romances, dolorous look,
    Your gude friend's fled;
For muckle pride in you she took.—   *great*
    Auld Esther's dead![20]

If her library had a "poet's nuik"—a poetry corner—then Esther's legacy was not forgotten. It lived on in poetry and in a tradition of female
librarianship. Her successor, Isaac Hatfield, died after only three years

in post, and (as Esther had done), Isaac's daughter inherited the job of librarian, or rather she was elected to this position by library members. Nearly eight decades later, in 1896 a Sheffield journalist noted that "Since Miss Hatfield's time, the librarian has always been a lady, her successors down to to-day being Mrs. Wells, Miss Lawton, Mrs. Greaves, and Miss Manlove."[21] This almost uninterrupted lineage of female librarians from 1777 until the end of the nineteenth century makes Sheffield unique in British librarianship, as well as notable in verse. Today Sheffield Central Lending Library remains headquartered on Surrey Street, close to the site where Esther Caterer worked.

As poets and other readers were well aware, often eighteenth- and early nineteenth-century libraries were called not "libraries" at all, but "book clubs" or "book societies." Some, such as the Penzance Ladies' Book Club, were single-sex ("no gentleman [to] be admitted as subscriber"), but others, such as Lancaster's Amicable Society with its "professional librarian, a Mrs Singleton," or the Yeovil Book Society in Somerset, whose president was Harriet Grove, were mixed-sex institutions.[22] Like her sister Charlotte, Harriet Grove was a diarist, but she had also been a poet's love and muse. Once engaged to her cousin Percy Bysshe Shelley, she was the dedicatee of *Queen Mab* and of several of his early lyrics, including "To Harriet," which celebrates her "look of love" and fears her "scorn," but says nothing of her librarianly gifts.[23]

Rather different, and far more interested in the library as an institution, is Charles Shillito's *The Country Book-Club*, published in 1788 with a comic frontispiece by Thomas Rowlandson. Above the Horatian motto "*Concordia Discors*," Rowlandson depicts several all-male, bewigged, bookish, and boozy book-club members sitting in a room on whose walls are pinned up such titles as "Th[omas] Glanvill on Witches" and "Liberty of the Press." These gents are being served drinks by an attendant female—more a barmaid than a Caterer-like librarian. Women as well as men subscribed to the publication of Shillito's witty poem, whose rhyming couplets present a "lowly, straw-roof'd cot" where "The motley members of the Book-club meet," glimpsed "Advancing slow, in literary pride / The Surgeon Barber by the Vicar's side." Described just before the outbreak of the French Revolution, this rural English book club is a relatively democratic space, accommodating not only to the formally educated but also to "A self-taught scholar: though of mean degree, / The hamlet boasts few men more wise than he." A classic of the genre of the "library poem," Shillito's piece catalogues some of the club's books and gets markedly lively when, after the members have done a good deal of drinking in their reading room, they start to hurl the book-stock at each other:

> Now books are made their *missile* force to try;
> Swift as artill'ry balls, huge volumes fly.[24]

Beautiful but apparently not a member of the book club, the woman who serves the refreshments fails to keep perfect order. *The Country Book-Club* is all the more enjoyable for growing rumbunctuous. As a library poem it is a milestone in its loving detailing of the book club itself, whose members include a bookseller with a taste for Bunyan, and a printer's "devil." Readers are assured that this latter printing technician with "shaggy hair" and "ink-bespatter'd garments," despite his appearance (and unlike "town-made printers, and their spies"), is guilty of "No flaming squib, no hot poetic brand." Shillito is a poet who loves not only books but also readers and the space in which they read, discuss "news" (i.e., "Scandal's tales"), and engage in book talk.

> And now a rustic messenger is seen;
> Weigh'd down by party pamphlets, Grub-street lays,
> Old magazines, gazettes, songs, speeches, plays,
> And half the learning of *High Holborn,* scann'd
> At cobwebb'd stalls, and purchas'd second-hand.[25]

After eyeing such publications from London, these rural bookmen get drunk. Theirs seems to be an all-male club, though they certainly welcome the landlord's "virgin daughter," "Isabel the gay," who pours drinks and encourages "the bowl" to circulate "with quicken'd speed, / That leaves no vacant time, to think, or *read.*" The entry of the landlord with "the last [i.e., latest] Reviews" causes anxiety to an aspiring writer in their midst, but the sight of Isabel brings further toasts. Eventually, after she exits, drunkenness ensues, and the men fling books at one another:

> Congreve, and Bunyan, Chesterfield, and Carr,
> Light troops and heavy, wage promiscuous war.
> E'en airy *Yorick* falls like pond'rous lead,
> And cracks his joke on some rich peasant's head.[26]

Satirically, decades after Jonathan Swift's *Battle of the Books*, Shillito depicts his book club as "meeting to dispute, to fight, to plead, / To smoke, to drink,—do anything but read—."[27]

Such book clubs may have occasioned jokes, but poets knew their value. Their very disputatiousness would make them, like pubs and coffeehouses, significant institutions in the eighteenth-century public sphere. Unlike coffeehouses (which tended to be an urban phenomenon), book clubs and circulating libraries were found in the country as well as in the city, and several poets set them up. In early eighteenth-century Edinburgh the poet, anthologist, and dramatist Allan Ramsay established a pioneering circulating library, but perhaps a more striking library was that encouraged among rural working folk by Ramsay's greatest poetic admirer. Instrumental in developing the Monklands Friendly Society, a community "circulating library" promoting "improvement" among "the lower classes" in southwest Scotland, Robert Burns, using the pen-name "A PEASANT," wrote an account of its principles and influenced its book buying. Into its collection went Enlightenment philosophy as well as imaginative fiction from *Don Quixote* to Henry Mackenzie's recent sentimental novel *The Man of Feeling*, one of Burns's own favorites.[28] This astute poet was schooled not only by the libraries of his family and his patrons, but also by rural workingmen's book clubs. Burns's Enlightenment eagerness led him alike to circulate among friends philosophy by Adam "Smith wi' his sympathetic feeling, / An' [Thomas] Reid, to common sense appealing," but appealing also to democratic ideals. Familiar with the running of working-class libraries, and with the libraries of noblemen who patronized him, he wrote sarcastically in "The Book-Worms,"

> Through and through the inspired leaves,
>   Ye maggots, make your windings;
> But, oh! Respect his lordship's taste,
>   And spare his golden bindings.[29]

If Burns's sensibility made him attractive to Sheffield's John Holland, who elegized Esther Caterer, it also attracted fellow English poet George Crabbe, but not before Crabbe's 1781 poem *The Library* had praised the sympathetic power of reading to "lead us willing from ourselves, to see / Others more wretched."[30] Though this phrasing pre-dates that of Burns's "To a Louse," to modern ears it may sound like a recasting of his "*To see ourels as others see us!*"—itself a reworking of phrasing used in print in 1759 by Adam Smith in his *Theory of Moral Sentiments*.[31] To hear Crabbe's poem as part of a book-lined echo chamber is not entirely misleading. While in one sense *The Library* is unique as a book-length treatment of its subject in published English verse, nevertheless it is a poem markedly less sociable than either Holland's "Ode" or Shillito's "The Country Book-Club." Crabbe's library is certainly a place of books that—whether they be "mighty Folio's . . . Quartos . . . light Octavos" or "An humbler band of Duodecimos"—"all in silence, all in order stand."[32] Yet, however well stocked, it is less a space for socializing than for contemplation. *The Library* shows some awareness of its subject as a physical entity and as a place where the sexes might dream of meeting (in a later revision, Crabbe wrote that among heavy tomes, "ladies read the work they could not lift"), but this library is principally a place for the poet to ponder the status of poetry in a world often engrossed by the prosaic and resistant to the claims of the fiction-making play of imagination.[33] Expanding his poem later, Crabbe makes clear that for his poet as for other "devout" readers the library is less an energizing locus within the public sphere, than a "peaceful temple" where, early in the Romantic era, "the poet meets his favouring muse."[34]

In the 1781 version, however, there is an insistent sense (not lost in Crabbe's later expanded text) that the poet can still find in the library a site of struggle: not so much a contestation of political or religious ideologies as a less public but intense struggle over the nature of the poetic calling. The issue is not just that, faced with the great "Immortals" of literature, "Each in his sphere the literary Jove," the contemporary composer of verse feels small; it is also that, surrounded by "History" and "Science" and philosophy, medical tomes, theology, and "Abridgements of the Law," the poet fears his place may be where "Wits, Bards, and Idlers fill a tatter'd row."[35] Pondering the exciting yet perhaps outgrown attractions of romances' "worlds bewitch'd," Crabbe's poet-speaker feels the counterclaims of "Reason" and "Fiction." He grows "Pensive," fears criticism, and is "wrapt in thought profound" until he receives advice from a "pitying Power" who urges him to stay true to his poetic vocation:

> "Nor say the Muses' song, the Poet's pen,
> Merit the scorn they meet from little men.
> With cautious freedom if the numbers flow,
> Not wildly high, not pitifully low;
> If vice alone their honest aims oppose,
> Why so asham'd their friends, so loud their foes?
> Happy for men in every age and clime,
> If all the Sons of Vision dealt in rhyme.
> Go on then, Son of Vision! Still pursue
> Thy airy dreams; the world is dreaming too.
> Ambition's lofty views, the pomp of state,
> The pride of wealth, the splendour of the great,
> Stript of their mask, their cares and troubles known,
> Are visions far less happy than thy own:
> Go on! And, while the Sons of Care complain,
> Be wisely gay and innocently vain;
> While serious souls are by their fears undone,
> Blow sportive bladders in the beamy sun,
> And call them worlds! And bid the greatest show
> More radiant colours in their world below;
> Then, as they break, the slaves of care reprove,
> And tell them, such are all the toys they love."[36]

More fully than any previous English-language poet, Crabbe sets up the library in poetry as signifying a place of both challenge and confirmation for the poet. That is how many have regarded it ever since. Later nineteenth-century poets could follow Burns in mocking aristocratic book collecting ("Within his Gothic library / The portly Earl reclines" until, eventually, "A blue fly settles on his nose") or could figure the library, as Andrew Lang does, as a place haunted by (almost exclusively male) ghosts, among them the spirits of poets including bookish William

Drummond of Hawthornden, who had treasured his own book-lined Scottish tower house retreat centuries earlier. For the Victorian book-man Lang, surrounded in his library by "Octavo, quarto, folio," the library is a place to "muse" in, sensing how

> The new and elder dead are there—
>   The lords of speech, and song, and pen—
> Gambetta, Schlegel, and the rare
>   Drummond of haunted Hawthornden.[37]

If in later Victorian British poetry libraries came at times to mean places of haunted sleep, often the meaning of the library in American poetry carried more vigor. Robert Burns's admirer Walt Whitman, conscious both that the library was a place in need of enlivening and an institution that could still seem fogged with quasi-aristocratic pride, arrived not as a supplicant to the muses' temple of books, but with more of a challenging democratic swagger. In the wake of the American Civil War, Whitman is sure that he is just what the library needs:

> Shut not your doors to me, proud libraries,
> For that which was lacking on all your well-fill'd shelves, yet needed
>   most, I bring;
> Forth from the war emerging—a book I have made,
> The words of my book nothing, the drift of it every thing;
> A book separate, not link'd with the rest, nor felt by the intellect,
> But you, ye untold latencies, will thrill to every page.[38]

Throughout mid-nineteenth-century America, "Culture and libraries" (as for Ralph Waldo Emerson) certainly went together; and so, increasingly, did libraries and women.[39] If the leisured British bookman Lang can make the library sound like a gentlemen's club, then, on hearing reports about librarianship abroad, librarians at the 1880 Edinburgh meeting of the Library Association were struck by one delegate's statement that "He found lady librarians in Sweden, and this was a concession to the claims of women's rights which might be beneficial; it was, at any rate, economical."[40] Three years earlier a Philadelphian, Lloyd B. Smith, at the Conference of Librarians in London, "drew attention to the employment of ladies in libraries in America," though "He regretted to say they were underpaid."[41]

Yet American libraries seem to have been more progressive than many in Britain. In 1877, speaking in London, the recently appointed librarian of Harvard, Justin Winsor, both a founder and the president of the new American Library Association, was reported as announcing with some pride that at Harvard,

> they take lady assistants into the library at £100 a year, and gradually raise their salaries to as high as £200, and £240 in exceptional cases. They obtain ladies having a fair knowledge of Latin, Greek, French and German, and a usable knowledge for library work of Italian. . . . They had present, he was glad to say, a representative of the American lady librarians (loud cheers), one who had been librarian of Wellesley College, eight miles from Boston, where the president is a lady, all the professors are ladies, and 400 ladies are the students.[42]

Alert to what we would now call the politics of gender, as well as to its economics, Winsor had previously worked as a librarian in Boston, a city famed for its book culture. His enthusiasm for "lady librarians" may be matched by that of Oliver Wendell Holmes, who ends his 1888 paean "For the Dedication of the New City Library, Boston" with words that might be read as celebrating not only learning but also the profession of librarianship that was increasingly open to American women:

> Here shall the sceptred mistress reign
>   Who heeds her meanest subject's call,
> Sovereign of all their vast domain,
>   The queen, the handmaid of them all![43]

In Britain library handmaids (as some still thought of female librarians) were still relatively rare. The 1899 International Congress of Women was told by "Miss Toulmin Smith (librarian of Manchester College, Oxford)" that

The chief opportunities for women at present were among public libraries as assistants and librarians. America with its 5,000 libraries offered plentiful provision for women, by whom they were chiefly served, but, with different circumstances, something had been done in England too. Women had been employed at Bristol and Manchester for the last 20 years, 35 at various grades now at Bristol and 85 at Manchester. In 1894 18 libraries in England and Scotland employed women assistants, and about 21 or 22 women were librarians.[44]

One of the best known of these was Minnie Stewart Rhodes James, librarian of the People's Palace for East London. With its "great lofty-domed room," this free library for impoverished working-class people had a collection of around half a million books and was rich in "fiction, poetry, history, and all the branches of arts and science."[45] A report on it given to the Library Association in 1892 was prefaced with a Wordsworthian poetic flourish,

> Books we know
> Are a substantial world, both true and good;
> Round these, with tendrils strong as flesh and blood,
> Our pastime and our happiness will grow.[46]

Prose fiction was the genre demanded most by People's Palace readers, but "among the poets" taken out around this time "Shakespeare and Byron" were "the most popular, Milton and Longfellow coming next."[47] However, Minnie James noted that "the pay, as a rule," was "poor" for women librarians in Britain and, expressed frustration that "so few women have been employed in British libraries in really responsible positions."[48]

After serving as curator of the Library Association museum in London and helping pioneer in Britain the Library Association's professional educational program, Minnie James emigrated to Boston, becoming an active member of the American Library Association and librarian of Boston's Library Bureau.[49] In London she had been encouraged by the ideals of the poetry-loving novelist Walter Besant, founder of the Society of

Authors. She may have stocked poetry on the shelves of the People's Palace, but she could be impatient with those who sought to use her library for poetic purposes. In 1890, she told members of the Library Association how in the People's Palace reading room

> A young lady recently asked for information on the edelweiss, so we gave her a botanical description of that Alpine flower. No, she did not want that, but some poetry about it. This was produced, but unfortunately failed to be sufficiently sentimental, and after a long search she was obliged to indite her epistle of love minus the edelweiss effusion.[50]

If the library in America, and, to a lesser extent, in Britain, could be seen as a portal of emancipation for women as well as men, in poetry it came to be seen so around the globe. Yet sometimes there is also a sense of the way in which, as it had been for George Crabbe and other poets, the library could be a subduing space. It might counter as well as spur imagination. Radical Australian poet and artist Lesbia Harford (1891–1927) writes in "Closing Time—Public Library" of how, when a "great gong" is beaten at ten o'clock,

> I push back my chair,
> And all the people leave their books. We flock,
> Still acquiescent, down the marble stair
> Into the dark where we can't read. And thought
> Swoops down insatiate through the starry air.[51]

If there is ambivalence as well as book-hunger in Harford's poem, then as the twentieth century progresses a veritable flood of library poems ensues. Often, though by no means always, these involve a sense of the library as a place where men and women meet and sometimes bond. New Zealand–raised poet and librarian Fleur Adcock remembers a book given to her by her first husband and inscribed " 'To Fleur from Pete, on loan perpetual!' " Her elegiac poem, playing on the strangeness of the phrase "permanent loan," turns to lament; but for the biblioholic Glaswegian poet Frank Kuppner there may be a sense of resigned ruefulness in the observation, "Not many girls here in the library today, I see."[52]

Sometimes the library in modern poetry remains sepulchral, deathly, melancholy (in the "bowels of the Sterling Library" at Yale Susan Howe detects "loud sobbing"), but, more enliveningly, it is also a place for sexual liaisons.[53] For male poets the increasing success of female librarians can spur unmitigated lust. Eyeing one librarian, Charles Bukowski swerves aside from reading library copies of the *Kenyon Review*, and learning there about poetic composition, to wanting to "grab her panties."[54] Similar thoughts seem to have occurred to modern England's greatest poet-librarian, Philip Larkin, at least in his poem "Administration."[55] Sitting in the library at Duke University, the speaker in Harvey Shapiro's poem "Library" grows excited as he thinks of "Cynthia" who "got herself off in the stacks" of the University of California at San Diego and attributed her actions to "the heavy breathing of lit."[56] If all this tends toward what Thom Gunn calls "wet dreams, in libraries congealing," then there is an excited but gentler erotics at play in such poems as Jackie Kay's "Biography" with its love letters hidden in books in a "*so hot*" library, and a wittily mischievous one in J. V. Cunningham's "I, Too, Have Been to the Huntington," where that palatial book-hoard is one among whose surrounding statuary "David equally with Venus / Has no penis."[57]

In many modern poems the library, then, signifies a sometimes awkwardly eroticized space. However, it remains, too, a place of death. "Here is the body of knowledge at rest," writes Sean O'Brien in "Notes on the Use of the Library (Basement Annexe)."[58] O'Brien is a northern English poet whose imagination seems haunted by book repositories—so much so that he has tried to exorcise his demon in a poem entitled simply "Hatred of Libraries." Where Stanley Kunitz in America imagined Abraham Lincoln's blood leaking in the "Great Hall of the Library" of Congress, O'Brien, an aficionado of Newcastle's Literary and Philosophical Society with its historic reading room, imagines scholarly library users as "wasters" who pass "notes to the dead."[59] It may be that notions of mausoleum-like libraries lead not only to laments for the famously cremated Library at Alexandria, a trope invoked repeatedly in modern verse, but also to the occasional celebration of library destruction. The American Weldon

Kees has readers "Burning the books, one by one" to keep warm, while in the 1980s Scotland's Edwin Morgan (who has his own poem about the "fearsome" destruction of the Alexandrian Library) writes with disconcerting post-Futurist glee about an imagined "conflagration / that laid the new British Library in ashes"—a spectacle his poem's speaker finds "unusually riveting."[60]

Perhaps to protect themselves against the mausoleum aspects of many older libraries, poets can resort to imaginatively liberating bad behavior. "I remember the thin librarian's look of hate / as we left holes in her shelves, like missing teeth," recalls Alastair Reid in a poem clearly based on his time as a student at the University of St. Andrews, whose historic King James Library had been for centuries a strictly policed book room. The same poet, who hosted Borges in St. Andrews and translated some of the great Argentinian's poems, writes with awe and delight about watching a man who spends his life in the library with a pencil, filling in the letter *O* with "o-so-patient shading" in book after book after book.[61] "The O-Filler" presents a very differently imagined book-hoard from the twenty-first-century vision of "The Digital Library, St. Andrews" where the present writer, one of Reid's countrymen, sees how "laptops open like thick-leaved books / The flatpack wealth of nations."[62] And both of these versions of the library seem as far from either Larkin's dour confronting of "the toad *work*" as from his lyrical celebration of Hull University's architecturally distinctive Brynmor Jones Library as "lifted study-storehouse" by day and "flattened cube of light" by night.[63]

In the poetic experiments of the Cambridge college librarian and English don J. H. Prynne and in those of the mid-twentieth-century poet Veronica Forrest-Thomson readers may sense readily how learned libraries can fuel bookish verse as one discourse is spliced with another. Yet, perhaps most appropriately, it falls to Alastair Reid's friend and Larkin's former library colleague Douglas Dunn—a librarian on both sides of the Atlantic and later a poet and professor at St. Andrews—to catch in his poem "Libraries. A Celebration" something of the combined enjoyments and drabness that adhere to the meaning of the library in modern verse. Most celebrated for his deeply moving 1985 collection *Elegies*, Dunn was awarded the Queen's Medal for Poetry in 2013. He presents traditional libraries and librarianship as still to be relished. Unlike Archibald MacLeish, that poet who was Librarian of Congress but who never used the word "library" in his collected verse, Dunn writes with aplomb about everything from "prayers to the Nine Muses" to "The Scottish Association of Assistant Librarians' / Weekend Conference at The Covenanters' Inn." His libraries may be less eroticized than those of some other poets, but he sings of them with "permanent devotion," whether winking toward Glasgow's Mitchell Library, for long Europe's largest open-access public library, or Hull's Brynmor Jones elevated book cube, or Akron Public Library in Ohio.[64] Then, when, in another, more somber poem, "December's Door," he elegizes his old friend Philip Larkin and watches "rubescent figments vitrify / On library windows," that image, mixing crematorium-like burning with a sense of awed beauty and something gracefully lasting, sums up lyrically at least some of the meanings of the library in recent English-language poetry.[65]

NOTES

1. *Johannis Amos Comenii Opera Omnia*, vol. 23, *Clamores Eliae*, ed. Julie Novakova (Prague: Academia Pragae, 1992), 43.

2. Goran Simić, *Sprinting from the Graveyard*, English version by David Harsent (Oxford: Oxford University Press, 1997), 14; D. J. Enright, *Collected Poems* (Oxford: Oxford University Press, 1998), 84.

3. Matthew Battles, *Library: An Unquiet History* (London: William Heinemann, 2003).

4. Kathleen Jamie, *The Queen of Sheba* (Newcastle: Bloodaxe, 1994), 11, 10; Les Murray, *The People's Otherworld* (North Ryde, New South Wales: Angus and Robertson, 1983), 60.

5. James W. P. Campbell, *The Library: A World History*, with photographs by Will Pryce (London: Thames and Hudson, 2013), 15.

6. Jorge Luis Borges, *Selected Poems*, ed. Alexander Coleman (London: Allen Lane, 1999), 282, 283, 199.

7. Jorge Luis Borges, *The Total Library: Non-Fiction, 1922–1986*, ed. Eliot Weinberger, trans. Esther Allen, Suzanne Jill Levine, and Eliot Weinberger (London: Allen Lane, 2000), 216.

8. Charles Bukowski, *what matters most is how well you walk through the fire* (New York: Viking Press, 1999), 325–26.

9. Rita Dove, *On the Bus with Rosa Parks* (New York: W. W. Norton, 1999), 32, 33.

10. Abraham Cowley, *The Works: Poems, Miscellanies* (Cambridge: Cambridge University Press, 1905), 409.

11. Margaret Cavendish, *Poems and Phancies* (London: William Wilson, 1664), 209.

12. *Apollos of the North: Selected Poems of George Buchanan and Arthur Johnston*, ed. Robert Crawford (Edinburgh: Polygon, 2006), xlix and 142–43.

13. Cowley, *The Works: Poems, Miscellanies*, 409.

14. Henry Vaughan, *Thalia Rediviva* (London: Robert Fawlet, 1678), 11.

15. Don Paterson, *Nil Nil* (London: Faber and Faber, 1993), 28, 29; *The Poems of Emily Dickinson, Reading Edition*, ed. R. W. Franklin (Cambridge, MA.: Belknap Press of Harvard University Press, 1999), 256.

16. John Donne, *The Poems*, ed. Herbert Grierson (Oxford: Clarendon Press, 1973), 162.

17. *The Poems of Alexander Pope*, ed. John Butt (London: Methuen, 1965), 389.

18. T. A. Ward, *A Short Account of the Sheffield Library, Its Founders, Presidents, and Librarians* (Sheffield: H. A. Bacon, 1825), 6, 5.

19. Ibid., 5, 6, 7, 9, 10.

20. Ibid., 8–9, with some readings from the text in William Hudson, *The Life of John Holland, of Sheffield Park* (London: Longmans, Green, 1874), 29–30.

21. [Anon.] "The Sheffield Library," *Sheffield and Rotherham Independent* June 3, 1896, 5.

22. David Allan, *A Nation of Readers: The Lending Library in Georgian England* (London: British Library, 2008), 40, 84, 88.

23. *The Complete Poetical Works of Percy Bysshe Shelley*, ed. Thomas Hutchinson (Oxford: Humphrey Milford, 1914), 518.

24. Charles Shillito, *The Country Book-Club: A Poem* (London: The Author, 1788), 15, 16, 9, 20, 38.

25. Ibid., 26, 27, 28, 30.

26. Ibid., 31, 6, 38.

27. Ibid., 39.

28. See Robert Crawford, *The Bard: Robert Burns; A Biography* (London: Jonathan Cape, 2009), 312.

29. Robert Burns, *Poems and Songs*, ed. James Kinsley (Oxford: Oxford University Press, 1969), 180, 718.

30. [George Crabbe], *The Library, A Poem* (London: J. Dodsley, 1781), 5.

31. Burns, *Poems and Songs*, 157.

32. [Crabbe], *The Library* (1781), 10.

33. See the later 1807 text as given in *The Poetical Works of George Crabbe*, ed. A. J. Carlyle and R. M. Carlyle (London: Henry Froude, 1908), 27.

34. Ibid., 26.

35. [Crabbe], *The Library* (1781), 9, 18, 11.

36. Ibid., 27, 28, 30, 31, 33–4.

37. Edmund John Armstrong, *Poetical Works*, ed. George Francis Armstrong (London: Longmans, Green, 1877), 381; Andrew Lang, *Poetical Works*, 4 vols. (London: Longmans, Green, 1923), 2: 97, 99.

38. Walt Whitman, *Complete Poetry and Prose*, ed. Justin Kaplan (New York: Library Classics of the United States, 1982), 175.

39. Ralph Waldo Emerson, *Complete Works*, Concord edition, vol. 9 (New York: Houghton Mifflin, 1904), 194.

40. "The Library Association," *Times* October 7, 1880, 6.

41. "Librarians in Congress," *Times* October 6, 1877, 10.

42. Ibid.

43. Oliver Wendell Holmes, *The Writings: Complete Poetical Works* (Boston: Houghton Mifflin, 1891), 183.

44. "International Congress of Women," *Times* July 5, 1899, 10.

45. "Free Libraries," *Graphic* October 15, 1892, 464; "Women as Librarians, by One of the Librarians of the People's Palace," *Monthly Packet* July 1, 1892, 42.

46. "Free Libraries," *Graphic* October 15, 1892, 464.

47. "What Is Read at the People's Palace, A Chat with a Lady Librarian," *Pall Mall Gazette* October 2, 1889, 2.

48. M.S.R. James, "Correspondence," *Monthly Packet* August 1, 1892, 237; M.S.R. James, "Women Librarians and Their Future Prospects," *Library Association Record*, June 1900, 293.

49. Fernanda Helen Perrone, entry for Minnie Stewart Rhodes James in *Oxford Dictionary of National Biography*, ed. H.C.G. Matthew and Brian Harrison (Oxford: Oxford University Press, 2004).

50. "Lady Librarians," *Pall Mall Gazette* May 30, 1890, 3.

51. Lesbia Harford, *The Poems of Lesbia Harford* (Melbourne: Melbourne University Press, 1941), vi.

52. Fleur Adcock, *Poems 1960–2000* (Newcastle: Bloodaxe, 2000), 162; Frank Kuppner, *A Bad Day for the Sung Dynasty* (Manchester: Carcanet, 1984), 64.

53. Susan Howe, *Pierce-Arrow* (New York: New Directions, 1999), 5.

54. Charles Bukowski, *War All the Time* (Santa Barbara: Black Sparrow Press, 1984), 211.

55. Philip Larkin, *Collected Poems*, ed. Anthony Thwaite (London: Faber and Faber, 1988), 161.

56. Harvey Shapiro, *A Day's Portion* (Brooklyn, NY: Hanging Loose Press, 1994), 30.

57. Thom Gunn, *The Man with Night Sweats* (London: Faber and Faber, 1992), 45; Jackie Kay, *Other Lovers* (Newcastle: Bloodaxe, 1993), 46; J. V. Cunningham, *The Collected Poems and Epigrams* (Chicago: Swallow Press, 1971), 80.

58. Sean O'Brien, *Cousin Coat: Selected Poems* (London: Picador, 2002), 85.

59. Stanley Kunitz, *The Lincoln Relics* (Port Townsend, WA: Graywolf Press, 1978), 8; Sean O'Brien, *HMS Glasshouse* (Oxford: Oxford University Press, 1991), 9.

60. Weldon Kees, *Collected Poems*, 3rd edition, ed. Donald Justice (Lincoln: University of Nebraska Press, 2003), 175; Edwin Morgan, *Collected Poems* (Manchester: Carcanet, 1990), 481, 482.

61. Alastair Reid, *Inside Out: Selected Poetry and Translations* (Edinburgh: Polygon, 2008), 85, 86.

62. Robert Crawford, *Full Volume* (London: Cape, 2008), 43.

63. Larkin, *Collected Poems*, ed. Thwaite, 89, 220.

64. Douglas Dunn, *Dante's Drum-kit* (London: Faber and Faber, 1993), 18.

65. Douglas Dunn, *Northlight* (London: Faber and Faber, 1988), 31.

CHAPTER 9

❦

The Library in Film

ORDER AND MYSTERY

Laura Marcus

This chapter focuses on a cluster of interrelated aspects of the library in film: the filmic representation of the space of the library, which will include the image of the haunted library and the library as labyrinth; the figure of the librarian; and the book in the library. It is, to a significant extent, concerned with the opposition and relationship between order and mystery or confusion. Fundamental to representations of the library is the contrast between the ordered rationality of the library as system and the hidden spaces of the library, including its underground stacks, which are frequently represented as the repositories of secret or occulted knowledge. From such representations, it is not a far step to images of the library at night and of the haunted library, played out in the ghost and Gothic fictions of the late eighteenth and the late nineteenth centuries: the latter of these the juncture at which film as a medium entered the scene.

Photography was, of course, the precondition for film, and it revealed, from its inception, a particular fascination with the book as object. The pioneer William Fox Talbot's 1839 photograph *Bookcase* (at Laycock Abbey) was made in the first year of photography: it is an interior shot, representing a wall of books. As Fox Talbot wrote to the scientist and astronomer Sir John Herschel, "there is not enough light for *interiors* at this season of the year, however I intend to try a few more. I find that a *bookcase* makes a very curious & characteristic picture: the different bindings of the books come out, & produce considerable illusion even with imperfect execution."[1] It was followed a year later by *A Scene in a Library* (see plate 26) included in *The Pencil of Nature*, the volume in which he juxtaposed passages of explanatory text with photographic plates to produce the earliest photographically illustrated book. *A Scene in a Library* shows two shelves of books, "arrayed in a mixture of orderliness and disorder," in Carol Armstrong's words, not all of whose inscriptions are fully legible. [2] They have, however, been identified as including three volumes of Wilkinson's *Manners and Customs of the Ancient Egyptians*, *Philological Essays*, *Miscellanies of Science*, *Botanische Schriften*, *La storia pittorica dell'Italia de Luigi Lanzi*, the first three volumes of the *Philosophical Magazine* (which contained numerous essays by Fox Talbot), and three volumes of Thomas Gaisford's edition of *Poetae Minores Graeci*.[3] For André Jammes, who has researched the holdings in Fox Talbot's library, the photograph could be understood as a self-portrait: Fox Talbot's wide ranging interests included philosophy, Egyptology, classical mythology, and scientific experiment. For *A Scene in a Library* (and similar images taken at this time), Fox Talbot photographed the books outdoors, setting them up on artificial shelves. The clarity of the books' appearance as individuated objects seems to have been particularly striking to contemporary viewers.

The passage of prose that accompanied the plate *A Scene in a Library* described an imagined "curious *experiment or speculation*" in which the "invisible rays" (what we would now term ultraviolet) that lie beyond the solar spectrum would be passed into an adjoining apartment through an aperture in a wall or screen:

> This apartment would thus become filled (we must not call it *illuminated*) with invisible rays, which might be scattered in all directions by a convex lens placed behind the aperture. If there were a number of persons in the room, no one would see the other: and yet nevertheless if a *camera* were so placed as to point in the direction in which any one were standing, it would take his portrait, and reveal his actions
>
> For, to use a metaphor we have already employed, the eye of the camera would see plainly where the human eye would find nothing but darkness.

Alas! that this speculation is somewhat too refined to be in-troduced with effect into a modern novel or romance; for what a *dénouement* we should have, if we could suppose the secrets of the darkened chamber to be revealed by the testimony of the imprinted paper.[4]

Carol Armstrong reads this enigmatic passage, and the opacity of its relationship to the image that it accompanies, as an analogy for the complex text-image relationship in *The Pencil of Nature*: "the text thematizes subjectivity—the subjectivity of the 'darkened chamber' described by the camera and attached to photography, whereas the photograph, exchanging places with the text, thematizes the library and with it, readership. . . . The 'testimony of the imprinted paper' that is photography breeds a whole new library with a new kind of publication in it, a new, as yet un-realized apparatus of the printed book."[5]

The very concept of "the pencil of nature" reminds us of the etymology of "photography" as "light-writing": Fox Talbot's fascination with scripts of many kinds, hieroglyphic and phonetic, is revealed in a number of his photographs, which include images of pages written in Middle Eastern languages and of hieroglyphic tablets, as well as photographs of the objects and artifacts that he collected. The "imprinted paper" of the photographic image is a mode of written text, but it is one captured by an "eye" that can penetrate beyond the human capacities of sight and it can "inventory" groups of objects in the simultaneity of their coex-istence, rather than having to submit to the linearity and sequence of cursive inscription.

Alain Resnais's 1956 documentary film of the former Bibliothèque nationale in Paris, *Toute la mémoire du monde*, opens in a subterranean space, where we begin to see, as if our eyes were becoming accustomed to the dark, the emerging outlines of what appear to be a camera and a mi-crophone. As in Fox Talbot's "speculation," the camera, without apparent human agency, has entered the space of the darkened chamber and will reveal its secrets: "panning upward from a dusty, haphazard pile of old books (which has served as background for the credits)."[6] The light that flashes on is further reminiscent of the torchlight shone through aper-tures to illuminate the treasures of walled-up Egyptian tombs, as in the highly charged moment in 1922 in which the torch of the archaeologist

Howard Carter revealed the tomb of King Tutankhamun and its contents.[7] This Egyptological echo is reinforced by the presentation of the underground library's contents as grave objects. It emerges in other library films, both through reference to the scrolls of the great library at Alexandria and to the hieroglyphic scripts that became, in the earliest theorizations of cinema, represented as film's originary language, a pictorial script lying somewhere between word and image.

The Bibliothèque nationale is represented by Resnais as the repository of knowledge at once secret and universal. The film traverses, through its extensive use of tracking shots, both the interior and the exterior of the building. It also creates a striking interplay between the vertical and the horizontal spaces of the library: lifts move up and down between floors, and trolleys are pushed across the length of the library bays. Human figures are glimpsed only fleetingly. The architecture of the library must, in order to accommodate its ever increasing stock, the voice-over tells us, burrow ever further underground and reach ever higher toward the sky. At the heart of the library, "this gigantic memory," "a model memory," is the great catalogue, which classifies and inventories: "with no catalogue, this fortress would be a maze." Resnais observed of the film that his screenwriter, Remo Forlani, and he "wanted to insist on this very important notion of the usefulness of books and show the infinite, vertiginous aspect of memory."[8]

The focus is on the library's spatial organization, but this is not distinct from representation of time, and the movement through the library, and the concentration on its particular treasures, from the ancient to the modern, renders the library a kind of time machine. There are explicit references to time travel and the world of science fiction in the film: the humble book we follow from its arrival at the sorting depot of the library to its placement on the library shelves is called *Mars*, and glimpses of its content pages reveal that it includes a chapter entitled "X-ray" and one on H. G. Wells. More explicitly, the temperature and humidity control room of the library contains, we are told, "machinery resembling that of Captain Nemo," from the Jules Verne novel in which the library of the Nautilus appears. At the close of Resnais's film, the voice-over pronounces that the range of disciplinary knowledge held in the library gives us "a glimpse of a future in which all mysteries are resolved, the keys to this and other universes." Each reader "working on his slice of universal memory will lay the fragments of a single secret end to end—the secret of human happiness."

This utopian invocation (the sum of knowledge as human happiness) is to some extent at odds with the overall tenor of much of the film, in which library readers are referred to as "paper-crunching pseudo-insects" fed by the materials they call up and in which the library itself becomes a fortress built to contain the mass of words that threaten to overwhelm us. Resnais's focus on "memory," and on the library as a site of memory, would, in 1956, when the film was released, almost certainly have been linked to the short film he had made the previous year, *Nuit et brouillard* (*Night and Fog*), a desolating representation of the Nazi concentration camps of World War II in which Resnais used extensive archive material, including photographs and newsreels. The concept of the library, in *Toute la mémoire du monde*, as a space of transcendence (created by the panning upward of the camera, to capture the great dome of the library as well as the statues, figures of the French Enlightenment, that line its walls) would not have been free from the troubling issues of culture and barbarism that run through so much of the thought of the postwar period.

Resnais's film further suggests that camera movement is the only kind of vision capable of encompassing the complex spatiality of the library— its interiority and exteriority; its spaces underground and overhead; its long, empty stacks; its populated circular reading room. The role of cinema as a recording medium is also highly significant; if the library is the site of memory, it is the province of film to preserve memory most completely. Fragile documents, including ephemera such as newspapers, are microfilmed; "Once captured on film—these pictures will perpetuate the memory of perishable documents. While this slow battle against death goes on, calls go out. Messages are endlessly spat forth across the labyrinth of stores."

Images of the library as maze or labyrinth have a long history, on which Jorge Luis Borges called in his story "The Library of Babel" (1941, published in English in 1962), and in the essay "The Total Library," which he published in 1939. Borges, himself a librarian (in 1955 he became director of the National Public Library in Buenos Aires), explored, in his short story, themes that would enter, more or less explicitly, into a range of texts and films: the infinite book and/or the infinite library; the universal library (which is the work of God) and Man, "the imperfect librarian"; the paradoxical understanding of the library as at once disorder and ultimate Order. Many of Borges's short stories inscribe the topoi and tropes that became central to postmodernist detective fiction—the labyrinth and the library, the book within a book, mirrors and doubles—and exploit the puzzle elements of the detective story genre, and the potential for both reading and misreading the nature of plot and pattern.

Umberto Eco's *The Name of the Rose* (1980, adapted for cinema in 1986) is a fiction woven around "The Library of Babel" and other Borges stories, including the representation of the architecture of the library, composed of a seemingly infinite series of hexagonal rooms, which Eco reconfigures as heptagons. As the detective figure, William of Baskerville, defines it: "The maximum of confusion achieved with the maximum of order: it seems a sublime calculation. The builders of the library were great masters."[9] William, accompanied by his young protégé, Adso, is investigating the murder of Venantius, a monk murdered in 1327 because he has located a valuable book hidden in the library of the monastery. Venantius had recorded the book's location in an encrypted message, which William must decipher in order both to solve the mystery of the murder—one of a series of murders in the monastery—and to find the hidden text. The detective's task is thus one of decipherment, and delay is the product of misreading and misinterpretation.

The encrypting of texts is also echoed in the space to which William is finally led—the library as labyrinth—while the letter literally kills, as the murderer, Jorge of Burgos, poisons the pages on which the secret and subversive book (an imagined treatise on comedy written by Aristotle) is written, thus destroying those who attempt to read it. The name of the murderer, and the attribute of blindness, are very close to the name and the identity of Jorge Borges. As Eco wrote in his postscript to the novel: "I wanted a blind man who guarded a library (it seemed a good narrative idea to me), and library plus blind man can only equal Borges, also because debts must be paid."[10] The concept of literary debt would in this instance seem a somewhat ambiguous one.

Resnais's film of the Bibliothèque nationale has, as we have seen, borrowed the terms of the fantastical, labyrinthine library as the repository of a universal knowledge to shape perceptions of an actual, existing library. Real libraries have featured in numerous films, from cinema's early years onward. Alfred Hitchcock's villain in *Blackmail* (1928) is chased by police through the sculpture galleries of the British Museum and the Reading Room of the former British Library, before falling to his death through the library's great glass dome. The British Museum Library was also a setting for the 1957 Jacques Tourneur horror film *Night of the Demon*, an adaptation by Hitchcock's screenwriter Charles Bennett of M. R. James's 1911 short story "Casting the Runes," in which a key scene takes place in the Special Manuscript Room of the British Library. The New York Public Library has frequently been represented in film (it features prominently in Blake Edwards's *Breakfast at Tiffany's* [1961]), and it plays a central role in the comic-horror film *Ghostbusters* (Ivan Rietman, 1984). The Library of Congress is depicted in a number of scenes in *All the President's Men* (Alan J. Pakula, 1976) (a fictionalized version of the Watergate scandal) and in Disney's *National Treasure: Book of Secrets* (2007), which creates a fictional XY classification and a secret compartment in the library's stacks for the volume of the title, a book containing the top secrets of the nation, to be viewed by its presidents alone.

Wim Wenders's *Wings of Desire* (*Der Himmel über Berlin*, 1987) used the space of the new Staatsbibliothek, in former West Berlin, inaugurated in 1978, and the film reveals the intimate relationship between architecture and cinema, a relationship that could be triangulated to include the space of the library. "Every librarian is, up to a certain point, an architect," asserts Michel Melot, director of the Centre Pompidou Library. "He builds up his collection as an ensemble through which the reader must find a path, discover his own self, and live."[11]

The links between the written or type-written word and the medium of film, like those between cinema and architecture, are of some complexity. Wim Wenders's film opens and closes with the angel, Damiel, reading and copying lines of poetry celebrating childhood. In interview, Wenders confirms that both the handwriting and the library were (in the interviewer's words) "gestures towards the written word." It is significant that Damiel, the angel who wishes to fall into the physicality of the world, takes up a pen (or the spirit of a pen), the instrument of writing, of inscription, from the library table. Such representations of "the written word" seem increasingly foregrounded in contemporary cinema, in which we frequently see a line of print-type or of hand-writing inaugurating, or perhaps even releasing, the visual images that follow.

For Wenders, writing and the book, memory, and public space come together in the "utopia" of the library. As he has written of *Wings of Desire*:

> When we were looking for a place in the city where the angels would live, would be at home, we looked for some time. Since angels are not really linked between people and God anymore we could not do a church, so we tried for another place. Then I remembered the ending of one of my favorite films, Truffaut's *Fahrenheit 451*, which is in this big open space, and there are all these people and everybody represents a book that they have learned by heart because books are persecuted and burned; and to me that was really a vision of paradise, with all these people walking around and sitting on benches in the park. I thought this is a heavenly place, a library, and then we found this big public library in Berlin, and it's really a wonderful place, with a lot of light, and built with a lot of respect for reading and books, and also so peaceful and quiet. There is also the whole memory and knowledge of mankind united there.[12]

In *Wings of Desire* (as in its Hollywood remake *City of Angels* [1998], which used the San Francisco Public Library as a setting) the library is the home of the angels who act as the comforters of the living and are able to listen in to their subconscious thoughts. Wenders has stated of the film that the camera was the eye of the angel, and the critic Ruth Perlmutter follows this in her suggestion that "the angels are cinema; theirs is the ideal ability to record and transmit, to access and represent individuals in their world and to save them from despair."[13] The open spaces of the library in the film become linked with the omniscient, aerial perspectives of the angels from the high places of the city and are contrasted with the enclosed spaces of small apartments, trains, and cars in which the city's inhabitants spend much of their lives. The library thus comes to represent a spatial freedom, a utopia (as Wenders suggests in his account of the influence of the close of *Fahrenheit 451*), made more charged by the dystopia of the divided city.

The library is also particularly important in relation to the film's soundscape. The interior monologues (which the angels are able to access) are those of the readers, so that a connection is set up between the book, the reader, and sound film's ability to represent interior monologue through voice-over. This takes on a very specific resonance in the library, which, as an institution, has a commitment to silence or, at least, to the whisper. Fragments of inner thoughts in the extended library scene in *Wings of Desire* include references to Walter Benjamin's purchase of Paul Klee's painting *Angelus Novus* in the 1920s: the image that informed Benjamin's allegory of the "angel of history," with his face turned toward the past, whose wreckage piles up before his feet: "The angel would like to stay, awaken the dead, and make whole what has been smashed. But a storm is blowing from Paradise and has got caught in his wings. . . . This storm drives him irresistibly into the future, to which his back is turned. . . . What we call progress is *this* storm."[14] There are also Benjaminian echoes in the film's figure of the storyteller—the old man called Homer—whom we see at the very end of the sequence, climbing up the library stairs. The old man represents not only storytelling but "collective memory, the spirit of history [and] the spirit of Berlin,"[15] and the library is his home.

Resnais's *Toute la mémoire du monde*, Truffaut's *Fahrenheit 451*, and Wenders's *Wings of Desire* are closely connected through their concerns with memory, and (to borrow the historian Pierre Nora's phrase), *lieux de mémoire*, sites of memory. Modern memory, claims Pierre Nora (who perceives "memory culture" as a result of the loss of living memory) "is, above all, archival. It relies entirely on the materiality of the trace, the immediacy of the recording, the visibility of the image. What began as writing ends as high fidelity and tape recording. . . . No longer living memory's more or less intended remainder, the archive has become the deliberate and calculated secretion of lost memory. It adds to life—itself often a function of its own recording—a secondary memory, a prosthesis memory." Writing of the paradoxical relationship in modern culture between the loss and the maintenance of memory (in archives and other forms of commemorative culture), Nora writes: "It is this very push and pull that produces *lieux de mémoire*—moments of history torn away from the movement of history, then returned; no longer quite life, nor yet death, like shells on the shore when the sea of living memory has receded."[16]

These issues are central to the final work of the German writer W. G. Sebald, the novel *Austerlitz* (2001), the story of Jacques Austerlitz, one of the Jewish children brought to Britain on the *Kindertransporte* of the 1930s and given a new identity. Throughout the course of the novel, Austerlitz narrates (to an unnamed interlocutor) the ways in which memories or "buried experiences" returned to him, in places of transit (notably the railway stations of Europe) and through his work as an architectural historian, in which he is driven by a particular fascination with the structures of fortresses and other historic and bureaucratically organized and ordered places of imprisonment. His quest is increasingly for his lost mother, who, he believes, was taken to the concentration camp at Teresienstadt and, subsequently, for his father, who might have escaped to France.

Toward the novel's close, Austerlitz speaks of his earlier studies in Paris and his work at the Bibliothèque nationale in rue Richelieu, in which he was engaged, like his fellow scholars, in researches at once meticulous and never ending. Some years later, he recounts, while watching "a short black and white film about the Bibliothèque Nationale . . . it struck me that the scholars, together with the whole apparatus of the library, formed an immensely complex and constantly evolving creature which had to be fed with myriads of words, in order to bring forth myriads of words in its own turn."[17] The reference is to Resnais's film *Toute la mémoire du monde*, and it is one of the many invocations of film, and of photography, in the novel, tied into its conceptual and perceptual network, in which questions of personal memory and historical evidence are central.

Austerlitz (and Sebald as his creator) also uses the memory of Resnais's film to draw the contrast to the old Bibliothèque nationale, now closed— "the domed hall with its green porcelain lampshades which cast such a soothing, pleasant light is deserted, the books have been taken off the shelves, and the readers, who once sat at the desks numbered with little enamel plates, in close contact with their neighbors and silent harmony with those who had gone before them, might have vanished from the face of the earth."[18] The new library, the Grande Bibliothèque, is, by contrast, a "hideous, outsize building, the monumental dimensions of which were evidently inspired by the late President's wish to perpetuate his memory whilst, perhaps because it had to serve this purpose, it was so conceived that it is, as I realized on my first visit, said Austerlitz, both in its outer appearance and inner constitution unwelcoming if not inimical to human beings, and runs counter, on principle, one might say, to the requirements of any true reader."[19] The towers of the new Grand Library "named in a manner reminiscent of a futuristic novel *La tour des lois*, *La tour des temps*, *La tour des nombres*, and *La tour des lettres*, make a positively Babylonian impression on anyone who looks up at their façades and wonders about the still largely empty space behind their closed blinds." [20]

While researching in this "Babylonian" library, President Mitterrand's self-monument, Austerlitz is approached by a member of the library staff, Henri Lemoine (whose name translates as "The Monk," thus forming a further connection with the monastery murder mystery *The Name of the Rose*), who once worked at the old library in rue Richelieu. In very close approximation to Pierre Nora's arguments about modern memory, Sebald writes "about the dissolution, in line with the inexorable spread of processed data, of our capacity to remember. . . . The new library building, which in both its entire layout and its near-ludicrous internal regulation seeks to exclude the reader as a potential enemy, might be described, so Lemoine thought, said Austerlitz, as the official manifestation of the increasingly importunate urge to break with everything which still has some living connection to the past."[21] Taking him up to the top of one of the library towers in order to look down at the city below, Lemoine tells Austerlitz of the underground warehouses used during World War II by the occupying Germans to store the valuables they took from the Jews before they were deported: "the whole affair is buried in the most literal sense beneath the foundations of our pharaonic President's Grande Bibliothèque, said Lemoine."[22]

In my discussion of Resnais's film, I pointed to the ambivalent, if not dystopian, elements of its representations of the library. For Sebald, it is this library, in part as it is represented in Resnais's film, which is experienced or remembered as a site of collaborative labors and collective memory. The new library, by contrast, is experienced as bombastic in its architecture and hostile to its users. Its external and internal structures are intended, Sebald suggests, to force a total break with the past, while its "near-ludicrous internal regulation" must summon up, for the reader, the novel's representations of the itemized and rationalized machinery of Nazi regimes of destruction. The highly charged nature of Austerlitz's depictions can stem only from the perceived barbarity of building a library, of all institutions, to the ends of self-aggrandizement, bureaucratic regulation, and the destruction of living memory.

Truffaut's *Fahrenheit 451*, invoked by Wenders as an inspiration for *Wings of Desire*, ties in a concern with memory culture particularly closely with the representation of technology. Television is perceived in entirely negative terms. Here, as elsewhere, it is implied that the medium of film is on the side of the book (and the library) not the mindless "sedative" of the television screen in the home. In Truffaut's film, as in the Ray Bradbury novel on which it is based (in turn indebted to Huxley's *Brave New World* [1932] and Orwell's *Nineteen Eighty-Four* [1949]), television (understood as the most significant threat to cinema in the second half of the twentieth century) comes to embody a society without memory, a present time without depth or ambition: books, by contrast, come to stand for memory, time, feeling, empathy, complexity. This is what film (marking an absolute distinction between itself and the continuous, memory-less present of television) allies itself to. In its attempt to burn all the books, the state seeks to destroy interior life and the freedom of human interactions. In the final scene of the film, to which Wenders alludes, we see the dissidents from this memory-less culture, the Book People, each learning a single book by heart before the volume is destroyed: the human mind and memory become living substitutes for the lost library. The central protagonist of the film, Montag (Oskar Werner), the former "Fireman," or destroyer of books, who joins the Book People, begins his apprenticeship to literature with Dickens's *David Copperfield* and, at the film's close, is shown beginning to learn and recite Poe's *Tales of Mystery and Imagination*.

If we turn to popular and Hollywood cinema, we find that libraries have been consistent settings in films from its early years onward, often sharing the emphases of the European films I have been discussing. James Bridges's *The Paper Chase* (1973) condenses the iconography of the library at night, the library as the repository of secrets, and the transmission of memory and knowledge. It offers a familiar image of the female librarian guarding the inner sanctum, followed by a nocturnal adventure by the film's central protagonist James Hart (Timothy Bottoms) and one of his fellow law students. Hart's torch shines into the dark, enclosed space of the library stacks to reveal its treasures: red archive boxes that take on tomb-like form and that contain the wisdom of the past, in the shape of the lecture notes taken by the feared and revered law professor Kingsfield (John Houseman) in his student days. At the close of the sequence, Hart, lying on his bed, performs his own writing on the wall, in a cinematic shadow play, inscribing the letter S, which is at once the initial of the woman with whom he is having an affair (Susan, Professor Kingsfield's daughter) and the Greek "sigma," understood here as a kind of hieroglyphic, the sign of an occulted, hieratic knowledge.

A loose archaism, a gesturing toward an undifferentiated "ancient world," again brings into being the Egyptological, and summons up the Library of Alexandria, the ambitions for which were that it would be, in the writer and bibliophile Alberto Manguel's words, "the storehouse for the memory of the world." As Manguel writes: "The heroes of Virgil, of Herman Melville, of Joseph Conrad, of most epic literature, embrace this Alexandrian belief. For them, the world (like the Library) is made up of myriad stories that, through tangled mazes, lead to a revelatory moment set up for them alone."[23] "Myriad stories," and storytelling, are also the narrative motors of the French director Jacques Rivette's *Céline and Julie Go Boating* (1974): in this film the library, in which one of the two young women protagonists works while the other makes her living as a magician, is the prelude to their entry into a mysterious alternative, and theatrical, world, whose plots they gradually learn to master and alter.

The representation of the library as the site and the container for secret and hidden knowledge is heightened in the ghost story. In M. R. James's ghost stories of the turn of the nineteenth century, an intimate relation of terror is drawn between the private library (with its antiquarian dimensions) and the book in the library, and haunted and secret spaces, including mazes and labyrinths. Books and engravings take on their own, malevolent life, frequently figured through forms of *vagina dentata*, opening up from within to pull those who read or look at them into the abyss. *Ghostbusters*, a spoof on the ghost story genre, begins with a scene in the New York Public Library, and a stereotypical representation of a female librarian as the embodiment of various forms of repression. The poltergeistic spraying out of the card catalogue turns the library's system into misrule: the cards fly like birds (there are echoes, indeed, of Hitchcock's *The Birds* [1963]), or small ghosts, in a demonstration of the precarious ways in which the library catalogue maintains order in the face of ever-threatening chaos. The personified library ghost, whom we see a little later, is also a female librarian, shelving books and dressed in the clothes of a previous century. She performs the stereotypical librarian's "Shhhh" to the Ghostbusters before turning toward them to reveal a horrendous skeletal figure.

The representation of libraries has also been central to science fiction cinema. I earlier noted the brief visual reference to H. G. Wells, and the invocation of Jules Verne, in Resnais's film. Libraries feature prominently in the various film versions of Wells's *The Time Machine*, expanding on the brief appearance of the decayed library in the novel:

> [W]e went out of that gallery and into another still larger, which at the first glance reminded me of a military chapel hung with tattered flags. The brown and charred rags that hung from the sides of it, I presently recognized as the decaying vestiges of books. They had long since dropped to pieces, and every semblance of print had left them. But here and there were warped boards and cracked metallic clasps that told the tale well enough.
>
> Had I been a literary man I might, perhaps, have moralized upon the futility of all ambition.[24]

The 2002 version of the film, directed by Wells's great-grandson Simon Wells, depicts the New York Public Library in 2023 and gives us Vox, a database hologram who claims to be the "compendium of human knowledge." Vox responds to the time traveller's question about time-travel logistics with information on H. G. Wells and the 1960 George Pal film version of *The Time Machine*. The hologram librarian is still in (virtual) existence when the traveller arrives in a time eight hundred thousand years beyond his own present. As one commentator has noted, libraries in science fiction films are almost invariably the sites in which the hero (time traveller or otherwise) discovers the secret that explains the basis of the dystopian society and its mechanisms of power.[25] This is the case for films including *The Time Machine*, *Zardoz*, *Soylent Green*, *Roller Ball*, *Logan's Run*, and *Battlefield Earth*. In John Boorman's 1974 film *Zardoz* (which owes a good deal to *The Time Machine*), for example, it is revealed that the central protagonist, Zed (Sean Connery), time travelling to the year 2239, had earlier found, in a forgotten, dust-covered library, the book that revealed to him the secrets of the film's eponymous godhead and the society over which he rules.

The 2002 version of *The Time Machine* also repeats the trope, found in Pal's film version, of the book that crumbles to dust under the time traveller's touch. This image comes to represent the irony and the pathos of a lost history and civilization, with the book again standing for memory and its erasure. The loss of the book and of the library is perceived as, or as the sign of, a culture's greatest tragedy (a theme that runs through to recent films such as *Agora* [2009], which represents the destruction of the great library at Alexandria). There is rarely any sense given in science fiction films that the futuristic technologies around which the films revolve have in any meaningful way replaced the book, or the library that held it, as the repository of knowledge.

In more general terms, there is a strikingly widespread presence of librarians and libraries in Hollywood cinema. It has been estimated that there are some five hundred films in which librarians feature or are mentioned. The stock characterization of the (usually) female librarian has been frequently noted. One of the least favored film representations among library professionals is the sequence in Frank Capra's *It's A Wonderful Life* (1946), in which the film's hero, George Bailey (James Stewart), is shown by the angel Clarence Odbody (Henry Travers), who has been sent down to Earth to dissuade George from suicide, that the "fate" of Mary (Donna Reed), George's wife, had he never lived, would have been to become the unmarried town librarian. It would certainly appear to be the case that the briefer the vignette, the more likely the film librarian is to conform to the familiar negative stereotype of the dowdy spinster, almost invariably "closing up the library" for the night. In more recent films, we find, however, fewer representations of the stereotypical spinster librarian and instances of anarchic young women becoming subject to the library's order and system, as in *Party Girl* (Daisy von Scherler Mayer, 1995), in which the wayward heroine takes a job as a library clerk in order to pay off a police fine and, coming to embrace her role as librarian, determines to master the Dewey Decimal System. In *Salmonberries* (Percy Adlon, 1991), the library comes to be associated with an active female sexuality and with relationships between women.

On occasion, earlier Hollywood films represented the bitterness and anger that was perceived to lie on the other side of repression, as in the 1932 film *Forbidden*, in which Barbara Stanwyck, playing a small-town librarian taunted by the local children, utters the striking line: "I wish I owned this library. . . . I'd get an axe and smash it to a million pieces, then I'd set fire to the whole town and play a ukulele while it burned." A different take on the beleaguered librarian emerged in the 1956 film *Storm Center*, in which the librarian, played by Bette Davis, encounters opposition from a blue-collar father whose son she is encouraging to read, and from the town as a whole, when she refuses to remove a book that supports communist ideals. The library is set on fire, and we see the titles of the books as they burn: at the close of the film the librarian declares her intention to rebuild the library. *Storm Center* was heavily criticized (and given a "separate classification") by the Legion of Decency for its "pro-communist leanings." In a very different cultural context, Tian Chuangzhuang's *The Blue Kite* (1993) narrates the story of ordinary lives destroyed by the Chinese Communist Party during the years of the Cultural Revolution, beginning with the life of Shalong (Pu Quanxin), a quiet and dedicated librarian whose colleagues sacrifice him to the "Rectification Movement" (the "Hundred Flowers Campaign") when they are forced to meet their quota of political renegades destined for "reeducation" by the party.

Representations of the library as a public space have been a key narrative motor in cinema. In Hollywood film, as in other national cinemas, the small-town library frequently becomes a synecdoche for the town itself, and beyond that for the nation. The library (like the schoolhouse) is at the heart of the concept of community. At the same time (and unlike the schoolhouse), it is a space into which strangers can (under certain conditions) enter. To explore this representation fully in Hollywood cinema would be to engage with the role of the public library, and the history of library provision in the United States, including the central role played by the Carnegie libraries. It would also open up the ways in which libraries come to represent issues of belonging and of exclusion in the broader society, based on class, race, and ethnicity, as in the films *Goodbye, Columbus* and *Sophie's Choice* (Alan J. Pakula, 1982), both of which depict deeply unsympathetic, "WASP," male librarians. In *Goodbye, Columbus* (Larry Peerce, 1969, adapted from Philip Roth's story) this negative representation is mitigated by the role of the central protagonist, Neil Klugman (Richard Benjamin), working as a library clerk, whose own "outsider" position gives him empathy with the young black boy from the ghetto who comes again and again to the public library to look at Gauguin's images of Tahiti and to dream of a better life.

In numerous films, the library (whether a private, small-town, city, or national library) and its holdings become the means by which protagonists can discover (often in the face of obstructive librarians, as in *Shadow of a Doubt* [Alfred Hitchcock, 1943] or *Chinatown* [Roman Polanski, 1974]) the secrets that drive the plot and will, in some cases, ultimately resolve it. Scenes in libraries (frequently involving searches through newspapers or legal documents) condense the processes of research and investigation and come to stand for the hermeneutics of the film as a whole.

One of the most striking filmic examples in this context is Orson Welles's *Citizen Kane* (1941). Searching for the meaning of the newspaper magnate Charles Kane's life in his dying word—"Rosebud"—the journalist Thomson gains entry into the inner sanctum of the Walter Parks Thatcher Memorial Library, in order to read the diary of Thatcher, Kane's former guardian. The library scene opens with a shot of a marble statue of Thatcher, panning down to its pedestal and inscription and, below it, a desk at which sits the library's female archivist. She is named in the film's screenplay as Bertha Anderson, "an elderly, mannish spinster," and her uniform and demeanor throughout the scene are suggestive of a prison commandant. She leads Thomson toward a heavy, embossed door, and there is a dissolve to the interior of the vault room, which resembles a mausoleum. The lighting in the scene, with beams of projected light, makes the link to the projection room in which the newsreel of Kane's life had earlier been screened to a group of editors and journalists, and to cinematic projection more generally. An armed guard in the vault brings out the journal from a wall safe, and Thomson is instructed by the archivist that he must confine his time-limited reading "to the chapter dealing with Mr. Kane."

As Thomson begins to read the journal, the camera moves onto the page of the manuscript, "following the words with the same action [as] the eye does the reading." There is then a dissolve from the white of the page to a field of white snow, and the film's foundational scene, in which Thatcher goes to take the young Charles Kane away from his parents' home and into his new life. This is followed by scenes of Kane as a young man, running his first newspaper, and scandalizing Thatcher in the process, before a dissolve back to the library and its vault room, from which Thomson is now ejected by the fierce librarian. The large portrait of Thatcher presiding over the room hints at the ways in which the picture of Kane in his journal has been filtered through Thatcher's perspectives, but the architecture of the vault and the library are also connected, through their monumentalism and the use of expressionist lighting and deep focus cinematography, to Kane's palace Xanadu. The library, like Xanadu, is a repository for hidden knowledge, while the manuscript pages of the journal provide access to scenes that are represented as the film and the spectator's realities, and not merely as those of Thatcher. The camera eye (rendered akin to the reading eye in the library scene), with its powers to transgress the "No Trespassing" sign with which the film opens and closes, has an intimate relationship to the manuscript through which we gain access to the past, moving us from the written word (the singularity of the handwritten, in contrast to the endlessly reproducible typewriting associated in the film with Kane) to the visual image. *Citizen Kane* is, finally, a quest narrative, one dimension of which is that the book in the library, as in a number of the films I've discussed, might hold the secrets for which answers or solutions are being sought. Ultimately, however, the film's central mystery—the meaning of a life—is never fully resolved.

"If there is a counterpart to the confusion of a library, it is the order of its catalogue," Walter Benjamin wrote in his essay, "Unpacking My Library."[26] The relationship between order and confusion is also at the heart of Alberto Manguel's writings on libraries, books, and the history of reading: "The order decreed by library catalogues is, at night, merely conventional; it holds no prestige in the shadows," he writes in his *The Library at Night* [27] and, in a discussion of classificatory systems in libraries, private and public, "Every library translates the chaos of discovery and creation into a structured system of hierarchies or a rampage of free associations."

For Adso, in *The Name of the Rose*, the discovery of the library gives him a new and frightening insight, into the nature of the world:

Until then I had thought each book spoke of the things, human or divine, that lie outside books. Now I realized that not infrequently books speak of books: it is as if they spoke among themselves. In the light of this reflection, the library seemed all the more disturbing to me. It was then the place of a long, centuries-old murmuring, an imperceptible dialogue between one parchment and another, a living thing, a receptacle of powers not to be ruled by a human mind, a treasure of secrets emanated by many minds, surviving the death of those who had produced them or had been their conveyors.[28]

These questions and representations might, at first glance, seem to be entirely the province of literature and not of cinema. But it is striking how so many films have taken up these questions of order and of mystery or confusion, as well as ideas of haunting in relation to the book and the library. The conceit of a "murmuring" among books, of which Eco writes, might translate, in rather literal terms, into the "whispering" in the stacks that denotes, in numerous films, the discovery of a secret in the library. It is there, in more subtle ways, in the "murmuring" of inner speech picked up by Wim Wenders's microphone, as by his cinematic angels.

In exploring the library in film we also begin to open up the complexities of the relationship between literature and cinema, the book and the film: the film that actualizes the book, the book that is the origin of the film. In its various representations of the library, film as a medium reveals its own complex, ambivalent relationships to the book and to the medium of print from which it both derives so much of its narrative drive and which it has, to some extent, come to replace. As film moves into its own digital era, the auratic representations of an earlier cinema, of the book, and of the library are likely to become ever more heightened.

NOTES

1. Henry Talbot to Sir John Herschel, December 7, 1839, quoted by Larry J. Schaaf in *The Photographic Art of William Henry Fox Talbot* (Princeton, NJ: Princeton University Press, 2000), 64.

2. Carol Armstrong, *Scenes in a Library: Reading the Photograph in the Book, 1843–1875* (Cambridge, MA: MIT Press, 1998), 125.

3. Schaaf, 190, drawing on André Jammes, "A Scene in a Library," *Photographie*, no. 1 (Spring 1983): 50.

4. William Henry Fox Talbot, *The Pencil of Nature* (London: Longman, Brown, Green and Longman's, 1844), plate VIII, 29–30.

5. Armstrong, *Scenes in a Library*, 129–30.

6. Noel Burch, "Four Recent French Documentaries," *Film Quarterly* 13.1 (Autumn 1959): 58.

7. "[A]s my eyes grew accustomed to the light, details of the room within emerged slowly from the mist, strange animals, statues, and gold—everywhere the glint of gold. For the moment—an eternity it must have seemed to the others standing by—I was struck dumb with amazement, and when Lord Carnarvon, unable to stand the suspense any longer, inquired anxiously, 'Can you see anything?' it was all I could do to get out the words, 'Yes, wonderful things.'" (Howard Carter, *The Tomb of Tutankhamen* (New York: Dutton, 1972, 1954), 35.

8. Quoted in Roy Armes, *The Cinema of Alain Resnais* (London: Zwemmer, 1968), 56.

9. Umberto Eco, *The Name of the Rose*, trans. William Weaver (London: Picador, 1983), 217.

10. Umberto Eco, *Postscript to "The Name of the Rose,"* trans. William Weaver (New York: Harcourt Brace Jovanovich, 1984), 28.

11. Michel Melot, *La sagesse du bibliothécaire*, quoted in Alberto Manguel, *The Library at Night* (New Haven, CT: Yale University Press, 2008), 133.

12. Ira Paneth, "Wim and His Wings," *Film Quarterly* 42.1 (Autumn 1988): 2–8.

13. Quoted in Robert Phillip Kolker and Peter Beicken, *The Films of Wim Wenders: Cinema as Vision and Desire* (Cambridge: Cambridge University Press, 1993), 143.

14. Walter Benjamin, "On the Concept of History," in his *Selected Writings*, ed. Michael W. Jennings. Vol. 4, 1938–1940 (Cambridge, MA: Harvard University Press, 2003), 392.

15. Kolker and Beicken, *The Films of Wim Wenders*, 141.

16. Pierre Nora, "Between Memory and History: *Les Lieux de Mémoire*," trans. Marc Roudebush, *Representations* 26 (Spring 1989): 12.

17. W. G. Sebald, *Austerlitz*, trans. Anthea Bell (London: Hamish Hamilton, 2001), 364.

18. Ibid., 385–86.

19. Ibid., 386.

20. Ibid., 389.

21. Ibid., 398.

22. Ibid., 403.

23. Manguel, *The Library at Night*, 27.

24. H. G. Wells, *The Time Machine* (New York: Henry Holt, 1895), 160.

25. Tom Goodfellow, *The Depiction of American Public Libraries in Film*, dissertation for MA in Information Services Management at University of North London, 2000. Ch.8, "Libraries and Science Fiction." Available online at http://www.angelfire.com/oz/tomgoodfellow/LibrariesinFilm.htm.

26. Walter Benjamin, "Unpacking My Library," in his *Selected Writings*, ed. Michael W. Jennings. Vol. 2, 1927–1934 (Cambridge, MA: Harvard University Press, 1999), 487.

27. Manguel, *The Library at Night*, 14.

28. Eco, *The Name of the Rose*, 286.

PART 3

THE LIBRARY NOW AND IN THE FUTURE

CHAPTER 10

"Casting and Gathering"

LIBRARIES, ARCHIVES, AND THE MODERN WRITER

Stephen Enniss

The recent decision to open the Man Booker Prize to any novelist writing in English is a reminder of the way language unites a global Anglophone community in a common culture. Our research libraries have long shared in this special relationship, as evidenced by the migration of rare books and manuscripts to America and, more recently, by the opportunities for new forms of cross-cultural collaboration. In the early years of the twentieth century, as literary studies shifted away from the classics and embraced English and American literary traditions, colleges and universities began establishing new departments of language and literature. For the first time in America, English and American authors began to appear on college examinations, and university libraries shifted their patterns of collecting to reflect these changes.

Before that time collecting had been largely the province of wealthy individuals. As late as the 1920s and 1930s collecting was still dominated by individual collectors. Henry Huntington established his great library in 1919, Pierpont Morgan in 1924, and in 1930 the cornerstone was laid for the Folger Shakespeare Library.

Henry and Emily Folger had begun building a collection devoted to Shakespeare and his age in the 1880s and bought at such an active pace that the editor and scholar Sidney Lee was warning just a few years later that Britain was being "drained of its First Folios."[1] A *Punch* cartoon from 1922 depicts Uncle Sam walking away with Gainsborough's *The Blue Boy* under one arm and a First Folio under the other (the first destined for the Huntington Library, the latter for the Folger) (see figure 10.1). Today the Folger Shakespeare Library holds the largest collection of early English books outside of Britain.

The Berg Collection at the New York Public Library was established in 1940 and, despite the war, grew dramatically in the years immediately following with the addition of the collections of W. T. Howe and Owen Young. Both men had assembled extraordinary collections of literary manuscripts of British and American authors, including rich manuscript holdings of Robert Burns, Sir Walter Scott, and Lewis Carroll.

With the growth of university English departments in America, the collecting of authors' papers became an institutional activity. As early as 1937 Charles Abbott of the State University of New York at Buffalo set out to build a collection of twentieth-century poets, including not only important editions of poetry in English but also working manuscripts of a wide range of contemporary authors. Abbott is said to have written to hundreds of poets to ask, quite literally, for the contents of their wastepaper baskets.

The dramatic expansion of special collections in America, however, got underway with the postwar growth of higher education in America and, more specifically, the growth of English literature programs in universities across the country.

Over a ten-year period, beginning in the late 1950s, the University of Texas at Austin committed $17 million to new collections,[2] all a result of the discovery of oil on a desolate spread of land owned by the university. The acquisition of the Hanley Collection in 1958 included a large collection of letters of George Bernard Shaw, the typescript of Dylan Thomas's *Under Milkwood*, the corrected proofs of James Joyce's *Ulysses*, and manuscripts of D. H. Lawrence. In the following years Texas added the manuscripts of E. M. Forster's *A Passage to India* and Joseph Conrad's *Victory* among many other stunning acquisitions. That same year the Lockwood Library at Buffalo purchased the archive of Sylvia Beach, with its own rich Joyce holdings, and two years later that of Robert Graves.

AUTOLYCUS, U.S.A.

UNCLE SAM. "NOW, THAT'S REAL DISAPPOINTING. I'D SET MY HEART ON THAT SKELETON."

SHADE OF SHAKSPEARE. "BUT ALL THE SAME I SHOULD FEEL MORE COMFORTABLE IF IT WAS INSURED."

Fig. 10.1. "Autolycus, U.S.A." Cartoon by Bernard Partridge in *Punch, or the London Charivari*, May 24, 1922. © Punch Limited and reproduced with permission.

A CASE STUDY: THE ARCHIVES OF
TED HUGHES AND SYLVIA PLATH

As the market for writers' papers grew, the writers themselves took no-
tice. In 1960 Sylvia Plath wrote to her mother that "Ted's been offered
160 pounds . . . for his manuscripts."[3] She was referring to the sale of
drafts of Ted Hughes's first two collections, *The Hawk in the Rain* and
Lupercal, the latter of which had only just been published. This set of
drafts, notes, and corrected page proofs was purchased by the London
dealer Ifan Kyrle Fletcher, who sold them on to the Lilly Library at Indiana University in Bloomington.

When Hughes and Plath separated in October 1962, Hughes sold
manuscript drafts of a number of recent poems to the London dealer
Bertram Rota, for as little as £5 a poem, and passed these earnings on to
his wife. One day, on his way to sell more, Hughes ran into the writer and
editor Ben Sonnenberg. "When he heard where I was going," Hughes
later recalled, "he gave me ten pounds for each of the three poems I had."[4]

After Plath's tragic death in 1963 Hughes became executor of her estate with responsibility for her papers as well. In the years following her
death he chose from her unpublished manuscripts a selection of poems
that he saw into print under the title *Ariel*, thus securing her posthumous
reputation as a major poet of her generation.[5]

In 1964 the collector Joseph Gold, who was then General Counsel
with the International Monetary Fund in Washington, wrote Hughes
offering to buy the manuscript of his poem "Pike." Hughes confessed
he had already sold it, having been "exceedingly pressed for cash."[6] "This
last year I've lost a lot of stuff," he explained, "manuscripts and so on.
I've started locking [them] in a chest—ridiculous business."[7] Over the
following months Hughes and Gold worked out an arrangement where
Gold would purchase manuscripts directly from Hughes. Writing to
the London manuscript dealer Winifred Myers, Hughes explained,

> "I am gradually being forced to realize that in time to come my
> manuscripts are going to be worth quite a lot. In the past, I've sold
> manuscripts for next to nothing—for less than I was paid merely
> for the publication of the poems. But now there seems to be a grow-

ing general opinion, here and in America and on the continent, that my work is permanent, and some of it possibly major."[8]

While Hughes increasingly took steps to keep his manuscripts safe, and those of his late wife as well, he still showed little awareness of the greater scholarly value that a larger archive might contain, indeed, just the opposite. He seems to have been content to let his early manuscripts be scattered widely among many different collectors and institutions.

In 1967 he published a manuscript edition of *Animal Poems*, thirty-six of which contained a single poem in his own hand. He followed this with other special manuscript editions that incorporated either fair copies of his poems in his hand, cannibalized working drafts, or, in the case of *Cave Birds*, facsimiles of the original manuscripts specially prepared for this purpose. This practice, which he began in 1967, was one he returned to repeatedly over his career, including in *Howls and Whispers* the limited edition companion volume to *Birthday Letters* published shortly before his death.[9] While these manuscript editions were a direct response to the market for handwritten poems, these editions had the effect of scattering his drafts even further among libraries and collections on both sides of the Atlantic.

In the 1970s a large cache of manuscripts and typescripts of *Cave Birds* went to the University of Exeter, and Hughes was still selling manuscripts casually for nominal sums to meet pressing immediate needs. A handwritten note in the Hughes archive lists potential buyers along with the prices he might expect from each. Among these buyers was the London bookselling firm Bernard Quaritch and the American rare book and manuscript dealer Marguerite Cohn of the House of Books in New York. "Market price of holograph of published poem—1 page—written out by author—£20. . . . Market price for manuscript pages of achieved poems—£35."[10] That impersonal self-reference, "written out by author," reveals a remarkable detachment from these transactions.

When it came time to consider what to do with Sylvia Plath's papers, Hughes confided to a friend, "I sold my own early papers years ago for a couple of hundred pounds—parts of them I know have since changed hands for vastly greater sums, but they can't help me anymore. They were probably my freshest, best work."[11] In the same letter Hughes proceeded to comment on the rapid growth of the manuscript trade in recent years: "I know Dylan Thomas' miraculous early notebooks,[12] from which he drew all his major poems, went for a few pounds—even as late as the fifties. While in 1963 Roethke's papers went for [a] quarter of a million $ [dollars]."

OPERATION MANUSCRIPT

Among those who took early note of this trade were Philip Larkin and Cecil Day-Lewis, both of whom were instrumental in organizing what Larkin called "Operation Manuscript." As Day-Lewis, noted, "we thought it wrong that so much material by contemporary British poets should be housed in American universities, while there was no similar collection over here."[13] With the help of a start-up grant from the Pilgrim Trust the Arts Council undertook a program to purchase worksheets of contemporary authors and to deposit them in the British Museum's Department of Manuscripts. It was a modest undertaking, but the organizers hoped to obtain some "good representative specimens," in the words of T. C. Skeat.[14]

Even as these fledgling efforts were getting underway, construction was being completed on the new Humanities Research Center at the University of Texas, a building conceived and designed to house the archives that were increasingly flowing to the Lone Star State.

In truth UK libraries were hardly in the game in the 1960s, or, as Larkin expressed it, "England is not really interested in the manuscripts of anyone not securely dead."[15] That situation would remain largely unchanged for more than three decades, prompting the manuscript dealer Roy Davids to quip, "Blessed Are the Dead."[16]

But before we condemn this trade as antithetical to our more pure interests, it is worth saying that it has provided a welcome subsidy to the writers themselves, while also serving as a reminder of our shared cultural values. When Hughes completed the sale of Sylvia Plath's papers to Smith College in 1981 he used some of the proceeds to pay school fees for his and Plath's two children. Plath would certainly have approved. It was she who had brought a business ethic to the couple's work, carefully noting on pink Smith College memorandum paper the circulation of her own and her husband's manuscripts: where they were accepted and what royalties had been paid.

Hughes began planning for the sale of his own archive in 1995, when he approached two appreciative scholars, Keith Sagar and Ann Skea, to help prepare a description of his papers. He soon decided, however, that this was a review that he needed to undertake himself, and he spent much of the following year going through his papers, months during which he was also writing many of the poems collected in *Birthday Letters*.

Hughes and I met for the first time at The George, a traditional thatched inn in Hatherleigh, not far from his home, Court Green, in nearby North Tawton. He spoke on that occasion about his recent travels in Bangladesh and Kenya, and the wildlife he had seen on those trips. He had hoped to see a tiger in Bangladesh, and, when I asked him if he had, he answered, "No, but I smelled one," an allusion to Yeats's response to E. R. Dodds when asked if he had ever seen a spirit. No, but I've often smelt them, Yeats replied.[17] Hughes was situating his own creative life not in Yeats's spirit world of ghosts and fairies, but in the natural world of lions and tigers.

Over the next two days Hughes spoke about the environment, the ecological damage we were doing to our rivers, the importance of memorization and of reading to children, the expressiveness of handwriting. He was working on an autobiographical poem sequence and was anticipating "dust storms," he confided.

At the time of our conversations the Churchill family was being criticized for the sale of the Winston Churchill papers for £12.5 million. Some objected on the grounds that Churchill's wartime speeches and other documents related to his service as prime minister should already be the property of the state; others were simply shocked at the price. The appeal that was made for government intervention raised the familiar specter that the papers might be sold abroad. The arguments, mostly at the expense of the Churchill family, had raged in the papers for months.

As poet laureate, Hughes hardly wanted to be the subject of similar recrimination. Besides, the National Heritage Memorial Fund was available only if one were dead. To sell his papers discreetly and for a competitive price, he would have to sell them abroad.

In the months following my visit to Devon the archive was transferred to Emory University and the announcement of the acquisition was greeted with great excitement by journalists who imagined new access to as-yet-undiscovered secrets of Hughes's private life. It would take much longer for scholars to begin the more painstaking study of the archive for new insights and understanding of Hughes's work and achievement.

When I saw Hughes in London in the summer of 1998, just a few short months before his death, he expressed a wish to visit the university since, as he put it, he would like to see the alligators. He was already undergoing treatment for cancer, and, in the end, he was unable to make that trip. Perhaps he would have been disappointed, since there were after all no alligators at the university. But had he visited he would have found his papers meticulously catalogued, well cared for, and open for research use.

He also would have found that his papers had been supplemented by a string of subsequent acquisitions that greatly expanded the university's Hughes holdings. His brother, Gerald, and sister, Olwyn, had both deposited family letters and other materials at Emory, as did his daughter, Frieda. His friends from university days Lucas Myers and Daniel Weissbort had done likewise, as did Emma Tennant, with whom he had had an affair in the 1970s, and the family of Assia Wevill, to name only some of the more noteworthy additions to the Hughes papers. Combined, these acquisitions—along with the acquisition of more than six thousand books from Hughes's personal library—give his papers a rich context.

After Hughes's death in the autumn of 1998 his daughter, Frieda, quarreled publicly with her stepmother over earnings from the Ted Hughes Estate, while at the same time the British Museum and the British Library quarreled over control of the Shaw Fund, a fund that had been established by a bequest of George Bernard Shaw to be split among the National Gallery of Ireland, the Royal Academy of Dramatic Art, and the British Museum, as Shaw had written, "in acknowledgement of the incalculable value to me of my daily resort to the Reading Room."[18]

Carol Hughes quietly sold a collection of Hughes's remaining papers (much of it material withheld from the Emory sale) to the British Library. The £500,000 purchase price was put together with support from the Friends of the National Libraries, the Friends of the British Library, and a £200,000 grant from the Shaw Fund (now restored to the British Library). The sum exceeded that paid by Emory for the larger archive eleven years earlier, and the sale had the effect of scattering further the already widely scattered Hughes papers.

There is nothing new, of course, about the movement of manuscript collections, and such material has often been split among institutions. One hoping to consult the papers of W. B. Yeats, for example, will need to visit the National Library of Ireland, the Harry Ransom Center at the University of Texas, the New York Public Library, Emory, Boston College, and literally scores of other libraries and archives across the UK, Ireland, and America.

This is not an anomaly. The notion of a "complete archive" may, in fact, be as illusory as the notion of an author's "original intent." Archives come to rest where there is a momentary convergence of vision, opportunity, and money.

When Andrew Motion was named poet laureate, following Hughes's death, he undertook a campaign to build support for collecting writers' archives in research libraries in the UK. His efforts heightened awareness of the unfavorable competitive position UK libraries often faced in seeking to build research collections of contemporary authors' papers, and his efforts led to the formation in 2005 of the UK Literary Heritage Working Group. The National Heritage Memorial Fund broke its long-standing policy prohibiting the use of its funds for a living author's papers, and funding for acquisitions doubled from £5 to £10 million.

The results of these and other related initiatives by the UK government have been significant. The British Library acquired the Harold Pinter papers for £1.1 million. Simon Armitage and Geoffrey Hill both sold their papers to the Brotherton Library in Leeds; Graham Swift's papers and Wendy Cope's went to the British Library, Douglas Dunn's to St. Andrews; and the Siegfried Sassoon papers went to Cambridge after a public campaign raised £1.25 million in support of the purchase.

Perhaps the most stunning acquisition, however, was the purchase of the archive of the publisher John Murray by the National Library of Scotland for a staggering £31.2 million.[19] In its long history the firm published many major British and American writers including work by Jane Austen, Lord Byron, Sir Walter Scott, and Washington Irving among many others.

All of us who care about our literary culture should applaud these acquisitions as I hope we can the recent acquisitions of the Ian McEwan papers by the University of Texas or Salman Rushdie's papers by Emory University. Each of the writers I have named has achieved something of the *permanence* that Hughes took note of so early in his career; each has been compensated for his or her work, and each of the libraries mentioned has made a substantial and open-ended commitment to the long-term preservation and care of these irreplaceable collections. In due course, researchers working in our libraries and archives will discover new insights into the development of these writers' novels, poems, and plays and, in time, develop a deeper understanding of our cultural moment.

I am confident that these are wise investments, whether paid in dollars or in pounds, and I applaud those librarians and archivists on both sides of the Atlantic who perform such valuable service to literature.

THE CHANGING NATURE OF THE MODERN ARCHIVE

When Emory entered into negotiation with Salman Rushdie for the purchase of his papers, the university soon learned that those "papers" included four discarded computers and an external hard drive on which Rushdie had downloaded the contents of his latest computer. "I email a lot, so there's all sorts of stuff there," Rushdie commented at the time, "but don't ask me to remember what it is."[20] During those negotiations, over the spring and summer of 2006, Rushdie's agent, Andrew Wylie, argued for the great value of Rushdie's digital remains. In the end, no precedent was set for the purchase of such material, because the agreement that was reached did not specify what portion of the total price paid was for the paper-based archive, what portion for the electronic archive, and what portion for a teaching appointment at the university.

Whatever else we may have to say about the trade in writers' archives, it is that trade that has ensured the survival of these often ephemeral materials. Before Ted Hughes and Sylvia Plath discovered a market for their manuscripts, they treated discarded drafts as scrap paper to be used up and disposed of. While the discovery of a market for their manuscripts eventually led to their papers being widely scattered, that market also ensured that their archive survived.

When Zadie Smith was asked what would likely become of her archive, she said, "I guess it will all go the way of everything else I write on the computer: oblivion."[21]

What institution will have the capacity to invest in the costly and painstaking work required to retain and preserve this highly unstable digital resource? Perhaps more to the point, will future researchers care that drawers of obsolete diskettes of this or that writer have been passed down to us? What new uses will be made of these electronic files if they have managed to survive?

If I had to hazard an answer to these questions, I would say that these challenges will be met imperfectly by a community of librarians and archivists working in widely scattered institutions. What successes there are will not be through the effort of any single institution—not the British Library alone, nor New York Public Library, nor the Beinecke or the Ransom Center alone. The successes are more likely to be piecemeal, through the work of librarians and archivists scattered among our national libraries, our archives and public record offices, and our universities.

In other words, the literary culture of our own time will survive as it has always survived, wherever there is that combination of vision, opportunity, and money. Addressing our present challenges will certainly require substantial investment and the best guidance of the profession working in collaboration with scholars and with writers themselves. It will also require a broad awareness of, and commitment to, the survival of our literary culture.

Casting and Gathering

In his poem "Casting and Gathering" Seamus Heaney describes two fishermen fishing the same river from opposite riverbanks. One casts and then gathers, only to have his movements mirrored by the other on the opposite bank. As the poem develops, it comes to seem a dance of two figures moving to the same motion.

Heaney wrote the poem for his close friend Ted Hughes, and the poem is a comment on their shared commitment to poetry. But that image might just as well serve as a metaphor for the work our libraries are engaged in on opposite sides of this even wider river. "Years and years ago, these sounds took sides," Heaney writes,

On the left bank, a green silk tapered cast
Went whispering through the air, saying *hush*
And *lush*, entirely free, no matter whether
It swished above the hayfield or the river.

On the right bank, like a speeded-up corncrake,
A sharp ratcheting went on and on
Cutting across the stillness as another
Fisherman gathered line-lengths off his reel.

I am still standing there, awake and dreamy,
I have grown older and can see them both
Moving their arms and rods, working away,
Each one absorbed, proofed by the sounds he's making.[22]

We will not catch and hold onto everything. An archive is also a record of absences at the very brink of oblivion. But by working together to meet these challenges I believe that much that is worthy of our attention will survive. No one library can contain a nation's literary or historical record, but collectively we can do a great deal, as the history of our libraries' growth over the past century demonstrates. By working together in common cause we may even discover, as Ted Hughes did when he was preparing his own archive for sale, "I found something I thought I had lost."[23]

NOTES

1. Quoted in "Notes on Rare Books," *New York Times*, December 15, 1929.

2. Cathy Henderson, "The Birth of an Institution," in *Collecting the Imagination*, ed. Megan Barnard (Austin: University of Texas Press, 2007), 28.

3. Sylvia Plath, *Letters Home*, ed. Aurelia Plath (London: Faber and Faber, 1975), 388.

4. Ted Hughes to Aurelia Plath, *Times Literary Supplement*, January 12, 1975, Ted Hughes papers, Emory University.

5. While Hughes has been vilified for the editorial decisions that he made, he and Plath had shared a remarkably collaborative creative relationship during

her lifetime. For a more full discussion of those issues, see Stephen Enniss, "Ted Hughes, Sylvia Plath, and the Myth of Textual Betrayal," *Papers of the Bibliographical Society of America* 101.1 (March 2007): 63–71.

6. Ted Hughes to Joseph Gold, March 19, 1964, Hughes papers, Emory University.

7. Ted Hughes to Joseph Gold, August 7, 1964, Hughes papers, Emory University.

8. Ted Hughes to Winifred Myers, ca. early 1960s, Hughes papers, Emory University.

9. *Howls and Whispers* was published in an edition of 110 copies, ten of which included a single manuscript of one of the poems.

10. Ted Hughes, "Possible Buyers," Hughes papers, Emory University.

11. Ted Hughes to Prouty Smith, May 12, 1975, Hughes papers, Emory University.

12. Hughes was referring to the sale of nine of Dylan Thomas's notebooks, including his early "red notebook," to the Lockwood Library at SUNY Buffalo.

13. C. Day-Lewis, Preface, *Poetry in the Making*, ed. Jenny Lewis (London: Turret Books, 1967), 9.

14. T. C. Skeat, Introduction. *Poetry in the Making*, ed. Jenny Lewis (London: Turret Books, 1967),12.

15. Philip Larkin, "Operation Manuscript," in *Poetry in the Making,* ed. Jenny Lewis (London: Turret Books, 1967), 18.

16. Roy Davids, "Blessed Are the Dead," *Author* (Society of Authors), Summer 2002. Online at http://www.roydavids.com/archives2.htm.

17. Louis MacNeice, *The Strings Are False* (London: Faber and Faber, 1996), 147–48.

18. Quoted in *Bernard Shaw*, by Michael Holroyd. (London: Vintage, 1998), 782.

19. The purchase was made possible with £17.7 million from the Heritage Lottery Fund, £8.3 million from the Scottish Executive, with the remainder to be covered by the National Library.

20. Rachel Donadio, "Literary Letters, Lost in Cyberspace," *New York Times Book Review* September 4, 2005, 15.

21. Ibid.

22. Seamus Heaney, "Casting and Gathering," *Seeing Things* (London: Faber and Faber, 1991), 13.

23. Ted Hughes in conversation with Ann Skea, August 1995. See Ann Skea's website, *Ted Hughes: Timeline* for 1995. Online at http://ann.skea.com/time line.htm.

CHAPTER 11

☙

Meanings of the Library Today

John P. Wilkin

I was tempted to subtitle this chapter "The more things change, the more they stay the same," but I actually intend to make a different point about libraries and constancy. "*Plus ça change, plus c'est la même chose*" suggests a sort of fatalism, and could be translated as "turbulent change only cements the status quo." I would like to argue a fundamentally different position. To define the meanings of the library (yesterday, today, and tomorrow) we need to tap into great truths. The library throughout time has actually had a sort of constancy in its role and function, a commitment to sustaining culture despite, and perhaps because of, changes occurring all around. The story of libraries, and particularly the one we see unfolding in the research library of today, is a story of abiding commitment to the record of the past and of the future. And the core function of libraries is to do more than preserve the cultural record: it is also to provide access to and ensure use of that record and, increasingly, to be involved in the *creation* of the cultural record as well.

LIBRARY MEANING: THE FOUR PILLARS

I have been asked occasionally to talk about my vision for a twenty-first-century research library. Most of the elements of that vision would be unsurprising to anyone reading this. Events of the last few years have created a very real sense of opportunities and of challenges. I would like to begin by sharing my "vision of the library" in a discussion that I have taken to calling, with my tongue in my cheek and with a nod to Ranganathan, the "four pillars of research libraries."[1]

There are four enduring areas of work for our libraries, areas that change in importance and complexion over time, but which are always part of the research library function. They are:

- Curation, by which I mean the selection, preservation, maintenance, collection and archiving of, and provision of access to, materials pertaining to the cultural record—for libraries, predominantly books and manuscripts, but often images and audio items also.
- Engagement with research and learning.
- Publishing, ranging from the most modest reproduction and dissemination of materials to full-blown editorial processes with peer review.
- Creating and managing spaces devoted to users and collections

Our engagement with each of these elements has ebbed and flowed over time, changing character as society and culture have themselves changed. In the twenty-first century these four areas of work remain applicable to the research library.

I would also like to consider each of these areas of research library work from the perspectives of "the network" and "the local." Some of a library's work can naturally be done more efficiently in a shared, networked context. Other work is best done locally. The best example of appropriately *local* work is the creation and management of spaces—we can create truly effective spaces only by paying attention to the geographic, disciplinary, and cultural elements that define them. The best example of an activity that can be done most appropriately in a *networked* context is curation. Here I would argue that a library's collection is not owned solely by the library, but by the society or culture that has collected it and put it in the library in the first place. We own the collection as a culture, and we must attend to it as a culture.

Neither of the activities in these examples is wholly "network" or wholly "local," of course. We can learn from the network how to make our local spaces better, and there are resources belonging to the wider cultural network that must receive local curatorial attention (rare books and manuscripts, for example). The key is to find the right balance between the two.

Curation

Libraries do curatorial work to preserve and provide access to the cultural record. Print collections continue to dominate our focus, but Big Data has made its way squarely into the library curatorial discussion, and that is as it should be. Other materials such as audio and video recordings also have their place in many of our research libraries. Various types of image resources are relevant too. And I would include conventional archival resources and archival organizations in this space: the curatorial aspect of the missions and functions of archives and libraries are roughly the same, and the curatorial methods are certainly the same, as well. Curation not only covers preservation and access, particularly for electronic resources, but also includes selection, description, and organization.

Libraries are best known to their constituencies and to the profession itself for their curatorial role. Curation provides the underpinnings for other things we do, and curating the collection is the most enduring part of our work. It is sometimes seen as the creation of truths, or at least as work that transcends bias. Yes, we select, and thus show bias, but a core tenet of collection development is acknowledging and surmounting bias.[2]

Although we are increasingly focused on the curation of digital resources, it is just as important that we get the print problem right as it is that we embrace responsibility for other types of communication. Words remain the basis of all scholarship, and formal communication through words in books and journals is at the core of the scholarly process. Although, as libraries, we need to turn our attention to new forms of communication, getting the print record right can only make work in the developing digital areas easier by forging a clear path and making it possible for us to shift from one resource format to another.

This *shift of resources* from print to digital is one of the greatest challenges facing libraries at the present time, as is the need to find more efficient ways of managing print so that attention can be devoted to other areas of library work. We know, for example, that there are more than a billion volumes stored in North American academic libraries. Emerging research at OCLC (the Online Computer Library Center, Inc.) suggests that roughly fifty million unique titles make up the corpus represented in these billion volumes. We cannot carry with us the cost burden of unnecessarily duplicated collections while we take on new costs, and we cannot walk away from the problem. The opportunity for doing things differently is evident—as is the fact that "doing differently" includes everything from storing, to describing, to various forms of document delivery or fulfillment. Doing things differently promises to help our users *and* save considerable resources that can assist us in other curatorial pursuits. As I will show, networked curation is key to our survival.

Engagement with Research and Learning

Although curation may be the most important area of work for libraries, the services we build around research and learning are often the most visible. These emerging services have their roots in the past but reflect new ways of operating.

- *Research*. Many academic libraries now have "field librarians," individuals who are embedded in academic departments, sharing the teaching load. Similarly, we find librarians embedded in clinical teams, conducting research and guiding collaborative strategies. In an increasing number of cases, we see librarians working with data, not just at the ingest and validation stages, but also as part of research teams shaping data organization and the use of community standards. This is a key way forward for libraries, connecting our information management activities to the mission of the institution.
- *Teaching and learning*. Increasingly librarians serve as instructional designers, collaborating in delivering online learning environments, and as collaborators in the classroom, developing and applying metrics to assess information literacy learning outcomes.

This aspect of the work of academic librarians will continue to be vital, and partnerships with primary academic constituencies will increasingly define what research libraries do. Although this work is conducted in local contexts, it relies more and more on the network (for example on shared, networked learning tools) for success.

Publishing

Not so long ago, the notion that publishing should be undertaken by libraries was controversial. In fact publishing has been a library function for a long time and has been apparent in low-level activities such as the collection and dissemination of dissertations, and in library printing shops. At a higher level, however, many actual university presses originated in libraries because there was a need to disseminate research products on a noncommercial basis. In his introduction to *Some Presses You Will Be Glad to Know About* (1937), Harry Miller Lydenberg comments:

> Just as the university came to see how unfair it was to expect the average publisher to market books possessed of so little popular appeal but at the same time of such real importance, some of the museums and similar institutions—libraries, for instance—found themselves faced with a kindred problem.
>
> The university is a place for teaching, also a place for the pursuit of truth, education and research. Which ranks first depends on your point of view.
>
> The museum and the library are neither teaching nor research centres. They are tool rooms for instruments of research.
>
> In the development of this useful function, however, some of them came to find they turned out certain results of study and research that seemed worthy of publication. But the trade publisher had no interest. So they, like the universities, started their own presses. Most of these presses began with slight equipment, slighter means. Growth came as the need voiced itself and the results of one effort justified the next.
>
> Even if these museums and libraries are not technically institutions of teaching and research the books they turn out plead for their recognition as institutions of learning.[3]

This narrative of the emergence of academic publishing from libraries in the earlier part of the twentieth century is considered in detail in an essay by Paul Courant and Elisabeth Jones, in the forthcoming book from the ACRL (Association of College and Research Libraries) *Getting the Word Out: Academic Libraries and Scholarly Publishing*, edited by Maria Bonn and Mike Furlough. As Courant and Jones note, "several of the earliest North American university presses—including those at Johns Hopkins, the University of California, the University of Toronto, the University of Washington, and the University of North Carolina—were initially created under the administrative aegis of the university library."[4] Their study confirms the long-standing connection between the library's role as curator of scholarly materials and its additional role as disseminator or publisher of those materials.

Whether we agree or not about the role of libraries in the past, libraries *are* publishing today and are frequently quite significant publishers. There are examples of university presses moving into libraries, and of electronic publishing initiatives such as *eScholarship*, the Digital Library of the University of California, and the *Scholarly Publishing Office* at the University of Michigan. Even institutional repositories can be considered publishers in this context. Increasingly, as a profession, we believe that by lashing together the publishing and curation roles, we can ensure greater integrity in the record and that the right sorts of "use" and "cost" models are part of the mix.[5] As we will see in a moment, the financial pressure of current commercial publishing on libraries is tremendous. A vigorous response by libraries is likely to help create a more sustainable future for research publishing, and this will in turn contribute to the sustainability of libraries and higher education.

In publishing, too, we can see an interesting interplay between "the local" and "the networked." A press's authors may be local yet often also belong to wider subject or discipline-based networks that might result in fruitful connections for the press. Clearly, too, a press's systems and services might benefit from being more fully networked with other similar publishing ventures, making the most of opportunities to share resources and costs.

Space

I believe very much in the value of library spaces for the life of the campus. The library is far more than a student union, no matter how many coffee shops and food courts we introduce. The proximity of user spaces to librarians and to collections or collection-related tools creates a very different kind of environment where our users, individually and collectively, engage with ideas and collaborate with one another in their research pursuits. The library is an important counterpart to the classroom. As long as the co-location of students on campuses is meaningful, the library space will be meaningful too. It is no accident that the library building is frequently at the heart of the campus.

CHALLENGES TO THE FOUR PILLARS

The work of libraries related to each of these four pillars is made increasingly difficult by the convergence of several trends: resources are flat or declining, costs are increasing, needs are increasing, and we face a rapidly changing set of environmental circumstances. We experience this as librarians, and although I probably need little evidence to support this argument, there is a real danger in using "felt experience" rather than data, so I will share some statistics.

The long-term decline in research libraries' funding can be measured in relative or absolute terms. Statistics from the Association of Research Libraries (ARL) show, for example, that between 1982 and 2009, U.S. academic research library expenditures as a percentage of total university expenditures declined from roughly 3.7 percent of the total budget of their institutions to just over 1.9 percent.[6]

That trend continues today. Looking across all U.S. higher education in more recent years, from 2008 to 2010, library expenditures fell from 1.33 percent to 0.62 percent of postsecondary expenditures.[7] Indeed, from 2008 to 2010, academic library funding was essentially flat, while expenditures continued to grow. The U.S. National Center for Education Statistics reported that total funding for academic libraries grew from $6.78 billion to $6.83 billion; adjusted for inflation, the dollar amount was unchanged.[8] This trend is further evidenced by ARL data for the last twenty-six years, with the last ten to twelve years being essentially flat.

In an era of constrained resources, a flat budget and increased demand is, I would argue, a vote of confidence. As librarians, we need only compare our situation to that of publishers or information technology organizations to appreciate how good we've got it. Still, the flat budget stands in stark contrast to rapidly growing costs: expenditures for licensed electronic resources during the same 2008 to 2010 period grew by 23 percent.[9] Journal subscription costs grew much faster than the rate of overall inflation. Of course we see these rising costs and diminished financial resources in the context of a rapidly evolving set of needs, an environment where demand for print and electronic resources remains high and where we strive to adapt to various changes. Many of our libraries report sustained levels of print borrowing, and "gate counts" continue to rise (up nearly 9 percent over 2008 rates).[10] At the same time, libraries are happily responding to the need for a variety of repository services, including digital object repositories, institutional repositories, and, in a few cases, data services and repository services for audio and video content. The costs for all these services are substantial, particularly for storage-intensive repositories like those for data and rich media.

I would like also to add some publishing data to this part of the conversation. Formal publishing has faced similar and yet greater challenges and is not faring well. While the director of publishing activities at Michigan, I watched as sales fell there and at the institutions of other AAUP (American Association of University Presses) members. By midyear in 2012–13, nearly two-thirds of these presses witnessed a decline over the previous year, continuing a general decline. Costs have been trimmed, but those that remain (for staff and services for example) continue to rise. In the face of these losses, U.S. university presses have witnessed a growing reluctance by university administrations to subsidize operations that are acting like "businesses." One response has been to move these organizations into libraries. At the last count, more than twenty AAUP presses reported to the library director and, in some cases, had become part of the library organization. In this, we can see both a vote of confidence for libraries and concerns about the "business" of academic publishing.

This complex interplay of roles is, I would argue, what "the library" currently means. To remove one of the four pillars I have described is to unbalance that meaning or identity, and to make the library's cultural role less compelling. We cannot succeed as libraries with flat or diminishing resources *without also adapting or changing the way we do our work*. A starvation diet, with a gradual diminution of resources in each of these four areas, will ultimately mean that we fail to fulfill functions such as curation and thus lose cultural responsibility. Curating the cultural record poorly or incompletely would undermine the record's integrity, and society would look for other ways to get the job done. As libraries, our response to the resource problem should not be to do less, but to do things differently, and particularly to do them more efficiently. This can be accomplished by working at scale.

WORK AT SCALE

The concept of scale is critically important to the success of libraries. Lorcan Dempsey writes very helpfully about scale and the way in which the library's work can be achieved more effectively through varieties of scale-enhanced work.[11] In brief, work at scale involves the consolidation of efforts in a sphere that cuts across institutions, for example through geographic, peer, or even broader alliances. By using scale-enhanced strategies, we shift resources and methods to a larger collaborative space. This is especially helpful in areas where the shift creates efficiencies, improves the service, or both, without changing the fundamental nature of the work. In libraries, scale opportunities abound—collection curation is one of the best examples of this, since curation at scale can be accomplished both more effectively and at a reduced cost.[12]

Success at scale is clearly exemplified by the HathiTrust, for which comprehensive overviews describing its purposes and economic model are available in print and online.[13] Here is an example of an organization that has managed an extraordinarily large body of content collectively, and in doing so has not simply driven costs down, but has also made participation affordable to member libraries.

The HathiTrust collection is vast by any measure, consisting of approximately eleven million volumes drawn from many of the partner libraries. Its size makes HathiTrust one of the ten largest research library collections in North America. The collection, too, reflects the rich diversity of the library collections on which it is based. Although the collection continues to evolve with the addition of new content, a few examples drawn from language and publication date data at the time of writing this chapter will help illustrate that richness and diversity.

- More than four hundred languages are represented in HathiTrust. Predictably, English is the language of the largest body of materials, but, even so, fewer than 50 percent of the materials are in English. Forty-eight percent of the books and journals are in English, 9 percent are in German, 7 percent are in French, 5 percent are in Spanish, and 4 percent are in Russian and Chinese. Indeed, the 3 percent identified as Urdu or the 2 percent identified as Tamil and Sanskrit represent relatively significant collections for most research libraries.

- By date, HathiTrust reflects the massive growth of publishing in history. Nearly 90 percent of the volumes held were published after the turn of the twentieth century. More than 10 percent of these were published after 2000. The smaller percentages published in earlier periods represent sizeable collections, with the more than one hundred thousand volumes published in the eighteenth century including significant numbers of volumes found in comprehensive publishing inventories such as the eighteenth-century portion of the *Eighteenth-Century Short Title Catalog.*

Other analytical approaches help emphasize how significant and representative the HathiTrust collection is. Work published by OCLC and performed in collaboration with HathiTrust shows the important overlap between HathiTrust and the collections of North American research libraries.[14] By 2010, with fewer than six million volumes online, nearly every ARL library could expect to find approximately 30 percent of its collection reflected in the digital copies held by HathiTrust. Now that HathiTrust in 2014 has approximately thirteen million volumes online, those same libraries can typically find substantially more than half of their print collections represented digitally in HathiTrust. Higher rates of overlap for smaller college libraries have been found by OCLC.

The precise way in which the collections of these libraries overlap with HathiTrust differs significantly by institution. For example, a large research library like Harvard, with a significant number of very specialized titles, will have fewer titles that overlap with other institutions. For Harvard, when there is overlap, it occurs with a small number of similarly large research libraries. Consequently, a smaller proportion of the titles

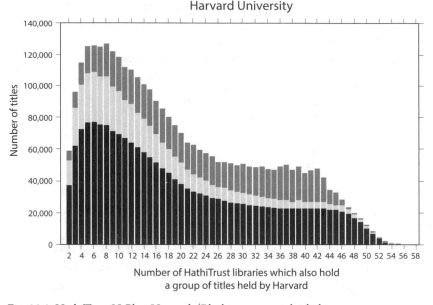

Harvard University

Number of HathiTrust libraries which also hold
a group of titles held by Harvard

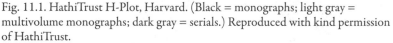

Fig. 11.1. HathiTrust H-Plot, Harvard. (Black = monographs; light gray = multivolume monographs; dark gray = serials.) Reproduced with kind permission of HathiTrust.

in the overlapping portion of Harvard's collection will be widely held. In the H-Plot in figure 11.1, the x-axis is the number of HathiTrust partner libraries that also hold a group of titles held by Harvard, and y-axis is the number of titles. The radical slope downward, from left to right, is distinctive of a large research library.

By contrast, the plot of holdings shown in figure 11.2 from Lafayette College in Pennsylvania shows a pattern more common among liberal arts colleges. More of Lafayette's volumes are widely held.

Other H-Plots in HathiTrust show fundamentally different patterns where, for example, medium-sized research libraries have relatively few titles widely or uniquely held.

These data help to emphasize how the problem of curating the published record is a shared one, whether the record is in print or electronic form. The HathiTrust digital collection is a reflection of the collections of each partner library. It serves each institution differently, even with the same body of materials. By aiming to build as comprehensive a *digi-*

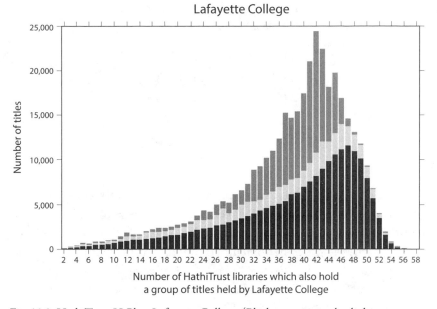

Lafayette College

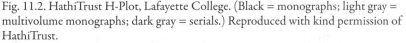

Number of HathiTrust libraries which also hold
a group of titles held by Lafayette College

Fig. 11.2. HathiTrust H-Plot, Lafayette College. (Black = monographs; light gray = multivolume monographs; dark gray = serials.) Reproduced with kind permission of HathiTrust.

tal collection as possible, we can also say that the *print* collections of the partner libraries reflect this interdependence. Despite differences, overlap between the institutions is significant, and an approach that manages the totality of our collections will significantly reduce our individual responsibilities, especially for lesser-used materials. Interestingly, relatively early (2010) analysis of the overlap between volumes in HathiTrust and volumes in the five most prominent shared print repositories in the United States (for example high-density print storage facilities such as ReCAP in New Jersey) confirms this by showing how the overwhelming majority of HathiTrust volumes exist in one or more of those print repositories. [15]

For HathiTrust, operation at scale has brought multiple benefits. The cost of storage per digitized volume in HathiTrust is, in absolute terms, lower than it would be for an individual institution, the result of both improved buying leverage and volume discounts. The cost of infrastructure generally is reduced through consolidation. The number of servers

Table 11.1. HathiTrust Cost of Operation, 2009–13.
(Data from HathiTrust)

2009	$1,932,830
2010	$1,364,750
2011	$1,969,476
2012	$2,034,749
2013	$1,724,396

needed can be reduced, as can the number of data centers, energy utilization, backup technologies, and, of course, the numbers of staff needed to support all these things.

Analysis of the scale phenomenon on HathiTrust's costs is interesting. Over the first few years, from 2008 to 2013, it saw phenomenal growth, storing roughly one million volumes at its inception, and approaching eleven million volumes by late 2013. Throughout this period of stunning growth, operations costs were remarkably flat. The total cost of operation (before additional strategic initiative fees) for the last four years decreased an average of 6.4 percent (see table 11.1).

Embedded in these numbers, of course, are too many variables to isolate scale alone as a cause of reduced cost: Moore's Law, strategic "banking" of replacement costs, and growing ambitions are all factors in the final cost of operation. Nonetheless, HathiTrust's costs are not in any way reflective of its dramatic growth. Growth was great; costs were flat.

Scale also brings with it important (even if obvious) opportunities for sharing those reduced costs. Over the seven years of its existence, HathiTrust has grown from fewer than twenty-five partner institutions to more than one hundred. The costs, which have increased with the content and not the size of the partnership, are shared among an increasingly large number of institutions. Over a period during which the content grew eleven-fold, costs for the University of California dropped nearly 25 percent, from over $600,000 per year to less than $500,000 per year. Even more dramatically, the costs for the CIC universities (the universities of the U.S. Committee on Institutional Cooperation) fell by over 50 percent, from roughly $1.5 million per year to approximately $700,000 per year. Notably, in both cases, the cost reduction is a result of a combination of a change in the cost model, from one that attributed institutional costs in a way that mimicked the cost of the institution operating in isolation from other libraries, to one that spread those costs over a growing number of partner institutions.[16]

Consider, then, the value of scale as seen through the example of HathiTrust. The published record is seen as a collective good (the "collective collection"), and responsibility and costs are shared. The benefits of the collaborative effort allow the partner institutions to see how their institutional needs are interdependent and mutual—serving the interests of one is likely to serve the interests of many. The collaboration also drives down costs, both in the aggregate and for individual institutions. Indeed, we see not only cost containment but also a reduction of costs through consolidation.

My focus here has been on cost and the way in which scale benefits us, but there are many other benefits that deserve more attention. One is impact, and very clearly HathiTrust has attracted attention in a way a single institution could not have done. By supporting this move to scale, librarians have also gained a much better understanding of the published record curated by the partner libraries, its distribution over time, for example, and what is held by individual institutions. Working at scale has, too, made some associated work easier. Reliable copyright determinations can now take place on a scale never before imagined, with hundreds of thousands of titles reviewed by partner institutions. Scale has changed the way the HathiTrust libraries do their work.

Conclusion

Curating, producing, and facilitating the use of the cultural record in all its myriad forms, the library is today a hub of intellectual life, as it has been in the past and will be in the future. The introduction of digital technologies has not changed the essential nature of the library but has created a path for increased vitality and long-term viability. While for some cultural agents digital technology is seen as a fundamental threat (publishing, for example, is struggling to find a way to maintain an economic model in the face of changes in the way writers write and readers read), the digital promises to make the cultural work of libraries easier and more sustainable. There are opportunities to establish a clearer sense of the nature and extent of the publishing record, as well as opportunities to distribute and coordinate print curation so that the print record is more persistent. There are also, of course, opportunities for shared efforts around digital curation. Technology also makes coordinated library efforts to support publishing more cost-effective, sustainable, and with greater reach. Technologically enhanced curation and publishing activities should allow libraries to shift resources to support more effective engagement with users in research and learning. This is an area of library work in which we should invest substantially. Indeed, the impact of such investment will also help libraries make better use of spaces, devoting a smaller footprint to less used (and undersupported) print collections and focusing attention on a smaller number of vital library spaces. These four complementary areas of library work are more likely to thrive as a result of the way in which technology fosters coordination, consolidation, and effective distribution.

I hope that there will in due course be consensus that scholarly publishing is a significant core responsibility of libraries. Much scholarly book publishing is not sustainable as a business and has not been for a very long time. As an enterprise its primary purpose is to validate scholarship and to share ideas, not to market those ideas. Libraries, therefore, must assert leadership in crafting sustainable economic models and engage faculty to help shape strategies that will support the long-term viability of the publishing endeavor. In publishing there is an opportunity to work at scale. A shared publishing platform, with ties to individual institutions, is the next great library frontier. Our success in this venture will help change the economics of scholarly publishing, will ensure broader access, and should ultimately reduce the cost of acquisitions. An "at-scale" approach to publishing by libraries can square the circle for cost-effective collection building, knitting together preservation and access (where the preservation copy and the access copy are the same thing), ensuring the lasting value of libraries and confirming their relevance.

Opportunities at scale made possible by digital technologies translate library work previously done in isolation to more effective, less costly, shared platforms that have greater impact. They allow us, as Lorcan

Dempsey has argued, to "transfer resource[s] away from 'infrastructure' and towards user engagement."[17] Curation is certainly one of the clearest examples of this. Publishing at scale, too, holds great promise and potential. The scale of library collaboration is changing. It is changing with economic pressures because we are no longer able to afford to do in isolation what we can do more cost-effectively together. It is changing with unforeseen opportunities as we craft new models of collaborative collection development and management. It is changing with new priorities, as we turn our attention to increasingly intensive partnerships with the communities of which we are a part, and away from those isolated and isolating activities that occupied us in the past. Technology has made much of this possible.

NOTES

1. Librarian and mathematician S. R. Ranganathan proposed the *Five laws of library science* in his 1931 publication of that title. First law: books are for use; second law: every reader his or her book; third law: every book its reader; fourth law: save the time of the reader; fifth law: the library is a growing organism.

2. There is little in library literature that argues that collection development is or could be without bias. However, the issue of bias underlies much literature, and that literature often reacts to the implicit notion that our work is free of bias. For example, Brian Quinn, in "Collection Development and the Psychology of Bias," *Library Quarterly* 82.3 (2012): 277–304, writes about our belief that we transcend bias, but that this attitude "ignores the psychological research on bias, which suggests that bias is a more complex and subtle phenomenon" (277). Elsewhere, Nicholas Joint, in his "Legal Deposit and Collection Development in a Digital World," *Library Review* 55.8 (2006): 468–73, argues that our inability to collect comprehensively necessarily leads to bias: "The important thing is to start the practical business of digital collection building with a view to creating a representative national archive, without worrying that a complete model of 'how to do it' is not yet in place. This may be a little worrying for a group as risk averse as the Library and Information Science profession, but it is in effect what we are doing already. So we should have the courage of our convictions that this is an area in which it is worth making honest mistakes and we should proceed to create models of good practice by seeing what works and what doesn't work, thereby establishing a way forward." That is, in a world

where bias is inevitable, we should do our best to represent the broadest and best, to be as neutral as possible despite the inevitability of bias.

3. Harry Miller Lydenberg, *Some Presses You Will Be Glad to Know About* (New York: University Books, 1937), 7–8.

4. Maria Bonn and Mike Furlough, eds., *Getting the Word Out: Academic Libraries and Scholarly Publishing* (Chicago: Association of College and Research Libraries, 2015).

5. The Library Publishing Coalition website (http://www.librarypublish ing.org/) provides a directory of libraries engaged in some support for publishing. By late 2013, there were more than one hundred North American libraries listed.

6. See Association of Research Libraries, *University and Library Expenditures* on the ARL Statistics website at http://www.arlstatistics.org/about/series /eg, and particularly the graph for "Library Expenditure as % of Total University Expenditure" at http://www.libqual.org/documents/admin/EG_2.pdf.

7. American Library Association, *State of America's Libraries Report, 2012,* on the website of the ALA at http://www.ala.org/news/mediapresscenter/ americaslibraries/soal2012.

8. Ibid.

9. Ibid.

10. Ibid.

11. For example, see Lorcan Dempsey's "Thirteen Ways of Looking at Libraries, Discovery, and the Catalog: Scale, Workflow, Attention," *Educause Review Online*, December 10, 2012.

12. Despite the value of scale in much library work, libraries have been reluctant to embrace that opportunity fully. I would argue that cataloging, which is often used as an example of library cooperation, is something of a counterexample. Cataloging records are shared, but they are *managed* locally, with significant redundant costs (e.g., for authority control and library management systems). Indeed, shared cataloging is emblematic of a tentativeness in libraries, where we are more likely to share software code and models for conducting work than we are to share systems that could reduce our costs and increase our impact.

13. HathiTrust includes many overview documents online at http://www .hathitrust.org/papers_and_presentations, including, e.g., Heather Christenson, "HathiTrust: A Research Library at Web Scale," *Library Resources and Technical Services* 55.2: 93–102. Online at http://www.hathitrust.org/documents /christenson-lrts-201104.pdf.

14. Constance Malpas, "Cloud-Sourcing Research Collections: Managing Print in the Mass-Digitized Library Environment." OCLC (Online Computer

Library Center, Inc.) Report, 2011. http://www.oclc.org/content/dam/re search/publications/library/2011/2011–01.pdf.

15. Constance Malpas, "Reconfiguring Academic Collections: The Role of Shared Print Repositories." Presentation to MLAC (Minnesota Library Access Center) Advisory Board, February 23, 2011. http://www.oclc.org/content/ dam/research/presentations/malpas/mlac2011.pdf.

16. Information regarding the HathiTrust cost model is available online on the HathiTrust website at http://www.hathitrust.org/cost, and the original rationale is provided at http://www.hathitrust.org/documents/hathitrust -cost-rationale-2013.pdf.

17. Lorcan Dempsey, "Sourcing and Scaling," *Lorcan Dempsey's Weblog*, February 21, 2010. http://orweblog.oclc.org/archives/002058.html.

CHAPTER 12

The Modern Library and Global Democracy

James H. Billington

Only one library building, as far as I know, has survived largely intact from classical antiquity. It is a small square structure in Ephesus in present-day Turkey. Its entrance is framed by four female statues signifying Wisdom, Character, Judgment, and Specialized Knowledge.[1]

Today, in our much more voluminous centers of learning, it sometimes seems as if only the last of these four Ephesian virtues—specialized knowledge—is still at the heart of the scholarly enterprise. Specialized knowledge is necessary for progress; but, if freedom is to survive and democracy to prevail in the modern and postmodern world, our educational establishment may need to rediscover the message suggested by those three other columns of the library at Ephesus. The human virtues of character within oneself, judgment about things beyond oneself, and the ripening of acquired knowledge into practical wisdom.

These remain the distinctive qualities of an ideal librarian. In this closing chapter I aim to show that:

1. librarians are becoming *more* rather than less important in this new age of instant electronic communication; and
2. libraries as *places* have a key role to play in building and sustaining participatory and accountable democratic societies—the kind that have historically not fought one another.

These ideal librarianly qualities seem likely to have been embedded in the founding of many of Britain's oldest libraries, reinforced in Scotland by the Calvinist heritage, and spread to America by the immigration of both settlers and ideas from the Scottish Enlightenment. I received my undergraduate education at Princeton when Presbyterian values were still part of the mix, and did my graduate work at Oxford's Balliol College, which, like Princeton, was founded by Scotsmen. My first job in Washington was to direct a new type of scholarly presidential memorial for the staunchly Presbyterian Woodrow Wilson; and, for the last twenty-seven years, I have been in charge of America's oldest federal cultural institution and the world's largest library. Like all Americans in this profession, I stand in the grateful shadow of yet another Scotsman, Andrew Carnegie, who did more than anyone else in our history both to build new libraries all over America and to engage local communities in sustaining and supporting them.

Libraries are places for the pursuit of truth. As librarian of Congress I am fortunate in my own working life to have responsibility for the world's largest foraging ground for this pursuit—a 158-million-item collection built by the Congress around the amazingly rich personal library of Thomas Jefferson. For him, the pursuit of truth was the highest form of the pursuit of happiness that he extolled in our Declaration of Independence. This pursuit differs from others in life, because it is inherently noncompetitive and communal. One person's discovery enriches another's search; and the ongoing pursuit of truth helps keep us from the pursuit of each other.

In our middle state, between the angels and the apes, we have to share truths even as we pursue them, because we can never possess Truth with a capital T. The great Jewish philosopher Franz Rosenzweig has been paraphrased as saying "Truth is a noun only to God; to men, it is really best known as an adverb."[2] In other words, it is properly attached to a verb— and, in the American and Scottish traditions, usually to an active verb.

The pursuit of truth is activated in special communities like those of the ancient universities. At a set-aside time in a set-aside place, a variegated group of reflective people can freely engage in this pursuit. Having written America's Declaration of Independence in his thirties, Jefferson left behind in his later years two great testaments to the modern ideal of knowledge-based democracy. He asked to be remembered on his tombstone not as a former president of the United States, but as the founder of a university. And his extraordinary personal library—involving sixteen languages and organized under the categories of memory, reason, and imagination—became the core of America's national library.

The Jeffersonian ideal was both uplifting and down-to-earth. He basically argued that if more people can have more access to more knowledge to use in more ways, then, whatever the problems of today, tomorrow can still be better than yesterday.

It has taken many years fully to open up either the horizons for, or the access to, institutions of higher learning. What I wish to explore in this essay is whether or not this quintessentially Enlightenment ideal is realistically sustainable in a globalized world experiencing the greatest revolution in generating and communicating knowledge since Gutenberg.

My text for giving a guardedly optimistic answer to this question comes from Ronald Cant's history of the University of St. Andrews. He points out that—even at its very beginnings in the fifteenth century—St. Andrews was different, both from "master universities" like Paris, which was a corporation of faculty, and from "student universities" like Bologna where the corporation consisted of students. There was, he says,

> little of the hard and fast distinction between "professor" and "student" to which we have become accustomed. . . . All were partners in the craft of scholarship and members of a single *society*.[3]

This medieval ideal that everyone in the community was engaged in the craft of scholarship was revived by the creation of the modern research university in the nineteenth century and by its global proliferation ever since. The college community built around the catechism and the classroom was largely superseded by the new university community built around the library and the laboratory. The model was the University of Berlin founded in 1810 and designed to out-enlighten the French, whose logic and language had been discredited by Napoleon's despotism. Everyone in this great new university—from its brilliant founding head, Alexander von Humboldt, to its most humble entering student—was regarded as a participant in pursuing truth along a variety of new pathways.

The emphasis on basic research has accounted for much of the progress and productivity of the modern world. But recent history suggests that such advances often come at the price of a kind of Faustian bargain.

The University of Berlin was the pure creation of a rising national state in its capital city. Educated Germans were among the freest and most reformist peoples in continental Europe in the first half of the nineteenth century. But as the German state grew in power, it subsequently descended into a repressive autocracy with more than a little help from its university graduates.

In times like these and in privileged places of study, I believe we have obligations as well as opportunities to seek tentative answers to important questions and not just definitive answers to trivial ones. We should not overindulge our human inclination to keep inserting our own view of what ought to be and should have been into the often exhausting search for what really is and was. Everyone in a democracy has a right to inject his or her opinion into the public dialogue. But within a community of scholars, truth is what we pursue rather than possess—particularly if we are to deal responsibly with the complex human problems of today and the multiple uncertainties of tomorrow.

Scholars, like all human beings, seek normative as well as descriptive truth. The question, "What is truth?" that the Gospel tells us Pilate asked Jesus was answered not by words, but by the life and sacrifice that embodied normative truth for those who founded—and many who have sustained—the ancient universities.

This is an unashamedly perfectionist norm, still affirmed under one label or another by nearly one-third of the world's population, but faithfully followed by painfully few. In the hundred years since the onset of World War I, we humans have proven ourselves a lot further from the angels and closer to the other animals than we like to admit. The great twentieth-century Christian theologian Karl Barth quietly suggested that even contemporary talk about God tends to be only talk about man in a loud voice.

In our imperfect middle status in the great chain of being, we still have the capacity to think—to remember, reason, and imagine. But, despite the enormous growth and spread of institutionalized cerebral activity since the founding of the University of Berlin two centuries ago, almost no one expected in advance or has clearly understood in retrospect that the two most consequential political upheavals of the late twentieth century were basically impelled by moral forces rooted in religion: the explosion of revolutionary Islamism and the implosion of the Soviet empire.

As a cultural historian, my own scholarly pursuit of truth began with reading Tolstoy's *War and Peace* as a schoolboy during World War II. It suggested to me that some deeper moral force embedded within the Russian people enabled them to resist Hitler, who like Napoleon had the most formidable army of that era and had previously conquered most of the rest of Europe. I sensed early in life that I might better understand the essence of what was happening in the world by reading yesterday's novel rather than today's newspaper.

I subsequently read Dostoevsky's *Possessed* at the outbreak of the Cold War; and it helped me understand how much of Stalin flowed from the ideology of Russian radicals in the 1870s, whom I later learned in my research to have been the first people in history to adopt the term "terrorist" as a badge of pride and used targeted and sustained political assassinations as a strategy for revolution.[4]

I was privileged to be in Moscow many years ago to witness the collapse of Soviet Communism at the very heart of its empire. One hundred and fifty armed defenders of the headquarters of Russia's first democratically elected president, Boris Yeltsin, and an unorganized ring of only a few thousand unarmed supporters miraculously prevailed against the largest array of uniformed military and security forces in human history—almost all of whom remained loyal to the hard-liners' coup attempt until it suddenly collapsed on the third day without a shot being fired.

People on both sides of the barricades were struggling not just to *discover* the freedoms of the West, but also to *recover* the moral bases of their own culture.

Still underappreciated in the West is the role that religion played in the serial unraveling of the Soviet empire, the world's first political system based on the systematic destruction of all religion. The process began with the total inability of the Communist overlords in Poland to crush, co-opt, or control in the largest Soviet satellite the Solidarity movement, rooted as it was in Catholic Christianity and in the working class. This was, in Arnold Toynbee's terms, the challenge to which an imperial system could not by its very nature find an effective response—and might therefore be fated to decline and fall.[5]

The indication that the final Soviet collapse in 1991 might give moral legitimacy to an otherwise unfamiliar democratic form of government came at the joint funeral of the three boys—two Christian and one Jew—who were accidentally run over by a tank during the stand-off. In contrast to a bureaucratized totalitarianism where no one accepted responsibility for what they actually did, a new leader took responsibility for something he could not possibly have prevented. There was hardly a dry eye in Russia when Yeltsin said to the parents of the boys, "Forgive me, your president, that I was unable to defend and save your sons."

"Forgive me," is what Russian Orthodox Christians often say to one another before taking communion, and the last words spoken by the tragic heroes of perhaps the two greatest Russian historical operas: Mussorgsky's *Boris Godunov* and Tchaikovsky's *Mazepa*.

Despite the crime, corruption, and neo-authoritarian tendencies that we have since seen in post-Communist Russia, I continue to be hopeful for the Russian future, in part because of the totally new perspective we have seen in the nearly seventeen thousand emerging young leaders we have brought from Russia to America under the Open World program, which our Congress created, whose board I chaired for its first decade, and which celebrated its fifteenth anniversary in 2014.

A key question for the future of European civilization is whether or not Russia will finally be able to zigzag its way into creating an accountable, participatory form of government cleansed by the antiseptic of openness. Russia has long borders with the two vast regions most resistant to democratic governance: the Middle East and China. If authoritarian nationalism continues to erode and effectively to erase Russia's post-Soviet hopes for democratic development in Eurasia, the threats to peace would be multiplied.

One of Russia's internal resources for democratic progress is its libraries and librarians. They provided refuges for scholars unwilling to become propagandists in the Soviet era. They quietly preserved and provided access both to the memory of Russia's pre-Communist past and to the experience of the post–World War II West. Despite much neglect in recent years, Russian libraries press on and have remained a resource and gathering place for people of all ages and backgrounds. Particularly remarkable has been the pioneering leadership of Yekaterina Genieva in the Library of Foreign Literature in Moscow, helping young Russians for two decades both to recover their own religious heritage and to discover the culture and experience of other countries.

In June 2009 I attended a dedication ceremony in the majestic former Synod Building in St. Petersburg of a new presidential library named after Boris Yeltsin. This highly electronic library was planned to develop branches in all political subdivisions of the Russian Federation. Whether or not it succeeds in doing so—and in providing open access to an ever widening range of knowledge and information—will be an important indicator of either progress toward, or regression from, a democratic future.

Hanging over any discussion of the future of libraries anywhere today is the seeming threat to their very existence posed by the great technological revolution of our times: the digitized generation and instant communication of knowledge and information. So far at least, the exploding virtual world has helped accelerate three kinds of human loss in the real world: of memory, of community, and of language.

The new technology proudly advertises its own capacity for memory, but it fosters a memory-free present-mindedness in its users. Its content is put on inherently perishable websites that face repeated obsolescence in the means of decoding. Sitting at a computer is a lonely activity, often isolating a person from face-to-face interaction through the local communities that have historically knit people together through family, school, and church, as well as business activities.

Communities are held together by communication; and the new online culture threatens to destroy reading among its younger addicts and, as a result, to dumb down the use of language. You cannot write if you do not read. The basic unit of human thought for the last two and a half millennia has been the sentence, which is largely obliterated in online chat rooms. The once elastic and rich English language is being replaced by a mushy mélange of abbreviations, acronyms, and the universalized pidgin English of air traffic controllers and computer programmers.

Despite these inherent cultural dangers, libraries within modern democracies have generally been early and active in bringing the new world of computer-born knowledge and information into their traditional world of books. And the Library of Congress, as the world's largest repository of human knowledge and creativity and as the de facto national library of the United States, has tried to help counter each of the threatening trends that I have mentioned.

The Library of Congress has used the new technology to put old cultural treasures with expert commentary in seven languages online free of charge for library and local use anywhere in the world. It began several years ago with a program called American Memory. It now offers a website containing more than 30 million important, multimedia items of American history and culture. More recently it has launched the World Digital Library, containing content from all 192 countries in UNESCO and much material from UNESCO's Memory of the World database.[6]

This World Digital Library is beginning to do for others what the Library of Congress has been doing for America—giving young people back their memory. It is helping to bring on to a single website historical and cultural documents that are widely scattered but that can help honor the distinct identities of different cultures and promote better international understanding.

The main aim of this digital outreach is educational—to stimulate students and lifelong learners and to empower teachers by providing variegated teaching plans for classroom and home use of these materials and for intergenerational reading and discussion.

Maps, music, movies, and manuscripts are being put online as well as rare original print materials in order to arouse curiosity and lead young people into reading and a better use of language. This is not just another form of distraction away from reading back into the passive spectatorism and shortening attention spans that television tends to produce. The online material is increasingly interactive like reading itself and is invariably explained clearly by authoritative curators in good English; and, in the World Digital Library, in six other languages as well.

Most important of all, perhaps, is the fact that primary documents of knowledge and creativity humanize the study of history and culture. Young people at a very early age can become motivated to ask questions of their own, look for answers in books, and enter actively into the learning process. The program is helping to develop capacity in less advanced regions and to repatriate in virtual form basic materials about their own countries from foreign repositories. Thus it can help bridge the digital divide within and between countries. Those with less literate backgrounds can have a more accessible initial entryway into education; and more people everywhere can gain a better understanding of their own heritage as well as of other cultures.

Contrary to the prophecy of many technological futurists, I believe that there can and should be increased importance in the twenty-first century for libraries as distinct places and librarians as knowledge navigators for the particular communities they serve. Libraries have historically been unifying gathering places for disparate people and interests in a given locality. The very inundation of unfiltered online information makes it urgent that every community have its own objective human guide to online information and knowledge that is reliable and relevant for their local concerns and, at the same time, to the broader perspectives that can be gleaned from books. Without the character and judgment of librarians able to integrate the artifactual with the virtual, future scholars will be hard-put to achieve in their work the results called for by the other two statues at Ephesus: specialized knowledge and higher wisdom.

There are many reasons for believing that the digital world will never fully replace the world of books. New technologies tend to *supplement* rather than supplant old ones. Movies did not obliterate plays; television did not destroy radio. Even as the Internet was exploding exponentially in the last decade, book publishing also increased worldwide by 40 percent. Online materials are perishable and manipulable in ways that are not yet generally understood; and digitization is still more a vehicle for communication than for preservation.

The values of the book culture are particularly important for us in the United States. We are the only world civilization whose governing institutions were shaped entirely in the age of print. The first meetings both of our Continental Congress in Philadelphia and of the Congress under its new Constitution in New York were held in libraries; and the first committee combining the two houses of Congress when it relocated to Washington, DC, was the Joint Committee on the Library of Congress. The word "liberty" is often connected in popular usage with *liber*, the Latin word for book. The future of democratic freedoms in our own more troubled times may depend on sustaining the values of the book culture even as we add on ever more gaudy technological innovations.[7]

Books are our guardians of memory, tutors in language, pathways to reason, and our golden gate to the royal road of imagination. Books take us to new places where boundaries are not set by someone else's pictures on a television screen and our thoughts are not drowned out by sounds on a boom box. Books help us to pose the unimagined question and to accept the unwelcome answer. Books convince rather than coerce. They are oases of coherence where things are put together rather than just taken apart. Good books take us away from the bumper cars of emotion and polemics in the media into trains of thought that can lead us into places we might not otherwise ever discover.

Reading a book can become a private conversation with someone from a time and place other than our own—a voyage into both mastery and mystery. The reader must both master enough of the language to understand the created object and, at the same time, wonder about the mystery of its creation—and perhaps about creation itself. And this may lead him or her back to the great founding books of world culture: the Vedas, Sutras, Analects, Torah, Koran, and Bible—preferably in the King James Version, which comes to us in the language of Shakespeare.

Libraries are antidotes to fanaticism. They are temples of pluralism, where books that contradict one another sit peacefully side by side on the shelves just as intellectual antagonists work peacefully next to each other in reading rooms.

In a speech on the American Great Plains some years ago, I praised librarians as gate keepers to knowledge. A native American Indian chief came up to me afterward and quietly explained that, long before European settlers brought books to North America, the elder of a tribe would preserve the knowledge of his people in his head the way librarians would later do in their collections. "But we didn't call him a gate keeper," he gently explained, "we called him the dream keeper." One of my favorite uses that teachers have made of our multiform, online American Memory materials is to ask students to reconstruct not just the accomplishments, but the dreams of some group of Americans from some time, region, or ethnicity other than their own.

The global information revolution makes it possible to dream of extending out far more broadly the model that Ronald Cant saw at the very founding of the university at St. Andrews, that of a community in which "all were partners in the craft of scholarship and members of a single society."[8] But we should still be haunted by the question T. S. Eliot asked long before information flooded onto the Internet:

> Where is the wisdom we have lost in knowledge?
> Where is the knowledge we have lost in information?[9]

He seems to suggest something of an answer in one of his greatest poems, written long before the digital age. Perhaps a mixture of humanity, nature, and electronics will somehow redeem the bellicosity and materialism of the modern world, which he had previously described as a waste land:

> The trilling wire in the blood
> Sings below inveterate scars
> Appeasing long forgotten wars . . .
>
> . . . .
>
> . . . We move above the moving tree
> In light upon the figured leaf
> And hear upon the sodden floor
> Below, the boarhound and the boar
> Pursue their pattern as before
> But reconciled among the stars.[10]

Whether or not we in the West can harness new technology at home to a better understanding of other cultures abroad, we will be ennobled by the effort to venture into the unknown worlds where books can lead us.

The most deeply bookish and most nearly successful effort to build an enduring cultural link between traditional China and the modernizing West of the high Renaissance ultimately ended in failure. But the great Jesuit mission to China left behind an epigraph written in a dead language by an unknown author to an unknown audience:

Abi viator,
congratulare mortuis,
condole vivis,
ora pro omnibus,
mirare e tace.

Move on, voyager,
congratulate the dead,
console the living,
pray for everyone,
wonder and be silent.

Wonder and silence are better for dream keepers than for image makers. Reading can balance our noisy, hurry-up, present-minded world with what Keats called "silence and slow time."[11] Whatever else you do in life, do not fail to experience the simple pleasure of being alone with a good book on a rainy day.

However great the confusion of our times and of the information in our minds, things can still come together in a book, just as the right and left halves of the brain come together in the miracle of the human mind, and the hemispheres—East and West, North and South—are all bound together on our single, fragile but glorious planet.

NOTES

1. *Sophia, Arete, Ennoia, Episteme*: four virtues attributed to Celsus, the Roman consul.

2. Jacob Agus, *Modern Philosophies of Judaism* (New York: Behrman's Jewish Book House, 1941), 191.

3. Ronald Gordon Cant, *The University of St. Andrews: A Short History* (Edinburgh: Scottish Academic Press, 1970), 70.

4. James H. Billington, *Fire in the Minds of Men* (New York: Basic Books, 1980), 405–14.

5. I wrote in February 1987, "It is not hard to imagine . . . that in the 21st century . . . even in the Soviet Union historians will look back on Solidarity as an anticipation if not a prototype of movements that . . . developed to transform

their own societies in ways radically different from the violent, secular revolutionary movements of the past." Steve W. Reiquam, ed., *Solidarity and Poland*, intro. James H. Billington, (Washington, DC: Wilson Center Press, 1988), 3.

6. See the World Digital Library website at http://www.wdl.org/en/ and the Memory of the World Project website at http://www.unesco.org/new/en/communication-and-information/flagship-project-activities/memory-of-the-world/homepage/.

7. Editor's note: in chapter 1, "Adventures in Ancient Greek and Roman Libraries," Edith Hall discusses the false etymology that links the Latin noun *liber* ("tree-bark," and hence eventually, "book" made of paper derived from bark) with the completely differently origined adjective *liber* ("free"), and explains why the link is a mistake (page XXX). The etymologically incorrect connection between "book" and "freedom" persists in popular understanding, however, and the two are so frequently paired together that the linkage has its own cultural history.

8. Cant, *The University of St. Andrews*, 70.

9. T. S. Eliot, "Choruses from 'The Rock,'" I (1934), *Collected Poems 1909–1935* (London: Faber and Faber, 1936), 157.

10. T. S. Eliot, "Burnt Norton," II, *Collected Poems 1909–1935* (London: Faber and Faber, 1936), 186–87.

11. John Keats, "Ode on a Grecian Urn," in *The Oxford Book of English Verse 1250–1900*, ed. Arthur Quiller-Couch (Oxford: Clarendon, 1919), 745.

SELECTED BIBLIOGRAPHY

Alexander, J.J.G., ed. *The Painted Page: Italian Renaissance Book Illumination 1450–1550*. London: Royal Academy of Arts, 1994.

Allan, David. *A Nation of Readers: The Lending Library in Georgian England*. London: British Library, 2008.

———. "Provincial Readers and Book Culture in the Scottish Enlightenment: The Perth Library, c. 1784–1800." *Library* 3 (2002): 367–89.

———. "The Scottish Enlightenment and the Politics of Provincial Culture: The Perth Literary and Antiquarian Society, ca. 1784–1790." *Eighteenth-Century Life* 27 (2003): 1–31.

Allen, Esther. "Michael Henry Heim: A Theory." In *The Man Between: Michael Henry Heim and a Life in Translation*, ed. Esther Allen, Sean Cotter, and Russell Scott Valentino. Rochester, NY: Open Letter, 2014.

American Library Association. *State of America's Libraries Report 2012*. Online at http://www.ala.org/news/mediapresscenter/americaslibraries/soal 2012/academic-libraries.

Armes, Roy. *The Cinema of Alain Resnais*. London: Zwemmer, 1968.

Armstrong, Carol. *Scenes in a Library: Reading the Photograph in the Book, 1843–1875*. Cambridge, MA: MIT Press, 1998.

Ashton, R. D. *Victorian Bloomsbury*. London: Yale University Press, 2013.

Baker, William. *The George Eliot–George Henry Lewes Library: An Annotated Catalogue of Their Books at Dr. Williams's Library, London*. New York: Garland, 1977.

———. *Wilkie Collins's Library: Reconstruction*. Westport, CT: Greenwood Press, 2002.

Battles, Matthew. *Library: An Unquiet History*. London: William Heinemann, 2003.

Beckwith, Frank. *The Leeds Library 1768–1968*, 2nd ed. Leeds: Leeds Library, 1994.

Bencheikh, Jamel Eddine, and André Miquel, trans., *Mille et une Nuits*. Paris: Gallimard, 2005.

Benjamin, Walter. "On the Concept of History." In his *Selected Writings*, ed. Michael W. Jennings. Vol. 4, 1938–1940. Cambridge, MA: Harvard University Press, 2003, 389–400.

———. "Unpacking My Library." In his *Selected Writings*, ed. Michael W. Jennings. Vol. 2, 1927–1934. Cambridge, MA: Harvard University Press, 1999, 486–93.

Bennett, Alan. "Baffled at a Bookcase." *London Review of Books* 33.15 (July 28, 2011): 3–7.

Berkovits, Ilona. *Illuminated Manuscripts from the Library of Matthias Corvinus.* Budapest: Corvina Press, 1964.

Bernstein, Susan David. *Roomscape: Women Writers in the British Museum from George Eliot to Virginia Woolf.* Edinburgh: Edinburgh University Press, 2013.

Berti, Monica, and Vergilio Costa, *La Biblioteca di Alessandria: Storia di un paradiso perduto.* Ricerche di filologia, letteratura e storia 10. Roma: Edizioni Tored, 2010.

Billington, James H. *Fire in the Minds of Men.* New York: Basic Books, 1980.

Bivens-Tatum, Wayne. *Libraries and the Enlightenment.* Los Angeles: Library-Juice Press, 2012.

Blake, N. F. *Caxton's Own Prose.* London: Deutsch, 1973.

Bonn, Maria, and Mike Furlough, eds. *Getting the Word Out: Academic Libraries and Scholarly Publishing.* Chicago: Association of College and Research Libraries, 2015.

Bonnet, Jacques. *Phantoms on the Bookshelves.* London: Quercus Books, 2013.

Borges, Jorge Luis. "The Library of Babel." In *Collected Fictions*, trans. Andrew Hurley. New York: Penguin, 1998, 112–18.

———. "The Library of Babel," trans. James E. Irby. In *Labyrinths*, ed. Donald A. Yates and James E. Irby. New York: Penguin, 1962, 78–86.

———. *Selected Poems*, ed. Alexander Coleman. London: Allen Lane, 1999.

———. *The Total Library: Non-Fiction, 1922–1986*, ed. Eliot Weinberger, trans. Esther Allen, Suzanne Jill Levine, and Eliot Weinberger. London: Allen Lane, 2000.

Borges, Jorge Luis, with Margarita Guerrero. *The Book of Imaginary Beings*, trans. Norman Thomas di Giovanni. New York: Penguin, 1967.

Burch, Noel. "Four Recent French Documentaries." *Film Quarterly* 13.1 (Autumn, 1959): 56–61.

Cadell, Patrick, and Ann Matheson, eds. *For the Encouragement of Learning: Scotland's National Library 1689—1989.* Edinburgh: HMSO, 1989.

Calvino, Italo. *Invisible Cities*, trans. William Weaver. London: Picador, 1974.

Cameron, Alan. *Callimachus and His Critics.* Princeton, NJ: Princeton University Press, 1995.

Campbell, James W. P. *The Library: A World History.* London: Thames and Hudson, 2013.

Canfora, Luciano. *The Vanished Library: A Wonder of the Ancient World,* trans. Martin Ryle. Berkeley: University of California Press, 1990.

Cant, Ronald Gordon. *The University of St. Andrews: A Short History.* Edinburgh: Scottish Academic Press, 1970.

Castillo, Debra A. *The Translated World: A Post-Modern Tour of Libraries in Literature.* Tallahassee: University of Florida Press, 1984.

Cavendish, Margaret. *Poems and Phancies.* London: William Wilson, 1664.

Chodorow, S. *Law Libraries and the Formation of the Legal Profession in the Late Middle Ages.* Austin: University of Texas Press, 2007.

Christenson, Heather. "HathiTrust: A Research Library at Web Scale." *Library Resources and Technical Services* 55.2: 93–102. Online at http://www.hathitrust.org/documents/christenson-lrts-201104.pdf.

Christiansen, A. K., L. B. Kantor, and C. B. Strehlke, eds. *Painting in Renaissance Siena 1420–1500.* New York: Metropolitan Museum of Art, 1988.

Clapinson, Mary. "The Bodleian Library and Its Readers, 1602–1652." *Bodleian Library Record* 19.1 (2006): 30–46.

Clark, J. W. *The Care of Books.* Cambridge: Cambridge University Press, 1901.

Clark, Peter. *British Clubs and Societies 1580–1800: The Origins of an Associational World.* Oxford: Oxford University Press, 2000.

Clegg, J. *The Medieval Church in Manuscripts.* London: British Library, 2003.

Colla, Elliott. "The Porter and Portability: Figure and Narrative in the Nights." In *Scheherazade's Children: Global Encounters with the Arabian Nights,* ed. Philip F. Kennedy and Marina Warner. New York: New York University Press, 2013, 89–107.

Connat, M., and J. Mégret. "Inventaire de la bibliothèque des du Prat." *Bibliothèque d'Humanisme et Renaissance* 3 (1943): 72–128.

Constans, L., ed. *Le Roman de Troie par Benoît de Sainte-Maure.* Société des anciens textes français. 6 vols. Paris: Firmin Didot, 1904–12.

Corpus of British Medieval Library Catalogues. London: British Library, 1990–.

Crabbe, George. *The Library, A Poem.* London: J. Dodsley, 1781.

Crawford, John C. "Leadhills Library and a Wider World." *Library Review* 46 (1997): 539–53.

Crawford, Robert, ed. *Apollos of the North: Selected Poems of George Buchanan and Arthur Johnston.* Edinburgh: Polygon, 2006.

———. *The Bard: Robert Burns; A Biography.* London: Jonathan Cape, 2009.

———. *Full Volume.* London: Cape, 2008.

Csapodi, Csaba. *The Corvinian Library: History and Stock.* Budapest: Akadémiai Kiadó, 1973.

Cunningham, J. V. *The Poems.* Chicago: Swallow Press, 1977.

Dalley, Stephanie. "Gilgamesh in the *Arabian Nights.*" *Journal of the Royal Asiatic Society.* 1.1 (April 1991): 1–17.

———, ed. and trans. *Myths from Mesopotamia: Creation, the Flood, Gilgamesh, and Others.* Oxford: Oxford University Press, 1989.

Darnton, Robert. *The Literary Underground of the Old Regime.* Cambridge, MA: Harvard University Press, 1982.

Davids, Roy. "Blessed Are the Dead." *Author* (Society of Authors), Summer 2002. Online at http://www.roydavids.com/archives2.htm.

De Hamel, Christopher. *A History of Illuminated Manuscripts,* 2nd ed. London: Phaidon, 1994.

Deliyannis, D. M. *Ravenna in Late Antiquity.* Cambridge: Cambridge University Press, 2010.

Dempsey, Lorcan. "Sourcing and Scaling." *Lorcan Dempsey's Weblog,* February 21, 2010. Online at http://orweblog.oclc.org/archives/002058.html.

———. "Thirteen Ways of Looking at Libraries, Discovery, and the Catalog: Scale, Workflow, Attention." *Educause Review Online,* December 10, 2012. Online at http://www.educause.edu/ero/article/thirteen-ways-looking-libraries-discovery-and-catalog-scale-workflow-attention.

Derolez, A. *Les Catalogues de bibliothèques.* Turnhout: Brepols, 1979.

———. *The Library of Raphael de Marcatellis.* Gent: E. Story-Scientia, 1979.

Derolez, A., et al. *Corpus Catalogorum Belgii.* Bruxelles: Paleis der Academiën, 1994.

De Strata, Filippo. *Polemic against Printing,* trans. Shelagh Grier, intro. Martin Lowry. Birmingham: Hayloft Press, 1986.

Dix, T. Keith. "Pliny's Library at Commum." *Libraries and Culture* 31.1 (1996): 85–102.

Donadio, Rachel. "Literary Letters, Lost In Cyberspace." *New York Times Book Review* September 4, 2005, 15.

Dupont, Florence *The Invention of Literature: From Greek Intoxication to the Latin Book,* trans. Janet Lloyd. Baltimore: Johns Hopkins University Press, 1999.

Eco, Umberto. *The Name of the Rose,* trans. William Weaver. London: Picador, 1983.

Eisenstein, Elizabeth. *The Printing Press as an Agent of Change: Communications and Cultural Transformations in Early Modern Europe.* Cambridge: Cambridge University Press, 1979.

————. *The Printing Revolution in Early Modern Europe*. Cambridge: Cambridge University Press, 1983.

Eliot, Simon. "Unequal Partnerships: Besant, Rice and Chatto, 1876–82." *Publishing History* 27 (1989): 73–109.

Eliot, Simon, and Jonathan Rose, eds. *A Companion to the History of the Book*. Malden, MA: Blackwell, 2007.

Enniss, Stephen. "Ted Hughes, Sylvia Plath, and the Myth of Textual Betrayal." *Papers of the Bibliographical Society of America* 101.1 (March 2007): 63–71.

Fischer, Steven Roger. *A History of Reading*. London: Reaktion, 2003.

Flavell, M. Kay. "The Enlightened Reader and the New Industrial Towns: A Study of the Liverpool Library, 1758–1790." *British Journal for Eighteenth-Century Studies* 8 (1985): 17–35.

"Free Libraries," *Graphic* October 15, 1892, 464.

Furneaux, Holly. *Queer Dickens: Erotics, Families, Masculinities*. Oxford: Oxford University Press, 2009.

Gabriel, A. L. *Student Life in Ave Maria College, Mediaeval Paris: History and Chartulary of the College*. Notre Dame, IN.: University of Notre Dame Press, 1955.

Gaiman, Neil. "Why Our Future Depends on Libraries, Reading and Daydreaming." theguardian.com, October 15, 2013. Online at http://www.theguardian.com/books/2013/oct/15/neil-gaiman-future-libraries-reading-daydreaming.

Gameson, R. "The Medieval Library (to c. 1450)." In *The Cambridge History of Libraries in Britain and Ireland I*. Vol. 1., ed. E. Leedham-Green and T. Webber. Cambridge: Cambridge University Press, 2006, 13–50.

————. "'Signed' Manuscripts from Early Romanesque Flanders." In *Pen in Hand: Medieval Scribal Portraits, Colophons and Tools*, ed. M. Gullick. Walkern: Red Gull Press, 2006, 31–73.

Genevois, A.-M., J.-F. Genest, and A. Chalandon. *Bibliothèques de manuscrits médiévaux en France*. Paris: Editions du CNRS, 1987.

George, Andrew, ed. and trans. *The Epic of Gilgamesh*. London: Penguin, 1999.

George, William, and Emily Waters, eds. *The Vespasiano Memoirs: Lives of Illustrious Men of the XV Century*. London: Routledge, 1926.

Goodfellow, Tom. *The Depiction of American Public Libraries in Film*. MA dissertation, University of North London, 2000. Online at http://www.angelfire.com/oz/tomgoodfellow/LibrariesinFilm.htm.

Gordan, Phyllis Walter Goodhart, ed. *Two Renaissance Book Hunters: The Letters of Poggius Bracciolini to Nicolaus de Niccolis*. New York: Columbia University Press, 1974.

Grego, Joseph. *Thackerayana*. London: Chatto and Windus, 1875.

Grendler, Marcella. "Book-Collecting in Counter-Reformation Italy: The Library of Gian Vincenzo Pinelli 1535–1601." *Journal of Library History* 16 (1981): 143–51.

———. "A Greek Collection in Padua: The Library of Gian Vincenzo Pinelli (1535–1601)." *Renaissance Quarterly* 33 (1980): 386–416.

Griest, G. L. *Mudie's Circulating Library and the Victorian Novel*. Bloomington: Indiana University Press, 1970.

Grossman, Richard H., and Andrew Wright. "Anthony Trollope's Libraries." *Nineteenth-Century Fiction* 31.1 (June 1976): 48–64.

Haddawy, Husain, trans. *The Arabian Nights*. New York: Norton, 1990.

Hall, Edith. *Introducing the Ancient Greeks: From Bronze-Age Seafarers to Navigators of the Western Mind*. New York: Norton, 2014.

———. *The Theatrical Cast of Athens*. Oxford: Oxford University Press, 2006.

———. "Tragic Theatre: Demetrios' Rolls and Dionysos' Other Women." In *The Pronomos Vase and Its Context*, ed. O. Taplin and R. Wyles. Oxford: Oxford University Press, 2010, 159–79.

Hamilton, Alastair. *The Arcadian Library: Western Appreciation of Arab and Islamic Civilization*. London: Arcadian Library in association with Oxford University Press, 2011.

Hamilton, David M. *The Tools of My Trade: The Annotated Books in Jack London's Library*. Seattle: University of Washington Press, 1986.

Hanink, Johanna. *Lycurgan Athens and the Making of Classical Tragedy*. Cambridge; Cambridge University Press, 2014.

Hanna, R. *A Descriptive Catalogue of the Western Medieval Manuscripts of St. John's College, Oxford*. Oxford: Oxford University Press, 2002.

Hapgood, Kathleen. "Library Practice in the Bristol Library Society, 1772–1830." *Library History* 5 (1981): 145–53.

Harden, Edgar. "The Writing and Publication of Esmond." *Studies in the Novel* 13 (1981): 79–92.

Harris, Michael H. *History of Libraries in the Western World*. Metuchen, NJ: Scarecrow Press, 1995.

Harrisse, Henry. *Excerpta Colombiniana: Bibliographie de 400 pièces du 16e siècle; précédée d'une histoire de la Bibliothèque colombine et de son fondateur*. Paris: Welter, 1887.

Haynes, I., A. Diaconescu, and A. Schafer. "Apulum: Romania." *Current World Archaeology* 10 (2005). Illustrated summary available online at http://www.world-archaeology.com/features/apulum-romania.htm.

Heaney, Seamus. *Seeing Things*. London: Faber and Faber, 1991.

Heller, B., and L. Stodulski. "Recent Scientific Investigation of the Detroit Saint Jérôme." In *Petrus Christus in Renaissance Bruges: An Interdisciplinary Approach*, ed. M. W. Ainsworth. New York and Turnhout: Brepols, 1995, 131–42.

Henderson, Cathy. "The Birth of an Institution." In *Collecting the Imagination: The First Fifty Years of the Ransom Center*, ed. Megan Barnard. Austin: University of Texas Press, 2007, 19–50.

Hill, Susan. *Howards End Is on the Landing: A Year of Reading from Home*. London: Profile Books, 2010.

Hillyard, Brian. "The Keepership of David Hume." In *For the Encouragement of Learning: Scotland's National Library 1689–1989*, ed. Patrick Cadell and Ann Matheson. Edinburgh: HMSO, 1989, 103–9.

Hilson, J. C. "More Unpublished Letters of David Hume." *Forum for Modern Language Studies* 6 (1970): 315–26.

Histoire des bibliothèques françaises (Centre national des Lettres). 4 vols. Paris: Promodis, 1988–92.

Hoare, Peter, ed. *The Cambridge History of Libraries in Britain and Ireland*. Cambridge: Cambridge University Press, 2006.

Hobson, Anthony. *Great Libraries*. London: Weidenfeld and Nicolson, 1970.

———. "A Sale by Candle in 1608." *Library*, ser. 5, 26 (1971): 215–33.

Horsfall, Nicholas. "Empty Shelves on the Palatine." *Greece and Rome*, 2nd ser., 40.1 (1993): 58–67.

Host, John. *Victorian Labour History: Experience, Identity and the Politics of Representation*. London: Routledge, 1998.

House, Humphry. *The Dickens World*. Oxford: Oxford University Press, 1941.

Houston, George W. "Tiberius and the Libraries: Public Book Collections and Library Buildings in the Early Roman Empire." *Libraries and the Cultural Record* 43.3 (2008): 247–69.

Hudson, William. *The Life of John Holland, of Sheffield Park*. London: Longmans, Green, 1874.

James, M.S.R. "Correspondence." *Monthly Packet* August 1, 1892, 237.

———. "Women Librarians and Their Future Prospects." *Library Association Record* June 1900, 293.

Jameson, Frederic. *The Cultural Turn: Selected Writings on the Postmodern 1983–1998*. Brooklyn: Verso, 1998.

Jammes, André. "A Scene in a Library." *Photographie* no. 1 (Spring 1983): 50.

Jensen, Kristian. "Universities and Colleges." In *The Cambridge History of Libraries in Britain and Ireland*. Vol. 1, to 1640, ed. Elizabeth Leedham-Green and Teresa Webber, 345–62. Cambridge: Cambridge University Press, 2006.

Joint, Nicholas. "Legal Deposit and Collection Development in a Digital World." *Library Review* 55.8 (2006): 468–73.

Jones, Arthur, and M. Barry King. "The Effect of Re-siting a Library." *Journal of Librarianship and Information Science* 11 (1979): 215–31.

Jourda, Pierre. "La bibliothèque d'un régent calviniste (1577)." In *Mélanges d'histoire littéraire de la Renaissance offerts à Henri Chamard*. Paris: Librarie Nizet, 1951, 269–73.

Kaufman, Paul. "The Community Library: A Chapter in English Social History." *Transactions of the American Philosophical Society* 57 (1967): pt. 7, 3–67.

Kelly, Thomas. *A History of Adult Education in Great Britain*, 2nd ed. Liverpool: Liverpool University Press, 1970.

Kennedy, Philip F., and Marina Warner, eds. *Scheherazade's Children: Global Encounters with the Arabian Nights*. New York: New York University Press, 2013.

Ker, N. R. *Medieval Libraries of Great Britain*, 2nd ed. London: Royal Historical Society, 1964; with *Supplement*, ed. A. G. Watson. London: Royal Historical Society, 1987.

Kessler, H. L. *The Illustrated Bibles from Tours*. Princeton, NJ: Princeton University Press, 1977.

Kilito, Abdelfattah. *Dites-moi le songe*. Arles: Actes Sud, 2010.

———. *L'oeil et l'aiguille: Essai sur 'Les mille et une nuits.'* Paris: Le Fennec, Editions de la Découverte, 1992.

Kingsley, Charles. *Hypatia*. London: Parker, 1853.

Klein, Lawrence E. *Shaftesbury and the Culture of Politeness: Moral Discourse and Cultural Politics in Early Eighteenth-Century England*. Cambridge: Cambridge University Press, 1994.

———. "The Third Earl of Shaftesbury and the Progress of Politeness." *Eighteenth-Century Studies* 8 (1974): 186–214.

Knowles, D., and C.N.L. Brooke, eds. *The Monastic Constitutions of Lanfranc*. Oxford: Oxford University Press, 2002.

Koch, Theodore W. "New Light on Old Libraries." *Library Quarterly* 4.2 (1934): 244–52.

Kolker, Robert Phillip, and Peter Beicken. *The Films of Wim Wenders: Cinema as Vision and Desire*. Cambridge: Cambridge University Press, 1993.

König, Jason, Katerina Oikonomopoulou, and Greg Woolf, eds. *Ancient Libraries*. Cambridge: Cambridge University Press, 2013.

Kunitz, Stanley. *Passing Through*. New York: Norton, 1995.

Labowsky, Lotte. *Bessarion's Library and the Biblioteca Marciana: Six Early Inventories*. Rome: Edizioni di storia e letteratura, 1979.

"Lady Librarians." *Pall Mall Gazette* May 30, 1890, 3.

Larkin, Philip. *Collected Poems*, ed. Anthony Thwaite. London: Faber and Faber, 1988.

———. "Operation Manuscript." *Poetry in the Making: Catalogue of an Exhibition of Poetry Manuscripts in the British Museum, April–June 1967*. London: Turret Books, 1967.

Leedham-Green, E. S. *Books in Cambridge Inventories: Book Lists from Vice-Chancellor's Court Probate Inventories in the Tudor and Stuart Periods*. Cambridge: Cambridge University Press, 1986.

Leedham-Green, E. S., and T. Webber, eds. *The Cambridge History of Libraries in Britain and Ireland. Vol. 1*. Cambridge: Cambridge University Press, 2006.

Lewis, C. Day. Preface, *Poetry in the Making: Catalogue of an Exhibition of Poetry Manuscripts in the British Museum, April–June 1967*. London: Turret Books, 1967.

Lively, Penelope. *Ammonites and Leaping Fish*. London: Fig Tree, 2013.

Loomis, L. H. "The Auchinleck Manuscript and a Possible London Bookshop of 1330–1340." *Proceedings of the Modern Language Association* 57 (1942): 595–627.

Lowell, M. *Enrichment: A History of the Public Library in the United States in the Twentieth Century*. Metuchen, NJ: Scarecrow Press, 1998.

Lydenberg, Harry Miller. *Some Presses You Will be Glad to Know About*. New York: University Books, 1937.

Lyons, Malcolm C., and Ursula Lyons, trans. *The Arabian Nights: Tales of 1001 Nights*, London: Penguin, 2009.

MacLeod, Colin. "Euripides' Rags." *Zeitschrift für Papyrologie und Epigraphik* 15 (1974): 221–22.

Magness, Jodi. *The Archaeology of Qumran and the Dead Sea Scrolls*. Grand Rapids, MI: William B. Eerdmans, 2002.

Mallett, Phillip, ed. *Thomas Hardy in Context*. Cambridge: Cambridge University Press, 2013.

Malpas, Constance. "Cloud-Sourcing Research Collections: Managing Print in the Mass-Digitized Library Environment." OCLC Report, 2011. Online at http://www.oclc.org/content/dam/research/publications/library/2011/2011-01.pdf.

———. "Reconfiguring Academic Collections: the Role of Shared Print Repositories." Presentation to MLAC (Minnesota Library Access Center) Advisory Board, February 23, 2011. Online at http://www.oclc.org/content/dam/research/presentations/malpas/mlac2011.pdf.

Manguel, Alberto. *The Library at Night*. New Haven, CT: Yale University Press, 2008.

Manley, Keith. "Lounging Places and Frivolous Literature: Subscription and Circulating Libraries in the West Country to 1825." In *Printing Places: Locations of Book Production and Distribution since 1500*, ed. John Hinks and Catherine Armstrong, 107–20. New Castle, DE, and London: British Library, 2005.

———. "Rural Reading in North West England: The Sedbergh Book Club, 1728–1928." *Book History* 2 (1999): 78–95.

Marsden, R. *The Text of the Old Testament in Anglo-Saxon England*. Cambridge: Cambridge University Press, 1995.

Marshall, Anthony J. "Library Resources and Creative Writing at Rome." *Phoenix* 30.3 (1976): 252–64.

Marzolph, Ulrich, and Richard van Leeuwen. *The Arabian Nights Encyclopedia*. Santa Barbara, CA: ABC-Clio, 2004.

Mathers, Powys, and J. C. Mardrus, trans. *The Arabian Nights: The Book of the Thousand Nights and One Night*. 6 vols. London: Folio Society, 2003.

McKendrick, S., J. Lowden, and K. Doyle, eds. *Royal Manuscripts: The Genius of Illumination*. London: British Library, 2011.

McKitterick, David. *Print, Manuscript and the Search for Order, 1450–1830*. Cambridge: Cambridge University Press, 2003.

Melot, Michel. *La sagesse du bibliothécaire*. Paris: L'Œil neuf, 2004.

Merwin, Dido. "Vessel of Wrath: A Memoir of Sylvia Plath." In *Bitter Fame*, by Anne Stevenson. Boston: Houghton Mifflin, 1989, 322–47.

Mitchell, Stephen. *Gilgamesh: A New English Version*. London: Profile Books, 2004.

Mittler, Elmar. *Bibliotheca Palatina: Katalog zur Ausstellung vom 8. Juli bis 2. November 1986*. Heidelberg: Braus, 1986.

Mojsov, Bojana. *Alexandria Lost: From the Advent of Christianity to the Arab Conquest*. London: Duckworth, 2010.

Mommsen, Theodor E. *Petrarch's Testament*. Ithaca, NY: Cornell University Press, 1957.

Morgan, Charles. *The House of Macmillan*. London: Macmillan, 1943.

Morgentaler, Goldie. "Meditating on the Low: A Darwinian Reading of *Great Expectations*." *Studies in English Literature, 1500–1900* 38.4 (Autumn 1998): 707–21.

Munby, A.N.L. "The Libraries of English Men of Letters." In *Essays and Papers*, ed. Nicolas Barker. Ukley: Scolar Press, 1977.

————, ed. *Sale Catalogues of Libraries of Eminent Persons*. 12 vols. London: Mansell, 1971–75.

Murray, Stuart. *The Library: An Illustrated History*. New York: Skyhorse; Chicago: ALA Editions, 2009.

Mynors, R.A.B., ed. *Cassiodori Senatoris Institutiones*. Oxford: Clarendon Press, 1937.

Naddaff, Sandra. *Arabesque: Narrative Structure and the Aesthetics of Repetition in the 1001 Nights*. Evanston, IL: Northwestern University Press, 1991.

Newton, F. *The Scriptorium and Library at Monte Cassino 1058–1105*. Cambridge: Cambridge University Press, 1999.

Nora, Pierre. "Between Memory and History: *Les Lieux de Mémoire*," trans. Marc Roudebush. *Representations* 26 (Spring 1989): 7–25.

Novakova, Julie, ed. *Johannis Amos Comenii Opera Omnia, 23, Clamores Eliae*. Prague: Academia Pragae, 1992.

Oliphant, Margaret. "The Library Window: A Story of the Seen and the Unseen." *Blackwood's Magazine* 159 (January 1896): 1–30.

Online Library of Liberty, available at http://oll.libertyfund.org/.

Oswald, Alice. *Memorial*. London: Faber and Faber, 2011.

Paneth, Ira. "Wim and His Wings." *Film Quarterly* 42.1 (Autumn 1988): 2–8.

Pettegree, Andrew. *The Book in the Renaissance*. London: Yale University Press, 2010.

————. "Rare Books and Revolutionaries: The French Bibliothèques Municipales." In his *The French Book and the European Book World*. Leiden: Brill, 2007, 1–16.

Pettegree, Andrew, and Malcolm Walsby, eds. *Netherlandish Books: Books Published in the Low Countries and Dutch Books Printed Abroad before 1601*. Leiden: Brill, 2011.

Philip, Ian. *The Bodleian Library in the Seventeenth and Eighteenth Centuries*. Oxford: Clarendon Press, 1983.

Plath, Sylvia. *Letters Home,* selected and ed. Aurelia Schober Plath. London: Faber and Faber, 1975.

Polastron, Lucien X. *Books on Fire: The Tumultuous Story of the World's Great Libraries*. London: Thames and Hudson, 2007.

Price, Leah. *How to Do Things with Books in Victorian Britain*. Princeton, NJ: Princeton University Press, 2012.

Pseudo-Plutarch. *Lives of the Ten Orators*. "Lycurgus" 841F.

Quinn, Brian. "Collection Development and the Psychology of Bias." *Library Quarterly* 82.3 (2012): 277–304.

Ranganathan, S. R. *The Five Laws of Library Science*. Madras: Madras Library Association; London: Goldston, 1931.

Reiquam, Steve W., ed. *Solidarity and Poland*, intro. James H. Billington. Washington, DC: Wilson Center Press, 1988.

Rodenbeck, John. "Literary Alexandria." *Massachusetts Review* 42.4 (2001–2): 524–72.

Rouse, E. P. "Old Halifax Circulating Library, 1768–1866." *Papers, Reports, etc. Read before the Halifax Antiquarian Society*, 1911, 45–60.

Sandars, Nancy K., ed. and trans. *The Epic of Gilgamesh*. London: Penguin, 1960.

Sanders, James A. "The Dead Sea Scrolls: A Quarter Century of Study." *Biblical Archaeologist* 36.4 (1973): 109–48.

Schaaf, Larry J. *The Photographic Art of William Henry Fox Talbot*. Princeton, NJ: Princeton University Press, 2000.

Scott, Patrick. "Book Ownership and Authorial Identity: Reconstructing the (Im)Personal Library of Arthur Hugh Clough." Available on the *Selected Works of Patrick Scott* website, online at http://works.bepress.com/patrick_scott/230/.

———. "Tennyson's Celtic Reading." *Tennyson Research Bulletin* 1.2 (1968): 4–8.

Sebald, W. G. *Austerlitz*, trans. Anthea Bell. London: Hamish Hamilton, 2001.

Shaver, Chester L., and Alice C. Shaver, eds. *Wordsworth's Library: A Catalogue*. New York and London: Garland, 1979.

Shaw, George Bernard. *Caesar and Cleopatra*. New York: Brentano's, 1906.

Sherman, C. R. *Imaging Aristotle: Verbal and Visual Representation in Fourteenth-Century France*. Berkeley and Los Angeles: University of California Press, 1995.

Sherwin-White, N. *The Letters of Pliny*. Oxford: Clarendon Press, 1966.

Shillito, Charles. *The Country Book-Club: A Poem*. London: The Author, 1788.

Sider, S. "Herculaneum's Library in 79 A.D.: The Villa of the Papyri." *Libraries and Culture* 25.4 (1990): 534–42.

Simić, Goran. *Sprinting from the Graveyard*, English version by David Harsent. Oxford: Oxford University Press, 1997.

Smith, Janet Charlotte. "The Side Chambers of San Giovanni Evangelista in Ravenna: Church Libraries of the Fifth Century." *Gesta* 29.1 (1990): 86–97.

Staikos, Konstantinos Sp. *A History of the Library in Western Civilization*. New Castle, DE.: Oak Knoll Press, 2004–12.

Starr, Raymond J. "Trimalchio's Libraries." *Hermes* 115.2 (1987): 252–53.

St. Clair, William. *The Reading Nation in the Romantic Period.* Cambridge: Cambridge University Press, 2004.

Stevens, G. P. "A Doorsill from the Library of Pantainos." *Hesperia* 18 (1949): 269–74.

Stevenson, Anne. *Bitter Fame.* Boston: Houghton Mifflin, 1989.

Stone, Harry. *The Night Side of Dickens: Cannibalism, Passion, Necessity.* Columbus: Ohio State University Press, 1994.

Stonehouse, J. H. *Catalogue of the Library of Charles Dickens and W. M. Thackeray.* London: Piccadilly Fountain Press, 1935.

Streeter, B. H. *The Chained Library: A Survey of Four Centuries in the Evolution of the English Library.* London: Macmillan, 1931.

Sutherland, J. "*Cornhill*'s Sales and Payments: The First Decade." *Victorian Periodicals Review* 19.3 (Fall 1986): 106–8.

———. "Michael Sadleir and His Collection of Nineteenth-Century Fiction." *Nineteenth-Century Literature* 56.2 (September 2001): 145–59.

———. *Victorian Novelists and Publishers.* London: Athlone Press, 1976.

Symington, John Alexander. *Catalogue of the Museum and Library, the Brontë Society.* Shipley: Caxton Press, 1927.

Talbot, William Henry Fox. *The Pencil of Nature.* London: Longman, Brown, Green and Longmans, 1844.

Tanner, Marcus. *The Raven King: Matthias Corvinus and the Fate of his Lost Library.* New Haven, CT: Yale University Press, 2008.

Thackeray, William Makepeace. "Nil Nisi Bonum." *Cornhill Magazine* (February 1860): 129–34.

Thomas, E. C., ed. *Philobiblon*, rev. M. Maclagan. Oxford: Basil Blackwell, 1960.

Thomson, Christopher. *The Autobiography of an Artisan.* London: Chapman, 1847.

Thornton, D. *The Scholar in His Study: Ownership and Experience in Renaissance Italy.* New Haven, CT, and London: Yale University Press, 1997.

Thorp, N. *The Glory of the Page: Medieval and Renaissance Illuminated Manuscripts from Glasgow University Library.* Glasgow and London: Miller, 1987.

Too, Yun Lee. *The Idea of the Library in the Ancient World.* Oxford: Oxford University Press, 2010.

Trypucko, Josef. *The Catalogue of the Book Collection of the Jesuit College in Braniewo Held in the University Library in Uppsala.* Warsaw and Uppsala: Uppsala Universitetsbibliotek and Biblioteka Narodowa, 2007.

Wagner, Klaus. "Le commerce du livre en France au début du XVIe siècle d'après les notes manuscrites de Fernando Colomb." *Bulletin du bibliophile* 2 (1992): 305–29.

———. "Judicia Astrologica Colombiniana. Bibliographisches Verzeichnis einer Sammlung von Praktiken des 15. und 16. Jahrhunderts des Biblioteca Colombina Sevilla." *Archiv für Geschichte des Buchwesens* 15 (1975): cols. 1–98.

Ward, T. A. *A Short Account of the Sheffield Library, Its Founders, Presidents, and Librarians.* Sheffield: H. A. Bacon, 1825.

Warner, Marina. *Stranger Magic: Charmed States and the Arabian Nights.* London: Vintage, 2012.

"What Is Read at the People's Palace, A Chat with a Lady Librarian." *Pall Mall Gazette* October 2, 1889, 2.

Wilberg, Wilhelm. *Forschungen in Ephesos.* Vol. 5.1, *Die Bibliothek.* Vienna: A. Holder, 1953.

Wilson, Charles. *First with the News: The History of W. H. Smith, 1792–1972.* London: W. H. Smith, 1985.

"Women as Librarians, by One of the Librarians of the People's Palace." *Monthly Packet* July 1, 1892, 42.

Wuttke, D., ed. *Sebastian Brant: Das Narrenschiff; Faksimile der Erst-ausgabe Basel 1494.* Baden-Baden: Koerner, 1994.

Zeri, F., with E. E. Gardner. *Italian Paintings: A Catalogue of the Collection of the Metropolitan Museum of Art; North Italian School.* New York: Metropolitan Museum of Art, 1986.

CONTRIBUTORS

David Allan is Reader in History at the University of St. Andrews. His books include *A Nation of Readers: The Lending Library in Georgian England* (British Library, 2008), *Making British Culture: English Readers and the Scottish Enlightenment* (Taylor and Francis, 2008), and *Commonplace Books and Reading in Georgian England* (Cambridge University Press, 2010).

James H. Billington has been the Librarian of Congress since 1987. He previously taught history at Harvard and at Princeton University and directed the Woodrow Wilson International Center for Scholars. His books include *The Icon and the Axe* (Knopf, 1966), *Fire in the Minds of Men* (Temple Smith, 1980), and *The Face of Russia* (TV Books, 1998), which was a major PBS television series. He has established both the Library of Congress's American Memory National Digital Library and the World Digital Library.

Alice Crawford is Digital Humanities Research Librarian at the University of St. Andrews Library. She is the author of *New Directions for Academic Liaison Librarians* (Chandos, 2012) and *Paradise Pursued: The Novels of Rose Macaulay* (Fairleigh Dickinson University Press, 1995).

Robert Crawford is Professor of Modern Scottish Literature and Bishop Wardlaw Professor of Poetry at the University of St. Andrews. Among his books are *Devolving English Literature* (Oxford University Press, 1992), *Scotland's Books* (Penguin, 2007), and *The Bard: Robert Burns; A Biography* (Princeton University Press, 2009). A Fellow of the British Academy and of the Royal Society of Edinburgh, he is writing a biography of T. S. Eliot. His seventh collection of poems, *Testament*, was published by Jonathan Cape in 2014.

Robert Darnton is Harvard's University Librarian and Carl H. Pforzheimer University Professor. He is author of numerous books and articles on publishing and cultural history, especially on eighteenth-century France. These range from *The Business of Enlightenment: A Publishing History of the Encyclopédie* (Harvard University Press, 1979) to *The Great Cat Massacre* (Allen Lane, 1984), *The*

Case for Books (Public Affairs, 2009), and *Censors at Work: How States Shaped Literature* (New York: Norton, 2014).

Stephen Enniss is Director of the Harry Ransom Center at the University of Texas at Austin. He did his undergraduate studies at Davidson College, followed by a library degree from Emory University, and a PhD in English from the University of Georgia. Before coming to the University of Texas, he held previous appointments at the Folger Shakespeare Library and at Emory University's Manuscript, Archives, and Rare Book Library. His research interests are in twentieth-century poetry, and he has written on Ted Hughes, Sylvia Plath, and Seamus Heaney, among other figures. He has curated a number of major exhibitions including "No Other Appetite: Sylvia Plath, Ted Hughes, and the Blood Jet of Poetry." He is recipient of a Leverhulme Fellowship for the recently published biography *After the Titanic: A Life of Derek Mahon* (Gill and Macmillan, 2014).

Richard Gameson, Professor of the History of the Book at Durham University, specializes in the history of the book from Antiquity to the Renaissance, and in medieval art. He has published over eighty studies on medieval manuscripts, book collections, art, and cultural history. His most recent books are *Manuscript Treasures of Durham Cathedral* (Third Millennium, 2010), *The Cambridge History of the Book in Britain,* volume 1(Cambridge University Press, 2012), and *From Holy Island to Durham: The Contexts and Meanings of the Lindisfarne Gospels* (Third Millennium, 2013). He is currently completing a descriptive catalogue of the medieval manuscripts of Trinity College, Oxford.

Edith Hall is Professor of Classics at King's College London. Her books include *Introducing the Ancient Greeks* (Norton, 2014), *Adventures with Iphigenia in Tauris* (Oxford University Press, 2012), *Greek Tragedy: Suffering under the Sun* (Oxford University Press, 2010), and, with Fiona Macintosh, *Greek Tragedy and the British Theatre* (Oxford University Press, 2005). She is cofounder and Consultant Director of the Archive of Performances of Greek and Roman Drama at Oxford, and Chairman of the Gilbert Murray Trust. She has been awarded the Erasmus Medal in 2015 by the European Academy for her research.

Laura Marcus is Goldsmiths Professor of English Literature and Professorial Fellow of New College at the University of Oxford. Her interests are in nineteenth- and twentieth-century literature, including life-writing, modernism, Virginia Woolf and Bloomsbury culture, contemporary fiction, and literature and film. Her book publications include *Auto/biographical Discourses: Theory, Criticism, Practice* (Manchester University Press, 1994), *The Tenth Muse:*

Writing about Cinema in the Modernist Period (Oxford University Press, 2007; awarded the 2008 James Russell Lowell Prize of the Modern Language Association), *Dreams of Modernity: Psychoanalysis, Literature, Cinema* (Cambridge University Press, 2014), and, as coeditor, *The Cambridge History of Twentieth-Century English Literature* (Cambridge University Press, 2004). She is a Fellow of the British Academy.

Andrew Pettegree, an expert on Europe during the Reformation and the history of communication, is Professor of History at the University of St. Andrews, where he was the founding Director of the St. Andrews Reformation Studies Institute. He is now also Director of the Universal Short Title Catalogue project (USTC), a survey of all books published in the first age of print. His many publications include *The Book in the Renaissance* (Yale University Press, 2010) and *Reformation and the Culture of Persuasion* (Cambridge University Press, 2005). His latest book, *The Invention of News: How the World Came to Know about Itself* (Yale University Press), was published in 2014.

John Sutherland is Emeritus Lord Northcliffe Professor at University College, London, and a specialist in Victorian fiction, twentieth-century fiction, and the history of publishing. A frequent columnist and reviewer in the *Guardian* and other newspapers, he has published prolifically, including *The Longman Companion to Victorian Fiction* (Longman, 1989; Pearson, 2009). His most recent works are *The Lives of the Novelists* (Profile, 2011), *A Little History of Literature* (Yale University Press, 2013), *Jumbo: The Unauthorised Biography of a Victorian Sensation* (Aurum, 2014), and *How to Be Well Read* (Random House, 2014).

Marina Warner is a writer of cultural history and fiction. Her works include the award-winning *Stranger Magic: Charmed States and The Arabian Nights* (Chatto and Windus / Harvard University Press, 2012), *From the Beast to the Blonde: On Fairy Tales and Their Tellers* (Chatto and Windus / Farrar, Straus and Giroux, 1994), and *Alone of All Her Sex: The Myth and the Cult of the Virgin Mary* (Weidenfeld and Nicolson, 1976; Oxford University Press, 2013). *Once upon a Time: A Short History of Fairy Tale* was published by Oxford University Press in 2014. She is a Fellow of All Souls College, Oxford, and Professor of English and Creative Writing at Birkbeck College, London. In 2005, she was elected a Fellow of the British Academy, and she was made DBE for services to literary scholarship in 2015.

John P. Wilkin is Juanita J. and Robert E. Simpson Dean of Libraries and University Librarian at the University of Illinois at Urbana-Champaign. He served previously as Executive Director of HathiTrust and as Associate University

Librarian for Publishing and for Technology at the University of Michigan, Ann Arbor. He was the primary investigator on a number of foundational grants and projects including a Mellon Foundation grant for creating an OAI (Open Archives Initiative) harvesting platform. He led the National Endowment for the Humanities–funded effort to convert and provide online access to the *Middle English Dictionary* and was also the principal investigator in the Making of America IV: The American Voice project, which won a grant from the Andrew W. Mellon Foundation, for the digital conversion of 7,500 nineteenth-century U.S. imprint monographs. He has researched and published widely in the fields of digital libraries, open source software, and multi-institution collaboration. He has worked extensively in transforming books to digital platforms and is one of the leaders in digital libraries.

INDEX

❦

Illustrations are indicated with *italic* page numbers.